WCF Multi-layer Services Development with Entity Framework

Fourth Edition

Create and deploy complete solutions with WCF and Entity Framework

Mike Liu

BIRMINGHAM - MUMBAI

WCF Multi-layer Services Development with Entity Framework

Fourth Edition

First published: December 2008

Second edition: June 2010

Third edition: December 2012

Fourth edition: October 2014

Production reference: 1241014

Published by Packt Publishing Ltd.
Livery Place
35 Livery Street
Birmingham B3 2PB, UK.

ISBN 978-1-78439-104-1

www.packtpub.com

Credits

Author
Mike Liu

Reviewers
Joe Enos

Joydip Kanjilal

Tarkan Karadayi

Jason De Oliveira

Jiri Pik

Commissioning Editor
Amarabha Banerjee

Acquisition Editor
Larissa Pinto

Content Development Editors
Pragnesh Bilimoria

Sweny M. Sukumaran

Technical Editor
Pramod Kumavat

Copy Editors
Dipti Kapadia

Deepa Nambiar

Project Coordinator
Rashi Khivansara

Proofreaders
Samuel Redman Birch

Ameesha Green

Linda Morris

Indexers
Monica Ajmera Mehta

Rekha Nair

Priya Sane

Graphics
Abhinash Sahu

Production Coordinator
Nitesh Thakur

Cover Work
Nitesh Thakur

About the Author

Mike Liu studied Mathematics and Software Engineering at Nanjing University and Brandeis University, where he graduated with a Bachelor's degree and a Master's degree, respectively. He is a Sun Certified Java Programmer (SCJP), Microsoft Certified Solution Developer for Visual Studio 6.0, and Microsoft Certified Solution Developer for .NET. He has been working as a software engineer/architect on various platforms (DOS, Unix, and Windows) using C/C++, Java, VB/VB.NET, and C#.

Mike started using C# for production development back in the year 2001 when C# was still in beta stage, and he is now working as a senior software engineer for an investment management firm in Boston, Massachusetts, US.

Mike had his first book, *MITT: Multi-user Integrated Table-processing Tool Under Unix*, *Beijing Hangtian University Press*, published in 1993, and second book, *Advanced C# Programming*, *Tsinghua University Press*, published in 2003. The previous three versions of this book were published in 2008, 2010, and 2012.

Many thanks to the editors and technical reviewers at Packt Publishing. Without their help, this book wouldn't be of such high quality. Also, thanks to my wife, Julia, and to my two sons, Kevin and James, for their consideration and sacrifices while I was working on this book.

About the Reviewers

Joe Enos works as a software engineer and architect, designing and building enterprise-level applications, mostly with .NET and SQL Server. He is the owner of No Edge Software and a co-owner of Blosme Software. He is passionate about providing organizations with the tools to improve their business and technical practices. He has spoken at developer events across the United States about build and deployment automation and is a strong advocate for building simple and reliable development and deployment strategies.

Joydip Kanjilal is a Microsoft Most Valuable Professional in ASP.NET, speaker, and author of several books and articles. Joydip has over 16 years of industry experience in IT with more than 10 years in Microsoft .NET and its related technologies. He was selected as MSDN Featured Developer of the Fortnight (MSDN) a number of times and also as Community Credit Winner at www.community-credit.com several times.

Joydip has authored/co-authored the following books:

- *Visual Studio 2010 and .NET 4 Six-in-One, Wrox*
- *ASP.NET 4.0 Programming, McGraw-Hill Osborne Media*
- *Entity Framework Tutorial, Packt Publishing*
- *Pro Sync Framework, Apress*
- *Sams Teach Yourself ASP.NET Ajax in 24 Hours, Sams Publishing*
- *ASP.NET Data Presentation Controls Essentials, Packt Publishing*

Joydip has reviewed the following books:

- *jQuery UI Cookbook, Packt Publishing*
- *C# 5 First Look, Packt Publishing*
- *jQuery 1.4 Reference Guide, Packt Publishing*
- *HTML 5 Step by Step, O'Reilly Media*

He has authored more than 250 articles for some of the most reputable sites such as www.msdn.microsoft.com, www.code-magazine.com, www.devx.com, www.ddj.com, www.aspalliance.com, www.aspnetpro.com, www.sql-server-performance.com, and www.sswug.org. A lot of these articles have been selected by www.asp.net (Microsoft's official site on ASP.NET).

Joydip also has years of experience in designing and architecting solutions for various domains. His technical strengths include, C, C++, VC++, Java, C# 5.0, Microsoft .NET, Ajax, WCF 4, ASP.NET MVC 4, ASP.NET Web API, REST, SOA, Design Patterns, SQL Server 2012, Google's Protocol Buffers, WPF, Microsoft Silverlight 5, Operating Systems, and Computer Architecture.

Joydip can be reached at the following links:

- Blog: http://aspadvice.com/blogs/joydip
- Website: www.joydipkanjilal.com
- Twitter: https://twitter.com/joydipkanjilal
- Facebook: https://www.facebook.com/joydipkanjilal
- LinkedIn: http://in.linkedin.com/in/joydipkanjilal

I would like to thank my family for providing me the support to make this book a success.

Tarkan Karadayi has been a professional software developer for over 15 years. He has a Master's degree in Computer Science and currently works as a principal software engineer.

I would like to thank my wife, Anna, and my sons, Taran, Kyle, and Ryan, for their love and support.

Jason De Oliveira works as the CTO for Cellenza (http://www.cellenza.com), an IT Consulting company specialized in Microsoft technologies and Agile methodology based in Paris, France. He is an experienced manager and senior solutions architect, with high skills in Software Architecture and Enterprise Architecture.

Jason works for big companies and helps them realize complex and challenging software projects. He frequently collaborates with Microsoft, and you can find him quite often at Microsoft Technology Center (MTC) in Paris.

He loves sharing his knowledge and experience via his blog, by speaking at conferences, writing technical books and articles in the technical press, giving software courses as Microsoft Certified Trainer (MCT), and coaching coworkers in his company.

Since 2011, Microsoft has awarded him with the Microsoft Most Valuable Professional (MVP C#) award for his numerous contributions to the Microsoft community. Microsoft seeks to recognize the best and brightest from technology communities around the world with the MVP Award. These exceptional and highly respected individuals come from more than 90 countries, serving their local online and offline communities and having an impact worldwide. Jason is very proud to be one of them.

Feel free to contact him via his blog if you need any technical assistance or want to exchange information or advice on technical subjects (http://www.jasondeoliveira.com).

Jason has worked on the following books:

- *.NET 4.5 Expert Programming Cookbook, Packt Publishing*
- *WCF 4.5 Multi-tier Services Development with LINQ to Entities, Packt Publishing*
- *.NET 4.5 Parallel Extensions Cookbook, Packt Publishing*
- *Visual Studio 2013: Concevoir, développer et gérer des projets Web, les gérer avec TFS 2013, ENI*

I would like to thank my lovely wife, Orianne, and my beautiful daughters, Julia and Léonie, for supporting me in my work and accepting long days and short nights during the weeks and sometimes even during the weekends. My life would not be the same without them!

Jiri Pik is a finance and business intelligence consultant, working with major investment banks, hedge funds, and other financial players. He has architected and delivered breakthrough trading, portfolio and risk management systems, and decision support systems across industries.

Jiri's consulting firm, WIXESYS, provides their clients with certified expertise, judgment, and execution at the speed of light. WIXESYS' power tools include revolutionary Excel and Outlook add-ons, available at http://spearian.com.

www.PacktPub.com

Support files, eBooks, discount offers, and more

You might want to visit www.PacktPub.com for support files and downloads related to your book.

Did you know that Packt offers eBook versions of every book published, with PDF and ePub files available? You can upgrade to the eBook version at www.PacktPub.com and as a print book customer, you are entitled to a discount on the eBook copy. Get in touch with us at service@packtpub.com for more details.

At www.PacktPub.com, you can also read a collection of free technical articles, sign up for a range of free newsletters and receive exclusive discounts and offers on Packt books and eBooks.

http://PacktLib.PacktPub.com

Do you need instant solutions to your IT questions? PacktLib is Packt's online digital book library. Here, you can access, read and search across Packt's entire library of books.

Why subscribe?
- Fully searchable across every book published by Packt
- Copy and paste, print and bookmark content
- On demand and accessible via web browser

Free access for Packt account holders

If you have an account with Packt at www.PacktPub.com, you can use this to access PacktLib today and view nine entirely free books. Simply use your login credentials for immediate access.

Instant updates on new Packt books

Get notified! Find out when new books are published by following @PacktEnterprise on Twitter, or the *Packt Enterprise* Facebook page.

Table of Contents

Preface

WCF is Microsoft's recommended model for building services, and Entity Framework is Microsoft's preferred ORM to access underlying data storages. Learning WCF and Entity Framework has become essential and critical for every software developer to survive in this SOA world.

This book is a step-by-step tutorial to guide you through learning WCF, Entity Framework, and LINQ to Entities. You will be guided through the creation of six WCF and Entity Framework solutions, of which four are multilayered real-world WCF service solutions, so you will not only be reading but also be coding through the book to gain practical experience in WCF and Entity Framework. Various test clients will be associated with each solution and all solutions can be built and run independently of other solutions. Clear instructions and relevant screenshots will make sure that you don't get lost in the world of WCF and Entity Framework. Configuration files, host applications, test clients, and WCF services for each solution will also be available for download for you to examine, modify, and debug from the outside in.

This book focuses on the essentials of using WCF and Entity Framework, rather than providing a reference for every single possibility. It leaves the reference material online where it belongs and instead concentrates on practical examples, code, and advice.

What this book covers

Chapter 1, Implementing a Basic HelloWorld WCF Service, introduces WCF and implements a simple HelloWorld WCF service.

Chapter 2, Hosting the HelloWorld WCF Service, discusses various hosting techniques of WCF services.

Chapter 3, Deploying the HelloWorld WCF Service, explores deployment options of WCF services.

Chapter 4, Debugging the HelloWorld WCF Service, discusses various debugging techniques of WCF services.

Chapter 5, Implementing a Three-layer WCF Service, explains how to create a layered WCF service with an interface layer and a business logic layer.

Chapter 6, Adding Database Support and Exception Handling, explains how to add a data access layer and fault message handling to the previously created WCF service.

Chapter 7, LINQ to Entities – Basic Concepts and Features, covers the basic concepts and features of LINQ to Entities such as LINQ to Entities designer, querying and updating tables, deferred execution, and lazy/eager loading.

Chapter 8, LINQ to Entities – Advanced Concepts and Features, covers advanced concepts and features of LINQ to Entities such as stored procedure, concurrency control, and transaction support.

Chapter 9, Applying LINQ to Entities to a WCF Service, discusses how to recreate the data access layer of a WCF service with LINQ to Entities.

Chapter 10, Distributed Transaction Support of WCF, explains how to add distributed transaction support to a WCF service.

Chapter 11, Building a RESTful WCF Service, converts the previously created WCF service to a RESTful WCF service and consumes it from a Windows 8 app.

Chapter 12, WCF Security, covers basic security features and settings of WCF and hosts a WCF service with basic authentication, SSL, and Windows authentication.

Chapter 13, Extending WCF Services, explains various extension points of WCF services and extends a WCF service with custom behaviors.

What you need for this book

You will need the following software for the examples explained in this book:

- Microsoft .NET Framework 4.5.1
- Microsoft Visual Studio 2013 Ultimate, Premium, or Professional
- Microsoft SQL Server 2012, 2008, 2005, or Express
- Internet Information Server 7.0, 7.5, or 8.0
- Windows 7 or Windows 8

Who this book is for

This book is for C#, VB.NET, and C++ developers who are eager to get started with WCF and Entity Framework and want a book that is practical and rich in examples from the very beginning.

Developers and architects evaluating SOA implementation technologies for their company will find this book particularly useful because it will get you started with Microsoft's tools for SOA and show you how to customize the examples explained in it for your prototypes.

This book presumes basic knowledge of C# or C++. Previous experience with Visual Studio will be helpful but is not required, as detailed instructions are given throughout the book.

Conventions

In this book, you will find a number of styles of text that distinguish between different kinds of information. Here are some examples of these styles, and an explanation of their meaning.

Code words in text, database table names, folder names, filenames, file extensions, pathnames, dummy URLs, user input, and Twitter handles are shown as follows: "Throughout this book, we will save our project source codes in the C:\SOAwithWCFandEF\Projects directory."

A block of code is set as follows:

```
namespace HelloWorldService
{
    [ServiceContract]
    public interface IHelloWorldService
    {
        [OperationContract]
        string GetMessage(string name);
    }
}
```

New terms and **important words** are shown in bold. Words that you see on the screen, in menus or dialog boxes for example, appear in the text like this: " If the **Open Project** dialog box pops up, click on **Cancel** to close it."

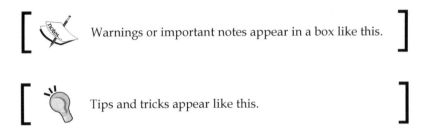

Warnings or important notes appear in a box like this.

Tips and tricks appear like this.

Reader feedback

Feedback from our readers is always welcome. Let us know what you think about this book—what you liked or may have disliked. Reader feedback is important for us to develop titles that you really get the most out of.

To send us general feedback, simply send an e-mail to feedback@packtpub.com, and mention the book title via the subject of your message.

If there is a topic that you have expertise in and you are interested in either writing or contributing to a book, see our author guide on www.packtpub.com/authors.

Customer support

Now that you are the proud owner of a Packt book, we have a number of things to help you to get the most from your purchase.

Downloading the example code

You can download the example code files for all Packt books you have purchased from your account at http://www.packtpub.com. If you purchased this book elsewhere, you can visit http://www.packtpub.com/support and register to have the files e-mailed directly to you.

Errata

Although we have taken every care to ensure the accuracy of our content, mistakes do happen. If you find a mistake in one of our books—maybe a mistake in the text or the code—we would be grateful if you would report this to us. By doing so, you can save other readers from frustration and help us improve subsequent versions of this book. If you find any errata, please report them by visiting http://www.packtpub.com/submit-errata, selecting your book, clicking on the **errata submission form** link, and entering the details of your errata. Once your errata are verified, your submission will be accepted and the errata will be uploaded on our website, or added to any list of existing errata, under the Errata section of that title. Any existing errata can be viewed by selecting your title from http://www.packtpub.com/support.

Piracy

Piracy of copyright material on the Internet is an ongoing problem across all media. At Packt, we take the protection of our copyright and licenses very seriously. If you come across any illegal copies of our works, in any form, on the Internet, please provide us with the location address or website name immediately so that we can pursue a remedy.

Please contact us at copyright@packtpub.com with a link to the suspected pirated material.

We appreciate your help in protecting our authors, and our ability to bring you valuable content.

Questions

You can contact us at questions@packtpub.com if you are having a problem with any aspect of the book, and we will do our best to address it.

1
Implementing a Basic HelloWorld WCF Service

Windows Communication Foundation (WCF) is Microsoft's unified programming model to build service-oriented applications. It is built on Microsoft's .NET framework and unifies a broad array of distributed systems capabilities in a composable, extensible architecture that supports multiple transports, messaging patterns, encodings, network topologies, and hosting models.

In this chapter, we will first learn basic WCF concepts and then implement a simple WCF service from scratch. We will build a HelloWorld WCF service by carrying out the following steps:

- Creating the solution and project
- Defining the WCF service contract interface
- Implementing the WCF service
- Hosting the WCF service in IIS Express
- Creating a client application to consume the WCF service

The basic WCF concepts

There are many terms and concepts surrounding WCF, such as address, binding, contract, endpoint, behavior, hosting, and channels. Understanding these terms is very helpful when using WCF, so let's first take a look at these terms.

Address

The WCF address is a specific location for a service. It specifies the path where a particular message will be sent. All WCF services are deployed at a specific address, and they listen at that address for incoming requests.

A WCF address is normally specified as a URL, with its first part specifying the transport mechanism and the next part specifying the unique location of the service. For example, `http://www.myweb.com/myWCFServices/SampleService.svc` is an address for a WCF service. This WCF service uses HTTP as its transport protocol, and it is located on the server, `www.myweb.com`, with a unique service path of `myWCFServices/SampleService.svc`.

Binding

Bindings are used to specify the transport, encoding, and protocol details required for clients and services to communicate with each other. Bindings are what WCF uses to generate the underlying representation of the endpoint (an endpoint is a place where clients can communicate with a WCF service; more details will follow). So, most of the details of the binding must be agreed upon by the parties that are communicating. The easiest way to achieve this for clients of a service is to use the same binding that the service uses.

A binding is made up of a collection of binding elements. Each element describes some aspect of how the service communicates with clients. A binding must include at least one transport binding element, at least one message-encoding binding element (which is provided by the transport binding element by default), and any number of other protocol binding elements. The process that builds a runtime out of this description allows each binding element to contribute code to that runtime.

WCF provides bindings that contain common selections of binding elements. These can either be used with their default settings, or the default values can be modified according to user requirements. These system-provided bindings have properties that allow direct control over the binding elements and their settings.

The following are some examples of system-provided bindings: **BasicHttpBinding**, **WSHttpBinding**, and **NetTcpBinding**. Each one of these built-in bindings has the predefined elements required for a common task and is ready to be used in your project. For instance, BasicHttpBinding uses HTTP as the transport to send SOAP 1.1 messages, and it has attributes and elements such as `receiveTimeout`, `sendTimeout`, `maxMessageSize`, and `maxBufferSize`. You can use the default settings of attributes and elements of BasicHttpBinding, or overwrite them as needed. We will explore all of the three bindings in this book.

Contract

A WCF contract is a set of specifications that defines the interfaces of a WCF service. A WCF service communicates with other applications according to its contracts. There are several types of WCF contract, such as service contract, operation contract, data contract, message contract, and fault contract. We define service contract and operation contract in the following sections of this chapter, and define more contracts throughout this book.

The service contract

A service contract is the interface of the WCF service. Basically, it tells us what the service can do. It can include service-level settings such as the name of the service, the namespace of the service, and the corresponding callback contracts of the service. Inside the interface, it can define a bunch of methods or service operations for specific tasks. A WCF service has to contain at least one service contract to service requests.

The operation contract

An operation contract is defined within a service contract. It defines the parameters and the return type of an operation. An operation can take data of a primitive (native) data type, such as an integer, as a parameter, or it can take a message, which should be defined as a message contract type. Just as a service contract is an interface, an operation contract is the definition of an operation. It has to be implemented in order for the service to function as a WCF service. An operation contract also defines operation-level settings such as the transaction flow of the operation, the direction of the operation (one-way, request/reply, or duplex callbacks), and the fault contract of the operation.

The message contract

If an operation contract needs to pass a message as a parameter or return a message, the type of these messages will be defined as message contracts. A message contract defines the elements of the message as well as any message-related settings, such as the level of message security and also whether an element should go to the header or to the body.

The data contract

Data contracts are the data types of the WCF service. All data types used by the WCF service must be described in the metadata to enable other applications to interoperate with the service. A data contract can be used by an operation contract as a parameter or return type, or it can be used by a message contract to define elements. If a WCF service uses only primitive (native) data types, it is not necessary to define a data contract.

The fault contract

In any WCF service operation contract, if an error is returned to the caller, the caller should be warned of that error. These error types are defined as fault contracts. An operation can have zero or more fault contracts associated with it.

Endpoint

Messages are sent between endpoints. Endpoints are places where messages are sent or received (or both), and they define all the information required for the message exchange. A service exposes one or more application endpoints (as well as zero or more infrastructure endpoints). A service can expose this information in the form of metadata that clients process to generate the appropriate WCF clients and communication stacks. When needed, the client generates an endpoint that is compatible with one of the service's endpoints.

A WCF service endpoint has an address, a binding, and a service contract (sometimes referred to as WCF ABCs).

Behavior

A WCF behavior is a type or setting to extend the functionality of a WCF component. There are many types of behaviors in WCF, such as service behavior, binding behavior, contract behavior, security behavior, and channel behavior. For example, a new service behavior can be defined to specify the transaction timeout of the service, the maximum concurrent instances of the service, and whether the service publishes metadata. Behaviors are configured in the WCF service configuration file. We will configure several specific behaviors in the chapters that follow. We will learn how to extend a WCF service with behaviors in *Chapter 13, Extending WCF Services*.

Hosting

The WCF service is a component that can be called by other applications. It must be hosted in an environment in order to be discovered and used by others. The WCF host is an application that controls the lifetime of the service. With .NET 3.0 and higher, there are several ways to host the service. We will explore various WCF hosting options in *Chapter 2, Hosting the HelloWorld WCF Service*.

Channels

As we have seen in previous sections, a WCF service has to be hosted in an application on the server side. On the client side, the client applications have to specify the bindings to connect to the WCF services. The binding elements are interfaces, and they have to be implemented in concrete classes. The concrete implementation of a binding element is called a channel. A binding element represents a configuration and a channel is the implementation associated with that configuration. Therefore, there is a channel associated with each binding element. Channels stack on top of one another to create the concrete implementation of the binding—the channel stack.

The **WCF channel stack** is a layered communication stack with one or more channels that process messages. At the bottom of the stack is a transport channel that is responsible for adapting the channel stack to the underlying transport (for example TCP, HTTP, SMTP, and other types of transport). Other channels provide a low-level programming model to send and receive messages.

Metadata

The **metadata** of a service describes the characteristics of the service that an external entity needs to understand in order to communicate with the service. Metadata can be consumed by the ServiceModel metadata utility tool (SvcUtil.exe) to generate a WCF client proxy and the accompanying configuration that a client application can use to interact with the service.

The metadata exposed by the service includes the XML schema documents that define the data contract of the service and WSDL documents that describe the methods of the service.

Though WCF services always have metadata, it is possible to hide the metadata from outsiders. If you do so, you have to pass the metadata to the client side by other means. This practice is not common but it gives your services an extra layer of security. When enabled through the configuration settings from metadata behavior, metadata for the service can be retrieved by inspecting the service and its endpoints. The following configuration setting in a WCF service configuration file will enable metadata publishing for the HTTP transport protocol:

```
<serviceMetadata httpGetEnabled="true" />
```

WCF environments

WCF was first introduced in Microsoft's .NET **Common Language Runtime (CLR)** Version 2.0. The corresponding framework at that time was .NET 3.0. To develop and run WCF services, Microsoft .NET Framework 3.0 or above is required.

Visual Studio is Microsoft's IDE to develop WCF service applications. Visual Studio 2008 and above support WCF service application development.

The following table shows all of the different versions of the .NET runtimes, .NET frameworks, and Visual Studio versions, along with their relationships:

CLR	.NET framework	Components				Visual Studio
CLR 4.0	.NET 4.5.1 .NET 4.5.2	Windows 8.1	Universal App		Type Script	2013
	.NET 4.5	Windows 8	HTML5		Portable Class Libraries	2012 or above
	.NET 4.0	Parallel Computing	Dynamic		Covariance and Contravariance	2010 or above
CLR 2.0	.NET 3.5 SP1	ASP.NET MVC	Entity Framework	LINQ to Entities	Cloud Computing	2008 or above
	.NET 3.5	LINQ / LINQ to SQL / LINQ to XML	LINQ to Objects	ASP .NET AJAX	REST / RSS	2008 or above
	.NET 3.0	WCF	WPF	WF	CardSpace	
	.NET 2.0	Winforms	ASP.NET		ADO.NET	2005 or above
CLR 1.0	.NET 1.1	Winforms	ASP.NET		ADO.NET	2003
	.NET 1.0					2002

Creating the HelloWorld solution and project

Now that we have a basic understanding of WCF concepts and terminologies, let's start building a simple HelloWorld WCF service. Before we can build the WCF service, we need to create a solution for our service project. We also need a directory in which we will save all the files. Throughout this book, we will save our project source codes in the `C:\SOAwithWCFandEF\Projects` directory. We will have a subfolder for each solution we create, and under this solution folder we will have one subfolder for each project.

> You don't need to manually create these directories with Windows Explorer; Visual Studio will create them automatically when you create the solutions and projects.

Now, follow these steps to create our first solution and the `HelloWorld` project:

1. Start Visual Studio 2013 (you can use Visual Studio Ultimate, Premium, or Professional throughout this book). If the **Open Project** dialog box pops up, click on **Cancel** to close it.

2. Go to menu **FILE** | **New** | **Project...**. The **New Project** dialog window will appear, as follows:

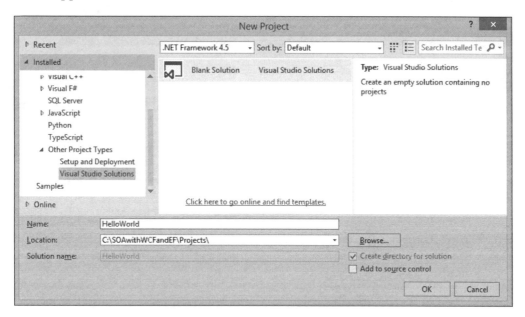

3. From the left-hand side of the window, expand **Installed | Templates
    | Other Project Types** and then select **Visual Studio Solutions** as the
    template. From the middle section of the window, select **Blank Solution**.

4. At the bottom of the window, type in HelloWorld in the **Name** field and
    enter C:\SOAwithWCFandEF\Projects\ in the **Location** field. Note that you
    should not enter HelloWorld within the location, because Visual Studio will
    automatically create a new folder for us inside the Projects folder.

5. Click on the **OK** button to close this window, and your screen should look
    like the following screenshot with an empty solution:

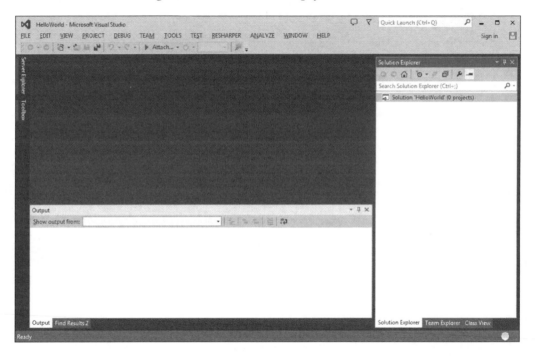

6. Depending on your settings, the layout might be different. However, you
    should still have an empty solution in your **Solution Explorer**. If you don't
    see the **Solution Explorer**, navigate to **VIEW | Solution Explorer** or press
    Ctrl + *Alt* + *L* to bring it up.

7. In the **Solution Explorer**, right-click on the solution and select **Add | New
    Project...** from the context menu. You can also go to **FILE | Add | New
    Project...** to get the same result. The following screenshot shows the context
    menu to add a new project:

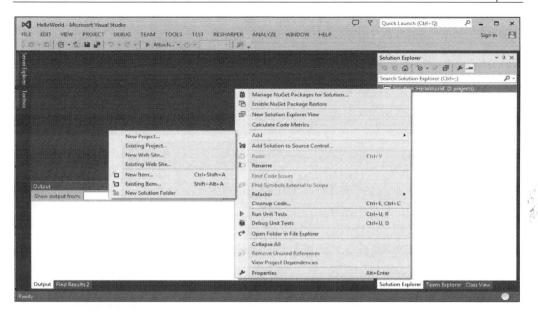

8. The **New Project** window should now appear on your screen. On the left-hand side of this window, select **Installed | Visual C#** as the template, and in the middle section of the window, select **Class Library**.

9. At the bottom of the window, type in `HelloWorldService` in the **Name** field. Leave `C:\SOAwithWCFandEF\Projects\HelloWorld` in the **Location** field. Again, don't add `HelloWorldService` to the location, as Visual Studio will create a subfolder for this new project (Visual Studio will use the `HelloWorld` folder as the default base folder for all the new projects added to the solution). Refer to the following screenshot:

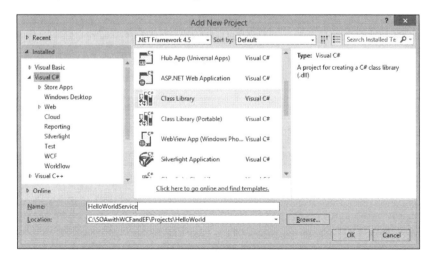

You might have noticed that there is already a template for a **WCF Service Application** in Visual Studio 2013. For this very first example, we will not use this template. Instead, we will create everything by ourselves to understand the purpose of each template. This is an excellent way for you to understand and master this new technology. In the next chapter, we will use this template to create the project, so we don't need to manually type a lot of code.

10. Now you can click on the **OK** button to close this window.

    Once you click on the **OK** button, Visual Studio will create several files for you. The first file is the project file. This is an XML file under our project's directory and it is called `HelloWorldService.csproj`.

    Visual Studio also creates an empty class file called `Class1.cs`. Later, we will change this default name to a more meaningful one.

    The window on your screen should now look like the one shown in the following screenshot:

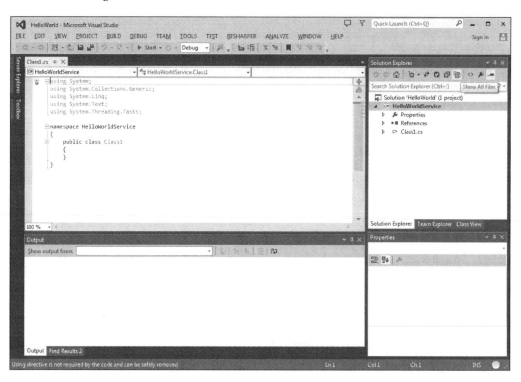

We have now created a new solution and a new project. Next, we will develop and build this project as a new service. However, before we go any further, we need to do one more thing to this project. Click on the **Show All Files** button on the **Solution Explorer** toolbar as shown in the preceding screenshot. Clicking on this button will show all files and directories in your hard disk under your project's folder—even those items that are not included in the project. Make sure that you don't have the solution item selected, otherwise you cannot see the **Show All Files** button.

Lastly, in order to develop a WCF service, we need to add a reference to the System. ServiceModel assembly. Perform the following steps:

1. In the **Solution Explorer** window, right-click on the **HelloWorldService** project and select **Add | Reference...** from the context menu. You can also right-click on **References** and select **Add Reference...** or go to **PROJECT | Add Reference...** to do this. The **Reference Manager** dialog window will appear on your screen as follows:

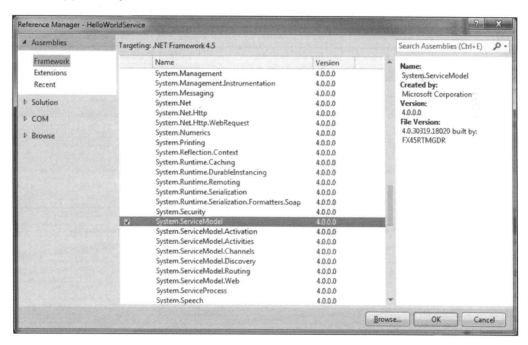

2. Check the checkbox in front of **System.ServiceModel** from the **Framework** tab under **Assemblies** and click on **OK**.

Now in **Solution Explorer**, if you expand the references of the **HelloWorldService** project, you will see that **System.ServiceModel** has been added under **References**. Also, note that **System.Xml.Linq** is added by default. We will use this later when we query a database.

Downloading the example code

You can download the example code files for all Packt books you have purchased from your account at http://www.packtpub.com. If you purchased this book elsewhere, you can visit http://www.packtpub.com/support and register to have the files e-mailed directly to you.

Defining the HelloWorldService service contract interface

In the previous section, we created the solution and the project for the HelloWorld WCF service. From this section onwards, we will start building the HelloWorld WCF service. First, we need to define the service contract interface. For this, perform the following steps:

1. In the **Solution Explorer**, right-click on the **HelloWorldService** project and select **Add | New Item...** from the context menu. The **Add New Item** dialog window shown in the following screenshot will appear on your screen:

2. On the left-hand side of the window, select **Installed | Visual C# Items** as the template, and from the middle section of the window, select **Interface**.

3. At the bottom of the window, change **Name** from `Interface1.cs` to `IHelloWorldService.cs`.

4. Click on the **Add** button.

Now an empty service interface file has been added to the project, which we are going to use as the service interface. Follow these steps to customize it:

1. Add a `using` statement:

   ```
   using System.ServiceModel;
   ```

2. Add a `ServiceContract` attribute to the interface. This will designate the interface as a WCF service contract interface:

   ```
   [ServiceContract]
   ```

3. Add a `GetMessage` method to the interface. This method will take a string as the input and return another string as the result. It also has an attribute called `OperationContract`:

   ```
   [OperationContract]
   string GetMessage(string name);
   ```

4. Change the interface to public.

The final content of the file, `IHelloWorldService.cs`, should look as follows:

```
using System;
using System.Collections.Generic;
using System.Linq;
using System.Text;
using System.Threading.Tasks;
using System.ServiceModel;

namespace HelloWorldService
{
    [ServiceContract]
    public interface IHelloWorldService
    {
        [OperationContract]
        string GetMessage(string name);
    }
}
```

Implementing the HelloWorldService service contract

Now that we have defined a service contract interface, we need to implement it. For this purpose, we will re-use the empty class file that Visual Studio created for us earlier and modify it to make it the implementation class of our service.

Before we modify this file, we need to rename it. In the **Solution Explorer** window, right-click on the **Class1.cs** file, select **Rename** from the context menu, and rename it as `HelloWorldService.cs`. Visual Studio is smart enough to change all the related files that are references to use this new name. You can also select the file and change its name from the **Properties** window.

Next, perform the following steps to customize the class file:

1. Open the `HelloWorldService.cs` file.

2. Make it implement `IHelloWorldService` implicitly as follows:

    ```
    public class HelloWorldService: IHelloWorldService
    ```

3. Add a `GetMessage` method to the class. This is an ordinary C# method that returns a string. You can also right-click on the interface link and select **Implement Interface** to add the skeleton of this method.

    ```
    public string GetMessage(string name)
    {
      return "Hello world from " + name + "!";
    }
    ```

The final content of the `HelloWorldService.cs` file should look like the following:

```
using System;
using System.Collections.Generic;
using System.Linq;
using System.Text;
using System.Threading.Tasks;
namespace HelloWorldService
{
    public class HelloWorldService: IHelloWorldService
    {
        public string GetMessage(string name)
        {
            return "Hello world from " + name + "!";
        }
    }
}
```

Now, build the project. If there is no build error, it means that you have successfully created your first WCF service. If you see a compilation error such as **'ServiceModel' does not exist in the namespace 'System'**, this is because you didn't add the `System.ServiceModel` namespace reference correctly. Revisit the previous section to add this reference and you are all set.

Next, we will host this WCF service in an environment and create a client application to consume it.

Hosting the WCF service in IIS Express

`HelloWorldService` is a class library. It has to be hosted in an environment where client applications can access it. In this section, we will learn how to host it using IIS Express. Later in the next chapter, we will discuss more hosting options for a WCF service.

Creating the host application

There are several built-in host applications for WCF services within Visual Studio 2013. However, in this section, we will manually create the host application so that you can have a better understanding of what a hosting application is really like under the hood. In subsequent chapters, we will learn and use the built-in hosting application.

To host the library using IIS Express, we need to add a new website to the solution. Follow these steps to create this website:

1. In the **Solution Explorer**, right-click on the solution **HelloWorld** and select **Add | New Web Site…** from the context menu (**Always show solution** must be enabled in **DEBUG | Options and Settings… | Projects and Solutions** in order to see the solution file). The **Add New Web Site** dialog window should pop up.

2. Select **Visual C# | ASP.NET Empty Web Site** as the template and leave the **Web location** field set to **File System**, but change the default address to `C:\SOAwithWCFandEF\Projects\HelloWorld\HostExpressServer` and click on **OK**.

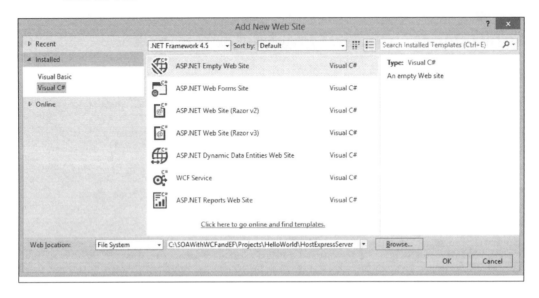

3. Now in **Solution Explorer**, you have one more item (**HostExpressServer**) within the solution. It will look like the following:

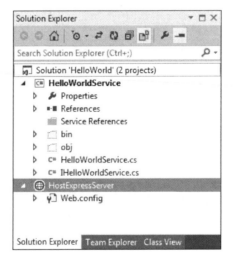

4. Next, we need to set the website as the startup project. In the **Solution Explorer**, right-click on the **HostExpressServer** website and select **Set as StartUp Project** from the context menu (or you can first select the website from **Solution Explorer** and then select the menu item **WEBSITE | Set as StartUp Project**). The **HostExpressServer** website should be highlighted in **Solution Explorer**, indicating that it is now the startup project.

5. As we will host `HelloWorldService` from this website, we need to add a `HelloWorldService` reference to the website. In the **Solution Explorer**, right-click on the **HostExpressServer** website and select **Add | Reference...** from the context menu. The **Reference Manager** dialog box should appear, as shown in the following screenshot:

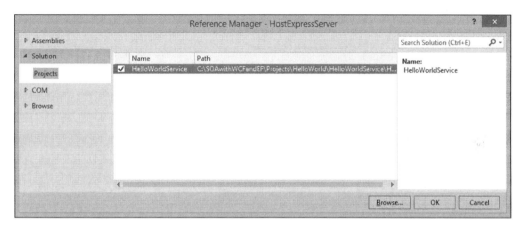

6. In the **Reference Manager** dialog box, click on the **Solutions** tab and then click on **Projects**. Check the **HelloWorldService** project and then click on **OK**. You will see that a new directory (`bin`) has been created under the `HostExpressServer` website and two files from the **HelloWorldService** project have been copied to this new directory. Later on, when this website is accessed, the web server (IIS Express) will look for executable code in the `bin` directory.

Testing the host application

Now we can run the website inside IIS Express. If you start the `HostExpressServer` website by pressing *Ctrl + F5* or by selecting **DEBUG | Start Without Debugging** in the menu, you will see an empty website in your browser with an error:

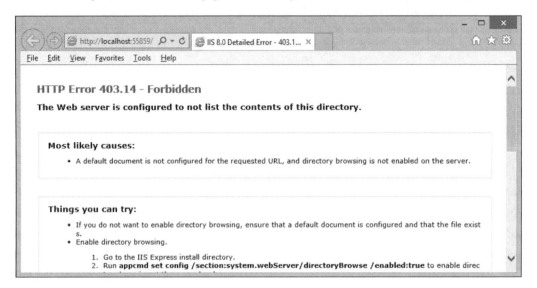

If you press *F5* (or select **DEBUG | Start Debugging** from the menu), you might see a dialog saying **Debugging Not Enabled**. Choose the **Run without debugging** (equivalent to *Ctrl + F5*) option and click on the **OK** button to continue. We will explore the debugging options of a WCF service later. Until then, we will continue to use *Ctrl + F5* to start the website without debugging.

IIS Express

At this point, you should have the `HostExpressServer` site up and running. This site actually runs inside IIS Express. IIS Express is a lightweight, self-contained version of IIS optimized for developers. This web server is intended to be used by developers only and has functionality similar to that of the **Internet Information Services (IIS)** server. It also has some limitations, for example, it only supports the HTTP and HTTPS protocols.

When a new website is created within Visual Studio, IIS Express will automatically assign a port for it. You can find your website's port in the **Properties** window of your website, as shown in the following screenshot:

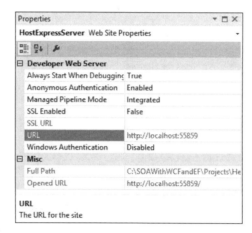

IIS Express is normally started from within Visual Studio when you need to debug or unit test a web project. If you really need to start it from outside of Visual Studio, you can use a command-line statement in the following format:

```
"C:\Program Files\IIS Express\iisexpress" /path:c:\myapp\ /port:[your_
port] /clr:v4.0
```

For our website, the statement should be as follows:

```
"C:\Program Files\IIS Express\iisexpress" /path:C:\SOAwithWCFandEF\
Projects\HelloWorld\HostExpressServer /port:55859 /clr:v4.0
```

 iisexpress.exe is located under your Program Files\ IIS Express\ directory. In an x64 system, it should be under your Program Files (x86)\ IIS Express\ directory.

Modifying the Web.config file

Although we can start the website now, it is only an empty site. Currently, it does not host our HelloWorldService website. This is because we haven't specified which service this website should host or an entry point for this website.

To specify which service our website will host, we can add a `.svc` file to the website. From .NET 4.0 onwards, we can also use the file-less (svc-less) activation service to accomplish this. In this section, we will take the file-less approach to specify the service.

Now, let's modify the `Web.config` file of the website to host our `HelloWorldService` (WCF service). Open the `Web.config` file of the website and change it to the following:

```xml
<?xml version="1.0"?>
<!--
  For more information on how to configure your ASP.NET application,
please visit
  http://go.microsoft.com/fwlink/?LinkId=169433
  -->
<configuration>
  <system.web>
    <compilation debug="true" targetFramework="4.5"/>
    <httpRuntime targetFramework="4.5"/>
  </system.web>

  <system.serviceModel>
    <serviceHostingEnvironment >
      <serviceActivations>
        <add factory="System.ServiceModel.Activation.
ServiceHostFactory"
        relativeAddress="./HostExpressServer/HelloWorldService.svc"
        service="HelloWorldService.HelloWorldService"/>
      </serviceActivations>
    </serviceHostingEnvironment>
    <behaviors>
      <serviceBehaviors>
        <behavior>
          <serviceMetadata httpGetEnabled="true"/>
        </behavior>
      </serviceBehaviors>
    </behaviors>
  </system.serviceModel>

</configuration>
```

Note that the `system.serviceModel` node is the only code that we have manually added to the `Web.config` file.

The `httpGetEnabled` behavior is essential because we want other applications to be able to locate the metadata of this service via HTTP. Without the metadata, the client applications can't generate the proxy and thus won't be able to use the service.

The following is a brief explanation of the other elements in this configuration file:

- The `configuration` node is the root node of the file.

- The `system.serviceModel` node is the top node for all the WCF service-specific settings.

- The `serviceHostingEnvironment` node is used to specify the hosting environment.

- The `serviceActivations` node is where you specify the service name and its relative address. This configuration element allows you to define the virtual service activation settings that map to your WCF service types. This makes it possible to activate services hosted in WAS/IIS without a `.svc` file.

- Within the `serviceBehaviors` node, you can define specific behaviors for a service. In our example, we have specified one behavior, which enables the service metadata exchange for the service.

Starting the host application

Now, if you start the website by pressing *Ctrl + F5* (don't use *F5* or the menu option **DEBUG | Start Debugging** until we discuss these later), you will still see the same empty website with the same error. However, this time we have a service hosted within this website, so just append `HostExpressServer/HelloWorldService.svc` after the address (it should look something like `http://localhost:55859/HostExpressServer/HelloWorldService.svc`). Then, you will get the description of this service, that is, how to get the `wsdl` file of this service and how to create a client to consume this service. You should see a page similar to the one shown in the following screenshot:

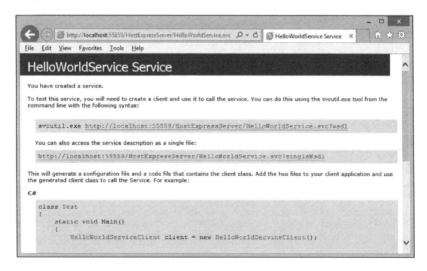

Now, click on the WSDL link on this page and you will get the WSDL XML file for this service. The wsdl file gives all of the contract information for this service. In the next section, we will use this wsdl file to generate a proxy for our client application.

Creating a client to consume the WCF service

Now that we have successfully created and hosted a WCF service, we need a client to consume the service. We will create a C# client application to consume HelloWorldService.

In this section, we will create a Windows console application to call the WCF service.

Creating the client application project

First, we need to create a console application project and add it to the solution. Follow these steps to create the console application:

1. In the **Solution Explorer**, right-click on the solution **HelloWorld** and select **Add | New Project...** from the context menu. The **Add New Project** dialog window should appear, as shown in the following screenshot:

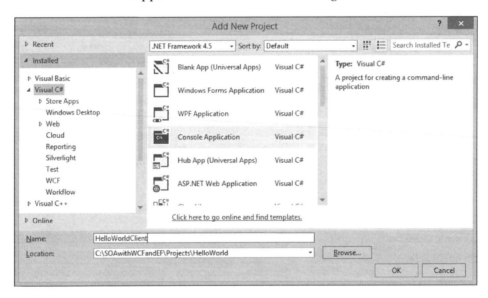

2. Select **Visual C# | Console Application** as the template, change the project name from the default value of `ConsoleApplication1` to `HelloWorldClient`, and leave the **Location** field as `C:\SOAwithWCFandEF\Projects\HelloWorld`. Click on the **OK** button. The new client project has now been created and added to the solution.

Generating the proxy and configuration files

In order to consume a SOAP WCF service, a client application must first obtain or generate a proxy class.

We also need a configuration file to specify things such as the binding of the service, address of the service, and contract.

To generate these two files, we can use the `SvcUtil.exe` tool from the command line. You can follow these steps to generate the two files:

1. Start the service by pressing *Ctrl + F5* or by selecting the menu option **DEBUG | Start Without Debugging** (at this point, your startup project should still be `HostExpressServer`; if not, you need to set this to be the startup project).

2. After the service has been started, open a command-line window, change the directory to your client application folder (that is, `C:\SOAwithWCFandEF\Projects\HelloWorld\HelloWorldClient`), and then run the command-line `SvcUtil.exe` tool with the following syntax (`SvcUtil.exe` might be in a different directory in your machine and you need to substitute `55859` with your service hosting port):

```
"C:\Program Files\Microsoft SDKs\Windows\v8.1A\bin\NETFX 4.5.1
Tools\SvcUtil.exe" http://localhost:55859/HostExpressServer/
HelloWorldService.svc?wsdl /out:HelloWorldServiceRef.cs
/config:app.config
```

You will see an output similar to that shown in the following screenshot:

Here, two files have been generated—one for the proxy (`HelloWorldServiceRef.cs`) and the other for the configuration (`App.config`).

If you open the proxy file, you will see that the interface of the service (`IHelloWorldService`) is mimicked inside the proxy class and a client class (`HelloWorldServiceClient`) is created to implement this interface. Inside this client class, the implementation of the service operation (`GetMessage`) is only a wrapper that delegates the call to the actual service implementation of the operation.

Inside the configuration file, you will see the definitions of `HelloWorldService` such as the endpoint address, binding, timeout settings, and security behaviors of the service.

> You can also generate a proxy class within Visual Studio, which we will do later in this book, but behind the scenes the same `SvcUtil.exe` tool is used by Visual Studio to generate the proxy class.
>
> In addition to generating a static proxy class at design time, you can also create a proxy dynamically at runtime or call the service through a Channel Factory instead of a proxy. Beware, if you go with the Channel Factory approach, you might have to share your interface DLL with the clients.

Customizing the client application

Before we can run the client application, we still have some more work to do. Follow these steps to finish the customization:

1. When you switch to Visual Studio 2013, you will be asked to reload the App.config file, as it has been changed. Click on **Yes** to reload it.

2. Add the proxy file to the project. In the **Solution Explorer**, first select the **HelloWorldClient** project and click on **Show All Files** to show all the files. Now, under the HelloWorldClient folder, you will see the proxy file (HelloWorldServiceRef.cs). However, this file is not yet included in the project. Right-click on it and select **Include In Project** to include it in the client project. You can also use the menu **PROJECT | Add Existing Item...** (or the context menu **Add | Existing Item...**) to add it to the project.

3. Add a reference to the System.ServiceModel namespace. From the **Solution Explorer**, just right-click on the **HelloWorldClient** project, select **Add | Reference...**, and check **System.ServiceModel** under **Assemblies | Framework**. Then, click on the **OK** button to add the reference to the project.

4. Modify program.cs to call the service. In program.cs, add the following line to initialize the service client object:

```
var client = new HelloWorldServiceClient();
```

 Using the default constructor on HelloWorldServiceClient means that the client runtime will look for the default client endpoint in the App.config file, which is present due to the use of SvcUtil.

Then, we can call the GetMessage method of our newly created object just as we would do for any other object:

```
Console.WriteLine(client.GetMessage("Mike Liu"));
```

Pass your name as the parameter to the GetMessage method so that it prints out a message for you.

Running the client application

We are now ready to run the client program.

First, make sure that the service host application, `HostExpressServer`, has been started. If you have stopped it previously, start it now (you need to set `HostExpressServer` as the startup project and press *Ctrl + F5* to start it in the non-debugging mode, or you can just right-click on the **HostExpressServer** project and select **View in Browser (Internet Explorer)** from the context menu).

Then, from the **Solution Explorer**, right-click on the **HelloWorldClient** project, select **Set as StartUp Project**, and then press *Ctrl + F5* to run it.

You will see an output as shown in the following screenshot:

Setting the service application to autostart

As we know we have to start the service host application before we run the client program, we can make some changes to the solution to automate this task, that is, to automatically start the service immediately before we run the client program.

To do this, in the **Solution Explorer**, right-click on solution, select **Properties** from the context menu, and you will see the **Solution 'HelloWorld' Property Pages** dialog box:

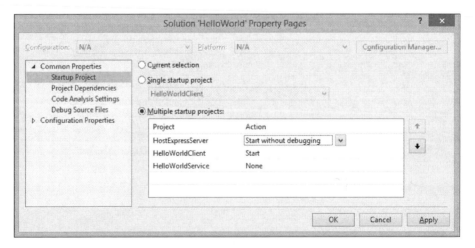

On this page, first select the **Multiple startup projects** option. Then, change the action of **HostExpressServer** to **Start without debugging**. Change **HelloWorldClient** to the same action.

 HostExpressServer must be above **HelloWorldClient**. If it is not, use the arrows to move it to the top.

To test it, first stop the service and then press *Ctrl* + *F5*. You will notice that HostExpressServer is started first, and then the client program runs without errors.

Note that this will only work inside Visual Studio IDE. If you start the client program from Windows Explorer (C:\SOAwithWCFandEF\Projects\HelloWorld\ HelloWorldClient\bin\Debug\HelloWorldClient.exe) without first starting the service, the service won't get started automatically and you will get an error message that says **There was no endpoint listening at http://localhost:55859/ HostExpressServer/HelloWorldService.svc**.

Summary

In this chapter, we implemented a basic WCF service, hosted it within IIS Express, and created a command-line program to reference and consume this basic WCF service. At this point, you should have a thorough understanding of what a WCF service is under the hood. You will benefit from this knowledge when you develop WCF services using Visual Studio WCF templates.

In the next chapter, we will explore more hosting options so that you can choose an appropriate hosting method for your WCF services.

2
Hosting the HelloWorld WCF Service

In the previous chapter, we built a basic HelloWorld WCF service and hosted it within IIS Express. In this chapter, we will explore more hosting options for WCF services, such as the following:

- Hosting a WCF service in a console application
- Hosting a WCF service in a Windows service application
- Hosting a WCF service in IIS using the HTTP protocol
- Hosting a WCF service in IIS using the TCP protocol
- Testing a WCF service

WCF hosting options

From the previous chapter, we know that a WCF service can be hosted within IIS Express. This method is the most convenient way to host a WCF service during the development stage.

Besides IIS Express, a WCF service can also be hosted in a managed application, such as a command-line application, a Windows service application, or on a website. This method is often referred to as a self-hosting method, as you have to write your own hosting application.

In addition to IIS Express and a managed application, IIS can also be used to host a WCF service. In fact, this is the most popular way to host a WCF service in production and, as we will learn soon in this chapter, you will benefit a lot from this hosting method.

In this chapter, we will explore all these options one by one in detail, except IIS Express, which has been covered in the previous chapter.

However, before we start exploring these options, I would like to point out some more options to host a WCF service:

- In Visual Studio, there is a built-in, general-purpose WCF service host (WcfSvcHost.exe), which makes the WCF host and development much easier. This host will be used by default if you create a WCF service using the WCF Service Library template. We will cover this feature in *Chapter 5, Implementing a Three-layer WCF Service*.

- Another option is to create a WCF service using the **WCF Service Application** template, in which case the WCF service project itself is a website and is ready to run within its own project folder. We will not cover this feature in this book as this kind of project is essentially a WCF service plus a WCF hosting website. You can try it and adopt it if it satisfies your needs.

- A WCF service can also be published to, and hosted in, the cloud. Microsoft Azure is such a platform. We will cover this feature in the next chapter.

Hosting the service in a managed application

First, let's create a .NET-managed application and host a WCF service within this application. The hosting application can be, for example, a command-line application, a Windows service application, a Windows Forms application, or a web application. This hosting method gives you full control over the lifetime of the WCF service. It is very easy to debug and deploy and supports all bindings and transports. The major drawbacks of these hosting methods are that you have to start the hosting application manually and that it provides only limited support for high availability, easy manageability, robustness, recoverability, versioning, and deployment scenarios. You could implement a hosting environment that provides all of these. However, it would cost you a lot in terms of effort and money to build something that is comparable to IIS.

Hosting the service in a console application

The following steps are needed to host a HelloWorldService in a command-line application. Note that these steps are very similar to the steps in one of the previous sections where we hosted a WCF service in IIS Express. However, the configuration file is called App.config and not Web.config.

If you want to host a WCF service in a Windows service application, a Windows Forms application, or a web application, you can follow the same steps that we have listed here, simply by creating the project using the appropriate project template:

1. Add a console application project to the solution:

   In the **Solution Explorer**, right-click on the solution file and go to **Add | New Project...** from the context menu. The **Add New Project** dialog box should appear. Select **Visual C# | Console Application** as the template. Then, change the name from `ConsoleApplication1` to `HostCmdLineApp` and click on the **OK** button. A new project is added to the solution.

2. Set the `HostCmdLineApp` project as the startup project:

   In the **Solution Explorer**, right-click on the **HostCmdLineApp** project and select **Set as StartUp Project** from the context menu. Alternatively, you can also select the project in the **Solution Explorer** and then select the menu item **PROJECT | Set as StartUp Project**.

3. Add a reference to the `HelloWorldService` project:

   In the **Solution Explorer**, right-click on the **HostCmdLineApp** project and go to **Add | Reference...** from the shortcut menu. The **Reference Manager** dialog box will appear. Click on **Projects** under the **Solution** tab, select and check the **HelloWorldService** project, and then click on **OK**. Now, **HelloWorldService** is under the `References` folder of this project.

4. Add a reference to `System.ServiceModel`:

   This reference is required as we will manually create a service host application and start and stop it in the steps that follow. In the **Solution Explorer** window, right-click on the **HostCmdLineApp** project and go to **Add | Reference...** from the context menu. You can also select the menu item **PROJECT | Add Reference...** to do this. Check **System.ServiceModel** from **Framework** under the **Assemblies** tab and click on **OK**.

5. Modify the configuration file to define the behavior of the service. We need to add a `serviceModel` node to enable the metadata for all services hosted within this application. The following is the full content of the `App.config` file:

   ```
   <?xml version="1.0" encoding="utf-8" ?>
   <configuration>
       <startup>
   ```

```
        <supportedRuntime version="v4.0"
          sku=".NETFramework,Version=v4.5" />
    </startup>

  <system.serviceModel>
    <behaviors>
      <serviceBehaviors>
        <behavior>
          <serviceMetadata httpGetEnabled="true"/>
        </behavior>
      </serviceBehaviors>
    </behaviors>
  </system.serviceModel>

</configuration>
```

6. Now, we need to modify the `Program.cs` file by writing some code in it to start and stop the WCF service. First, add a `using` statement, as follows:

```
using System.ServiceModel;
```

7. Then, add the following lines of code within the static `Main` method:

```
var host =
new ServiceHost(typeof(HelloWorldService.HelloWorldService),
new Uri("http://localhost:55859/HostCmdLineApp/HelloWorldService.
svc"));
host.Open();
Console.WriteLine("HelloWorldService is now running. ");
Console.WriteLine("Press any key to stop it ...");
Console.ReadKey();
host.Close();
```

As you can see from the preceding code snippet:

- We get the type of `HelloWorldService`
- We construct a base address for the WCF service and create a service host, passing the type and base address
- We call the `Open` method of the host to start the service
- To stop the service, we just call the `Close` method of the service host

The following code snippet shows the full content of the `Program.cs` file:

```
using System;
using System.Collections.Generic;
using System.Linq;
using System.Text;
using System.Threading.Tasks;
using System.ServiceModel;

namespace HostCmdLineApp
{
  class Program
  {
    static void Main(string[] args)
    {
      var host =
      new ServiceHost(typeof
      (HelloWorldService.HelloWorldService),
      new Uri("http://localhost:55859/
        HostCmdLineApp/HelloWorldService.svc"));
      host.Open();
      Console.WriteLine("HelloWorldService is
        now running. ");
      Console.WriteLine("Press any key to stop it
        ...");
      Console.ReadKey();
      host.Close();
    }
  }
}
```

After the project has been successfully built, you can press *Ctrl + F5* or just *F5* to start the service. You will see a command-line window indicating that `HelloWorldService` is available and waiting for requests:

Note that when you run the program, you might get an error message such as **System.ServiceModel.AddressAccessDeniedException, Your process does not have access rights to this namespace**. This is because Visual Studio has to register the namespace for the `HelloWorld` service and, by default, Windows runs applications under a limited-rights user account even when you are logged in to the computer as an administrator. You have to run Visual Studio as an administrator to solve this issue. Just right-click on the Visual Studio executable file, `devenv.exe`, and select **Run as administrator**, or change the **Privilege Level** property (from the **Compatibility** tab) to **Run this program as an administrator**, so you can always run Visual Studio as an administrator.

Alternatively, if you don't want to run Visual Studio as an administrator, you can manually register the namespace using tools such as `HttpSysConfig`. You can search for `Your process does not have access rights to this namespace` on the Internet, using your preferred search provider to see the various solutions for this issue.

Consuming the service hosted in a console application

To consume the service hosted in the previous console application, you can follow the same steps as described in the *Creating a client to consume the WCF service* section of *Chapter 1, Implementing a Basic HelloWorld WCF Service*; except here you will pass `http://localhost:55859/HostCmdLineApp/HelloWorldService.svc?wsdl` instead of `http://localhost:55859/HostExpressServer/HelloWorldService.svc?wsdl` to the `SvcUtil.exe` command when you generate the proxy class and the configuration file.

In fact, you can reuse the same client project because it is the same service, just hosted differently. To reuse the same client inside the `App.config` file of the `HelloWorldClient` project, consider the following line of code:

```
<endpoint address=
    "http://localhost:55859/HostExpressServer/HelloWorldService.svc"
```

Change this into the following line:

```
<endpoint address=
    "http://localhost:55859/HostCmdLineApp/HelloWorldService.svc"
```

Now, when you run the client program, it will use the WCF service hosted in the newly created command-line application and not the previously-created `HostExpressServer` application. You will get the same result as before when IIS Express was used to host the WCF service.

Hosting the service in a Windows service

If you don't want to manually start the WCF service, you can host it in a Windows service. In addition to the automatic start, the Windows service hosting gives you some other features, such as recovery ability when failures occur, security identity under which the service is running, and some degree of manageability. Just as with the self-hosting method, this hosting method also supports all bindings and transports. However, it also has some limitations. For example, you have to deploy it with an installer and it doesn't fully support high availability, easy manageability, versioning, and deployment scenarios.

The steps to create such a hosting application are very similar to what we did to host a WCF service in a command-line application, except that you have to create an installer to install the Windows service in the service control manager. You can refer to the following page on the Microsoft website in order to know how to create such a Windows service installer (`http://msdn.microsoft.com/en-us/library/9k985bc9(v=vs.110).aspx`).

Hosting the service in IIS using the HTTP protocol

It is a better option to host a WCF service within the **Internet Information Services (IIS)** server because IIS provides a robust, efficient, and secure host for WCF services. IIS also has better thread and process execution boundaries handling capability (in addition to many other features) compared to a regular managed application. Actually, web service development on IIS has been the domain of ASP.NET for a long time. When ASP.NET 1.0 was released, a web service framework was part of it. Microsoft leveraged the ASP.NET HTTP pipeline to make web services a reality on the Windows platform.

One thing you need to pay particular attention to when hosting WCF in IIS is that the process and/or application domain might be recycled if certain conditions are met. By default, the WCF service session's state is saved in memory; hence, all information will be lost in each recycle. This will be a big problem if you run a website in a load-balanced or web-farm (web-garden) environment. In this case, you should save the session's state in a SQL server database or in the ASP.NET state server.

Next, we will learn how to host `HelloWorldService` in IIS using the HTTP protocol. After this section, we will learn how to host it using the TCP protocol so that you can choose the appropriate protocol for your service according to your specific needs.

Preparing the folders and files

First, we need to prepare the folders and files for the host application. Follow the following steps to create the folders and copy the required files:

1. Create the folders:

    In Windows Explorer, create a new folder called HostIIS under
    C:\SOAwithWCFandEF\Projects\HelloWorld and a new subfolder
    called bin under this HostIIS folder. You should now have the following
    new folders: C:\SOAwithWCFandEF\Projects\HelloWorld\HostIIS and
    a bin folder inside the HostIIS folder.

2. Copy the files:

    Now copy the HelloWorldService.dll and HelloWorldService.pdb
    files from the HelloWorldService project folder located at
    C:\SOAwithWCFandEF\Projects\HelloWorld\HelloWorldService\bin\
    Debug\ to our new folder, C:\SOAwithWCFandEF\Projects\HelloWorld\
    HostIIS\bin.

3. Copy the configuration file:

    Copy Web.config from the HostExpressServer project folder located
    at C:\SOAwithWCFandEF\Projects\HelloWorld\ to our new folder,
    C:\SOAwithWCFandEF\Projects\HelloWorld\HostIIS.

    The files under the two new directories should now be something similar
    to the following (the parent folder here is C:\SOAwithWCFandEF\Projects\
    HelloWorld\):

    > Web.config under HostIIS
    >
    > HelloWorldService.dll and HelloWorldService.pdb under
    > HostIIS\bin

4. Create the Visual Studio solution folder:

    To make it easier to view and manage from the Visual Studio Solution
    Explorer, you can add a new solution folder, HostIIS, to the solution
    and add the Web.config file to this folder. Add another new solution
    folder, bin, under HostIIS and add the HelloWorldService.dll and
    HelloWorldService.pdb files under this bin folder. Your **Solution
    Explorer** should be as shown in the following screenshot:

5. Add the following post-build events to the `HelloWorldService` project;
    so next time, all the files will be copied automatically when the service
    project is built:

    ```
    xcopy "$(AssemblyName).dll" "C:\SOAwithWCFandEF\Projects\
    HelloWorld\HostIIS\bin" /Y
    xcopy "$(AssemblyName).pdb" "C:\SOAwithWCFandEF\Projects\
    HelloWorld\HostIIS\bin" /Y
    ```

6. Modify the `Web.config` file:

    The `Web.config` file that we have copied from `HostExpressServer`
    has a relative address, `HostExpressServer/HelloWorldService.svc`.
    For IIS hosting, we need to get rid of `HostExpressServer` from the path.
    Just open the `Web.config` file under the `HostIIS` folder and change the
    relative path from `HostExpressServer/HelloWorldService.svc` to
    `./HelloWorldService.svc`.

Starting IIS

By default, IIS is not running in Windows 7 and Windows 8. You can follow these steps to turn it on:

1. Go to **Control Panel | Programs | Turn Windows features on or off**.

2. From the **Windows Features** dialog box, check the checkbox for **Internet Information Services**.

3. Click on **OK**.

IIS is now running, but as Visual Studio was installed before IIS was turned on, IIS does not have any ASP.NET features enabled at this point. This means if you create an ASP.NET website within IIS now and try to access it, you will get an error.

There are two ways to enable WCF support from within IIS. The first is to follow these steps:

1. Run `aspnet_regiis.exe` to enable `aspnet_isapi` as a web service extension.

2. Run `ServiceModelReg.exe` to register the required script maps in IIS.

3. Manually create the application extension mapping and managed handlers for SVC files inside IIS.

The second and a much easier way is to reinstall the .NET Framework. After you have turned on the IIS features, as we just did previously in this section, uninstall and then reinstall .NET Framework 4.5.1. ASP.NET 4.5.1 will automatically be supported by IIS, once .NET 4.5.1 is reinstalled. I used this method as it is much easier.

> As the .NET Framework 4.5.1 SDK is included in Visual Studio 2013, you might need to repair Visual Studio 2013 to reinstall the .NET Framework 4.5.1 SDK, instead of uninstalling/reinstalling .NET Framework 4.5.1.
>
> If the latest .NET Framework installed on your machine is not 4.5.1 but 4.5.2 or later, uninstall and then reinstall 4.5.2 or later.

Enabling WCF services on Windows 8

On Windows 8, you have to enable WCF services in order to host a WCF service in IIS. You can go to **Control Panel | Turn Windows Features on or off**, and then check the checkbox for **HTTP Activation** by going to **.NET Framework 4.5 Advanced Features | WCF Services**. This will also turn on a few .NET 4.5 development features, including **.NET Extensibility 4.5**, **ASP.NET 4.5**, **ISAPI Extensions**, and **ISAPI Filters**.

Once you have turned on the **HTTP Activation** feature, you will be able to host a WCF service in IIS on a Windows 8 machine. In the next section, we will create a similar IIS application to host the `HelloWorldService` WCF service.

> You can explicitly enable WCF services on Windows 7 (**Control Panel | Turn Windows Features on or off | Microsoft .NET Framework 3.5.1 | Windows Communication Foundation HTTP Activation**), but WCF services will work fine on Windows 7 using the HTTP protocol even if you don't explicitly enable them.

Creating the IIS application

Next, we need to create an IIS application named `HelloWorldService`. Follow these steps to create an application in IIS:

1. Open the IIS Manager by going to **Control Panel | Administrative Tools** (or just type `start inetmgr` in the command prompt).

2. Expand the nodes of the tree in the left-hand side pane until the node named **Default Web Site** becomes visible.

3. Right-click on this node and select **Add Application...** from the context menu.

4. In the **Add Application** window, enter `HelloWorldService` in the **Alias** field.

5. Browse to or enter `C:\SOAwithWCFandEF\Projects\HelloWorld\HostIIS` in the **Physical path** field.

6. Leave **DefaultAppPool** as the **Application pool**. You can click on the **Select...** button to verify that this application pool is a .NET 4.0.30319 application pool. If it is not, you need to enable IIS to support .NET 4.0.30319, as described in the *Starting IIS* section. If you create your own application pool, make sure it is a .NET 4.0.30319 pool.

7. Finally, to finish adding the application, click on the **OK** button.

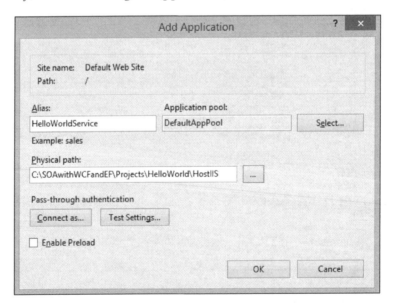

Starting the WCF service in IIS

Once you have copied the files to the `HostIIS` folder and have created the IIS application, the WCF service is ready to be called by the clients. When a WCF service is hosted within IIS, we don't need to explicitly start the service. As with other normal web applications, IIS will control the lifetime of the service. As long as the IIS service is started, client programs can access it.

> The deployment method we are learning about here is only one of the few deployment options to deploy a WCF service to IIS. We will discuss more deployment methods in the next chapter.

Testing the WCF service hosted in IIS using the HTTP protocol

To test the WCF service, open an Internet browser and enter the following URL in the address bar of the browser. You will get a screen that is almost identical to the one you got previously: `http://localhost/HelloWorldService/HelloWorldService.svc`.

Instead of the service description page, you may get an error page saying **Cannot read configuration file due to insufficient permissions**, such as the one shown in the following screenshot:

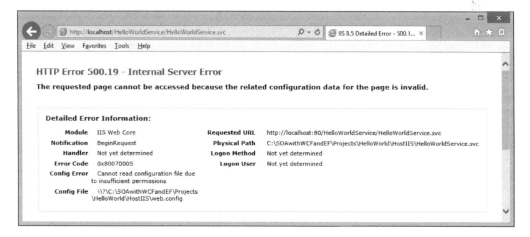

This is because the `HelloWorldService` hosting folder is not within the usual IIS's default hosting location, `C:\inetpub\wwwroot`, which by default is accessible to the IIS server. To make the `HelloWorldService` accessible to the IIS server, you just need to give your default application pool identity, normally `applicationPoolIdentity(IIS_IUSRS)`, read access to the `C:\SOAwithWCFandEF\Projects\HelloWorld\HostIIS` service folder. Here we will go one step further, that is, we will grant the `IIS_IUSRS` users read access to the parent folder, `C:\SOAwithWCFandEF\Projects\HelloWorld`, as later on we will host more services within this folder and we don't want to grant permissions to each subfolder.

The following screenshot shows how the IIS default app pool identity users' read access is given to the parent folder of the service folder:

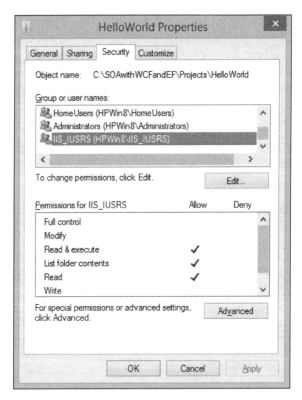

Different from being hosted within IIS Express, here you don't need to add a port after the host because it is now hosted in IIS with the default HTTP port, 80. This also means that you can access the service using your real computer (host) name or IP address and even outside of your computer if your computer is in a network. Two example URLs are as follows:

- `http://[your_pc_name]/HelloWorldService/HelloWorldService.svc`
- `http://[your_pc_name].[your_company_domain].com/ HelloWorldService/HelloWorldService.svc`

We can reuse the client program that we created earlier to consume this WCF service hosted within IIS. Refer to the following endpoint address:

```
<endpoint address=
  "http://localhost:55859/HostCmdLineapp/HelloWorldService/"
```

Change this to the following:

```
<endpoint address=
  "http://localhost/HelloWorldService/HelloWorldService.svc"
```

Now, when you run this client program, it will use the WCF service hosted within IIS instead of the previously created `HostCmdLineApp` application. You will get the same result as before, when the service was hosted in our own host application.

Hosting the service in IIS using the TCP protocol

Hosting WCF services in IIS using the HTTP protocol gives the best interoperability to the service, because the HTTP protocol is supported everywhere today. However, sometimes interoperability might not be an issue. For example, the service may be invoked only within your network with all Microsoft clients only. In this case, hosting the service by using the TCP protocol might be a better solution.

Benefits of hosting a WCF service using the TCP protocol

Compared to HTTP, there are a few benefits in hosting a WCF service using the TCP protocol:

- It supports connection-based, stream-oriented delivery services with end-to-end error detection and correction

- It is the fastest WCF binding for scenarios that involve communication between different machines

- It supports duplex communication, so it can be used to implement duplex contracts

- It has a reliable data delivery capability (this is applied between two TCP/IP nodes and is not the same thing as WS-ReliableMessaging, which applies between endpoints)

Preparing the folders and files

First, we need to prepare the folders and files for the host application, just as we did for hosting the service using the HTTP protocol. We will use the previous HTTP hosting application as the base to create the new TCP hosting application:

1. Create the folders:

    In Windows Explorer, create a new folder called `HostIISTcp` under `C:\SOAwithWCFandEF\Projects\HelloWorld` and a new subfolder called `bin` under the `HostIISTcp` folder. You should now have the following new folders: `C:\SOAwithWCFandEF\Projects\HelloWorld\HostIISTcp` and a `bin` folder inside the `HostIISTcp` folder.

2. Copy the files:

    Now, copy all the files from the `HostIIS` hosting application folder at `C:\SOAwithWCFandEF\Projects\HelloWorld\HostIIS` to the new folder that we created at `C:\SOAwithWCFandEF\Projects\HelloWorld\HostIISTcp`.

3. Create the Visual Studio solution folder:

    To make it easier to be viewed and managed from the Visual Studio Solution Explorer, you can add a new solution folder, `HostIISTcp`, to the solution and add the `Web.config` file to this folder. Add another new solution folder, `bin`, under `HostIISTcp` and add the `HelloWorldService.dll` and `HelloWorldService.pdb` files under this `bin` folder.

4. Add the following post-build events to the `HelloWorldService` project, so next time, all the files will be copied automatically when the service project is built:

```
xcopy "$(AssemblyName).dll" "C:\SOAwithWCFandEF\Projects\
HelloWorld\HostIISTcp\bin" /Y
xcopy "$(AssemblyName).pdb" "C:\SOAwithWCFandEF\Projects\
HelloWorld\HostIISTcp\bin" /Y
```

5. Modify the `Web.config` file:

The `Web.config` file that we have copied from `HostIIS` is using the default `basicHttpBinding` as the service binding. To make our service use the TCP binding, we need to change the binding to TCP and add a TCP base address. Open the `Web.config` file and add the following node to it under the `<system.serviceModel>` node:

```xml
<services>
  <service name="HelloWorldService.HelloWorldService">
    <endpoint address="" binding="netTcpBinding"
    contract="HelloWorldService.IHelloWorldService"/>
    <host>
      <baseAddresses>
        <add baseAddress=
        "net.tcp://localhost/HelloWorldServiceTcp/"/>
      </baseAddresses>
    </host>
  </service>
</services>
```

In this new `services` node, we have defined one service called `HelloWorldService.HelloWorldService`. The base address of this service is `net.tcp://localhost/HelloWorldServiceTcp/`. Remember, we have defined the host activation relative address as `./HelloWorldService.svc`, so we can invoke this service from the client application with the following URL: `http://localhost/HelloWorldServiceTcp/HelloWorldService.svc`.

For the file-less WCF activation, if no endpoint is defined explicitly, HTTP and HTTPS endpoints will be defined by default. In this example, we would like to expose only one TCP endpoint, so we have added an endpoint explicitly (as soon as this endpoint is added explicitly, the default endpoints will not be added). If you don't add this TCP endpoint explicitly here, the TCP client that we will create in the next section will still work, but on the client `config` file you will see three endpoints instead of one and you will have to specify which endpoint you are using in the client program.

The following is the full content of the `Web.config` file:

```xml
<?xml version="1.0"?>
<!--
  For more information on how to configure your ASP.NET
  application, please visit
  http://go.microsoft.com/fwlink/?LinkId=169433
  -->
<configuration>
  <system.web>
    <compilation debug="true" targetFramework="4.5"/>
    <httpRuntime targetFramework="4.5" />
  </system.web>

  <system.serviceModel>
    <serviceHostingEnvironment >
      <serviceActivations>
        <add factory="System.ServiceModel.Activation.
ServiceHostFactory"
          relativeAddress="./HelloWorldService.svc"
          service="HelloWorldService.HelloWorldService"/>
      </serviceActivations>
    </serviceHostingEnvironment>

    <behaviors>
      <serviceBehaviors>
        <behavior>
          <serviceMetadata httpGetEnabled="true"/>
        </behavior>
      </serviceBehaviors>
    </behaviors>

    <services>
      <service name="HelloWorldService.HelloWorldService">
        <endpoint address="" binding="netTcpBinding"
        contract="HelloWorldService.IHelloWorldService"/>
        <host>
          <baseAddresses>
            <add baseAddress=
            "net.tcp://localhost/HelloWorldServiceTcp/"/>
          </baseAddresses>
        </host>
      </service>
    </services>
  </system.serviceModel>

</configuration>
```

Enabling the TCP WCF activation for the host machine

By default, the TCP WCF activation service is not enabled on your machine. This means your IIS server won't be able to host a WCF service with the TCP protocol. You can follow these steps to enable the TCP activation for WCF services:

1. Go to **Control Panel | Programs | Turn Windows features on or off**.

2. Expand the **Microsoft .Net Framework 3.5.1** node on Windows 7 or **.Net Framework 4.5 Advanced Services** on Windows 8.

3. Check the checkbox for **Windows Communication Foundation Non-HTTP Activation** on Windows 7 or **TCP Activation** on Windows 8.

   The following screenshot depicts the options required to enable WCF activation on Windows 7:

The following screenshot depicts the options required to enable TCP WCF activation on Windows 8:

4.   Repair the .NET Framework:

After you have turned on the TCP WCF activation, you have to repair .NET. Just go to **Control Panel**, click on **Uninstall a Program**, select **Microsoft .NET Framework 4.5.1**, and then click on **Repair**.

Creating the IIS application

Next, we need to create an IIS application named `HelloWorldServiceTcp` to host the WCF service, using the TCP protocol. Follow these steps to create this application in IIS:

1.   Open IIS Manager.
2.   Add a new IIS application, `HelloWorldServiceTcp`, pointing to the `HostIISTcp` physical folder under your project's folder.
3.   Choose **DefaultAppPool** as the application pool for the new application. Again, make sure your default app pool is a .NET 4.0.30319 application pool.

4. Enable the TCP protocol for the application. Right-click on **HelloWorldServiceTcp**, select **Manage Application | Advanced Settings**, and then add `net.tcp` to **Enabled Protocols**. Make sure you use all lowercase letters and separate it from the existing HTTP protocol with a comma.

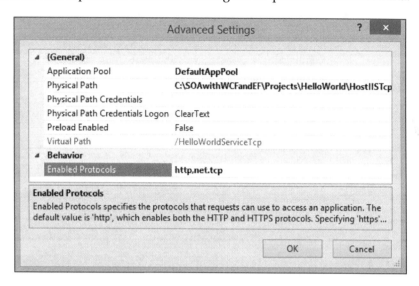

Now the service is hosted in IIS using the TCP protocol. To view the WSDL of the service, browse to `http://localhost/HelloWorldServiceTcp/HelloWorldService.svc` and you should see the service description and a link to the WSDL of the service.

Testing the WCF service hosted in IIS using the TCP protocol

Now, we have the service hosted in IIS using the TCP protocol; let's create a new test client to test it:

1. Add a new console application project to the solution, named `HelloWorldClientTcp`.

2. Add a reference to `System.ServiceModel` in the new project.

3. Add a service reference to the WCF service in the new project, naming the reference `HelloWorldServiceRef` and use the URL `http://localhost/HelloWorldServiceTcp/HelloWorldService.svc?wsdl`.

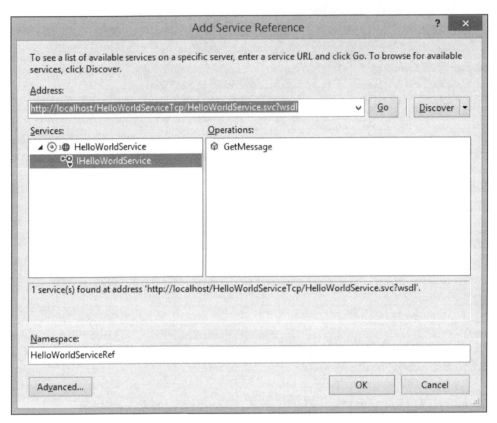

4. You can still use the `SvcUtil.exe` command-line tool to generate the proxy and config files for the service hosted with TCP, just as we did in previous sections. Actually, behind the scenes Visual Studio is also calling `SvcUtil.exe` to generate the proxy and config files.

5. Add the following code to the `Main` method of the new project:

```
var client = new HelloWorldServiceRef.HelloWorldServiceClient ();
Console.WriteLine(client.GetMessage("Mike Liu"));
```

6. Finally, set the new project as the startup project.

Now, if you run the program, you will get the same result as before; however, this time the service is hosted in IIS using the TCP protocol.

Summary

In this chapter, we hosted the HelloWorld WCF service in several different ways. We created a console application to host the service so that we can have full control of the hosting process. We also created two IIS applications to host the service, one with the HTTP protocol and another with the TCP protocol.

In the next chapter, we will learn how to publish a WCF service so that you know how to deploy a WCF service to a production environment.

3
Deploying the HelloWorld WCF Service

In the previous chapters, we built a basic HelloWorld WCF service and hosted it in a few different ways. In this chapter, we will learn how to deploy/publish this service.

In this chapter, we will cover the following topics:

- Publishing from Visual Studio to an on-premises computer
- Publishing from Visual Studio to the cloud
- Publishing using a deployment package

Publishing the HelloWorldService from Visual Studio

A WCF service can be published to another specific environment either from within Visual Studio or via a deployment package. The first one, publishing a WCF service right from within Visual Studio, works great if you need to deploy your WCF service to a test environment. The second one, deploying the WCF service using a deployment package, is often desirable when you need to deploy a service to staging or production environments. In this section, we will learn how to publish the HelloWorld WCF service with Visual Studio. In the next section, we will learn how to deploy the service using a deployment package.

Publishing from Visual Studio to an on-premise computer

From Visual Studio, you can publish a WCF service to IIS on your local computer, to IIS on another computer in your network, to the filesystem, to an FTP site, or to the cloud. In this section, we will publish the existing HelloWorld WCF service to an IIS server on a computer in your network, either your local computer or a remote computer. We will call this computer as the target computer going forward in this chapter. We will call the computer the service is publishing from as the source computer or the development computer.

> You can follow the same steps to publish the service to the
> filesystem, or to an FTP site. Later in this chapter, we will
> learn how to publish to the cloud.

Creating the publishing project

To publish the HelloWorld service to IIS, we first need to create a new hosting website to host the service and then publish from this new hosting website to the target computer.

We can reuse the existing website, HostExpressServer, but if you do so, as the relative address in the configuration file of the website HostExpressServer includes the word HostExpressServer, the final service endpoint address will also include this word, in addition to the published site name. This makes the endpoint address much longer and more confusing.

You can follow these steps to create the new hosting website:

1. Start Visual Studio as an administrator and open the HelloWorld solution.

2. Add a new website to the solution:

   In the **Solution Explorer**, right-click on the solution file and select **Add | New Web Site...** from the context menu. The **Add New Web Site** dialog box should appear. Select **Visual C# | ASP.NET Empty Web Site** as the template. Then, change the web location from the default one to C:\SOAwithWCFandEF\Projects\HelloWorld\HostBaseServer and click on the **OK** button. A new website is added to the solution.

3. Add a reference to the `HelloWorldService` project:

   In the **Solution Explorer**, right-click on the **HostBaseServer** project and select **Add | Reference...** from the shortcut menu. The **Reference Manager** dialog box will appear. Click on **Projects** under the **Solution** tab, select and check the **HelloWorldService** project, and then click on **OK**. Now, **HelloWorldService** is under the **References** folder of this project.

4. Copy the configuration file:

   Copy/overwrite the `Web.config` file from the `HostIIS` project folder to the new `HostBaseServer` project folder. We will reuse the same configuration file for the new website as the HostIIS web application.

Publishing the HelloWorldService

Now that we have created the publishing project, we can publish the service to an IIS instance on another computer from Visual Studio.

You can follow these steps to publish the service:

1. From the Visual Studio solution explorer, right-click on the new publishing website, **HostBaseServer**, then select **Publish Web Site** from the context menu. The **Publish Web** dialog box should appear:

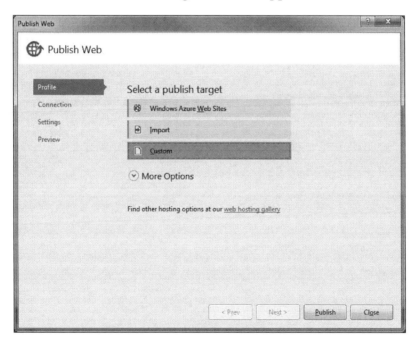

2. The **Profile** tab on the left-hand side of the dialog box should be selected. If not, click on the link **Profile** to select it.

3. In this dialog box, click on the **Custom** link in the publish target list. The **New Custom Profile** dialog box should appear.

4. Enter `HelloWorldLocal` as the profile name in this dialog box. Then, click on the **OK** button to close the **New Custom Profile** dialog box.

5. The wizard should automatically advance to the **Connection** step on the **Publish Web** dialog box. Enter the target computer name as the server name (or `localhost` if publishing to your local machine) and `Default Web Site/HelloWorldLocal` as the site name. Leave the default **Web Deploy** as the **Publish method**. Click on the **Validate Connection** button to make sure the entered server name and site name are correct.

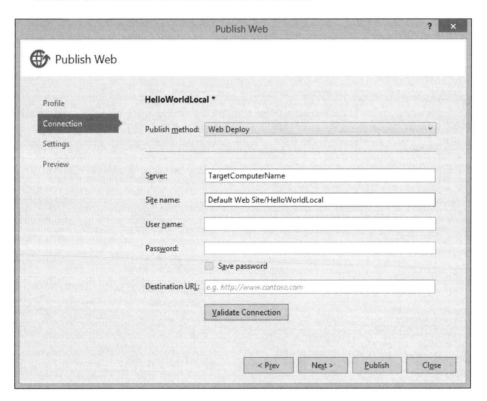

6. Click on the **Next** button to advance to the **Settings** step, then click on **Next** again to advance to the **Preview** step. On the **Preview** step, click on the **Start Preview** button to preview the files that will be deployed. As you can see from the following screenshot, two files will be deployed to the IIS server on the target computer.

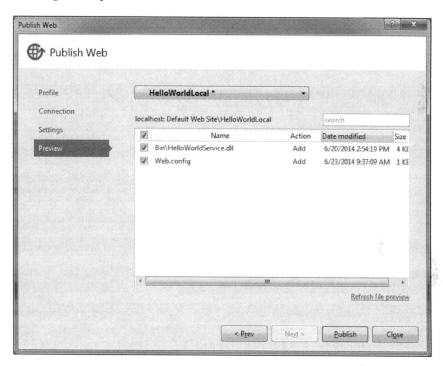

7. Click on the **Publish** button to publish the service. The existing `HelloWorld` WCF service should be published to the IIS server on the target machine with an application name, `HelloWorldLocal`.

If you try to publish to a remote computer in your network, you need to have Web Deploy installed on the remote computer, otherwise you will get an error that the Web deployment task failed (**Could not connect to the remote computer ("computer name")**). On the remote computer, make sure that Web Deploy is installed and that the required process ("Web Management Service") is started.

Testing the service

Now that we have published the service to the local IIS instance, we can test it with a browser or with the existing test client.

Within a browser, just enter the following address and you should see the service description page, same as before (you need to replace `TargetComputerName` with your remote computer name or with localhost if you have published to your local computer): `http://TargetComputerName/HelloWorldLocal/HelloWorldService.svc`.

To test the service with the existing client, just change the endpoint address to the following:

```
<endpoint address=
    "http://TargetComputerName/HelloWorldLocal/HelloWorldService.svc"
```

 Now, when you run this client program, it will use the WCF service hosted in IIS on the target computer, which we just published from Visual Studio.

Publishing to the cloud

Besides publishing a WCF service to a computer on-premises, we can also publish the service to the cloud. Unlike an on-premise service, which can only be accessed within the network, a service that is hosted in the cloud can be accessed over the Internet by clients more easily. You can also take advantage of the cloud infrastructure so that you don't need to worry about them. In this section, we will learn how to publish our WCF service to the cloud.

Before publishing to the cloud, you need to make sure you have a Microsoft Azure account. You can go to the Microsoft Azure home page `http://account.windowsazure.com/` to create a new account. If you are a MSDN subscriber, you can just enable your Microsoft Azure account and benefits.

Creating the profile to be published

We first need to create a new profile to publish the existing `HelloWorld` WCF service to the cloud. You can follow these steps to create this profile:

1. Start Visual Studio as an administrator and open the `HelloWorld` solution.

2. From the Visual Studio solution explorer, right-click on the **HostBaseServer** project, select **Publish Web Site**, and the **Publish Web** dialog should pop up.

3. As there is already a profile (`HelloWorldLocal`) defined in this project, you will be prompted to publish with this existing profile. We need to create a new profile as this time we want to publish to the cloud. So, click on the **Profile** link on the left-hand side of the dialog box and pick **<New Custom Profile ...>** from the profiles drop-down list.

4. Enter `HelloWorldCloud` as the profile name and click on the **OK** button to close the **New Custom Profile** dialog box.

Creating the cloud website

To publish to the cloud, we need to sign in to the cloud and select or create a cloud website. You can follow these steps to accomplish this task:

1. At this point, the wizard should have advanced to the **Connection** step automatically and it assumes this is a custom deployment to an on-premises server. As we intend to deploy to the cloud, click on the **Profile** link again to go back to the **Profile** step.

2. Now click on the **Windows Azure Web Sites** link as the publish target. After you click on this link, the **Select Existing Web Site** dialog will pop up. Within this dialog box, you need to sign in to Azure first. Click on the **Sign In...** button to sign in, as shown in following screenshot:

3. After signing in to Azure, choose an existing website if you have already created a website in Azure, otherwise you can click on the **New ...** button to create a new website. Here, we will create a new Azure website. Enter `HelloWorldCloud` as the **Site name** and choose your region. Then, click on the **Create** button to create the cloud website, as shown in following screenshot:

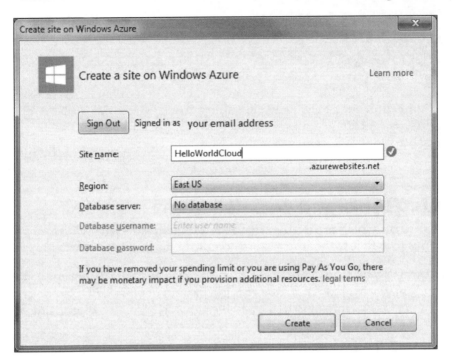

The site name must not be used by others, and it will be part of your WCF cloud service endpoint address URL.

As the site name, `HelloWorldCloud`, has been used in this book, obviously you cannot use it again. In this book, we will keep using this site for our example, and whenever you see it, you should substitute it with your own cloud website name.

Publishing the HelloWorldService to the cloud website

After you have clicked on the **Create** button, a new website will be created in the cloud. Next, we will publish the WCF service to this cloud website, using the following steps:

1. The wizard should have advanced to the **Connection** step automatically. Here, you can view the service hosting server, the site name of the service, the username, and password to log in to the server. Most importantly, you should copy and save the **Destination URL** of the service, which will be the end point to be used in the client application for your cloud service.

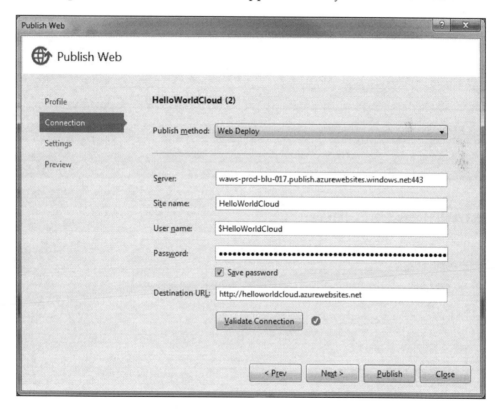

2. Click on the **Validate Connection** button to make sure this cloud service has been configured properly.

3. Now, click on **Next** until it reaches the **Preview** step. You can click on the **Start Preview** button to review the files that will be published to the cloud.

4. Finally, click on the **Publish** button to publish the service to the Azure cloud. An Internet explorer browser will pop up to tell you that the site has been created successfully.

Testing the service

Now that we have published the service to the cloud, we can test it with a browser or with the existing test client.

Within a browser, just enter following address and you should see the service description page, same as before: `http://helloworldcloud.azurewebsites.net/HelloWorldService.svc`.

 The site address of this end point is exactly the destination URL that we have copied from the publishing wizard.

To test it with the existing client, just change the endpoint address to the following:

```
<endpoint address=
    "http://helloworldcloud.azurewebsites.net/HelloWorldService.svc"
```

Now, when you run this client program, it will use the WCF service
hosted with Windows Azure in the cloud that we just published
from Visual Studio.

You can also log in to your Azure account management portal to view/change
settings for this cloud service.

In this section, we have published the HelloWorld WCF service
to the cloud as an Azure website. In addition to hosting a WCF
service in the cloud as a website, you can also create an Azure
cloud service directly from Visual Studio, or publish a WCF
service to the cloud as an Azure cloud service if you create your
WCF service using one of the WCF templates. We will create such
a WCF service in a following chapter, and at that time, you can try
to publish to the cloud as a cloud service.

Publishing the HelloWorldService using a deployment package

Now we have learned how to publish a WCF service right from within Visual Studio;
next we will learn how to deploy it by using a deployment package. This is often
desirable when you are deploying a service to staging or production environments,
as from Visual Studio you might not be able to access the staging or production
environment, for example, when the staging or production environment is outside a
firewall or in a different domain.

Creating the package

To deploy a WCF service with a package, we first need to create the package. You
can follow these steps to create a deployment package for the HelloWorld service.

1. Install Web Deploy. You need to have Microsoft Web Deploy installed on
    your computer in order to publish a website to a package. If you don't have
    it installed already, you can install Web Deploy Version 3.0 or any higher
    version from Microsoft's website.

2. Start Visual Studio as an administrator and open the HelloWorld solution.

3. From the Visual Studio solution explorer, right-click on the **HostBaseServer**
    project, select **Publish Web Site**, and the **Publish Web** dialog should pop up.

4. As there are already profiles defined in this project, you will be prompted to publish with one of the existing profiles. Again, we need to create a new profile, so click on the link **Profile** link on the left-hand side of the dialog box and pick **<New Custom Profile>** from the profile's drop-down list.

5. Enter `HelloWorldPackage` as the profile name and click on **OK** to close the **New Custom Profile** dialog box.

6. The wizard will advance to the **Connection** step automatically. **Web Deploy** is preselected for the **Publish method** as it assumes this is a custom deployment to an on-premise server. We want to create a package, not to deploy from Visual Studio, so select **Web Deploy Package** from the **Publish method** drop-down list.

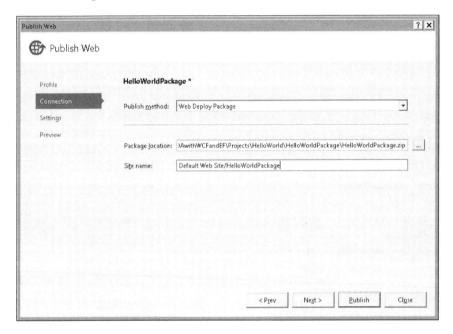

7. Enter `C:\SOAwithWCFandEF\Projects\HelloWorld\HelloWorldPackage\HelloWorldPackage.zip` as the package location and `Default Web Site/HelloWorldPackage` as the site name.

8. Click on the **Publish** button to create the package.

Installing the package

Now we have created the package; next we will install this package on the IIS server. You can install this package on your local computer or a remote computer and we will call this computer as the target computer in the following sections.

You can follow these steps to install this package:

1. First, make sure Web Deploy is installed on the target computer. Also, make sure that the version of the Web Deploy on the target computer is same as the one on the development computer.

2. Copy the package file, `HelloWorldPackage.zip`, from the development computer to the target computer.

3. Then, open the IIS manager.

4. Expand and select the **Default Web Site** node on the left-hand side of the **Connections** pane.

5. Click on **Import Application...** in the **Deploy** section on the bottom side of the **Actions** pane and on the right-hand side of the manager console.

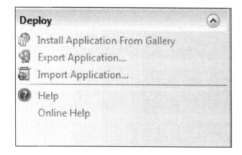

If the **Deploy** section is missing in the **Actions** pane in IIS manager, you can uninstall and then reinstall Web Deploy tool to fix it.

6. Now the **Import Application Package** dialog box should pop up. Choose the package ZIP file, `HelloWorldPackage.zip`, which was just copied from the development computer to this target computer.

7. Click on the **Next** button and accept the default selections of the package contents.

8. Then, leave the default `HelloWorldPackage` as the application path and click on **Next**.

9. If you have an existing website with the same name `HelloWorldPackage` on the IIS server, it will ask to overwrite existing files. Choose appending or deleting extra files and click on **Next** to continue.

10. The **Installation Progress and Summary** page should pop up to confirm that the package was installed successfully.

Testing the service

Now that we have installed the service to another computer with a package, we can test it with a browser or with the existing test client.

Do the same as we did before: within a browser, just enter the following address and you should see the service description page (you need to replace `TargetComputerName` with your remote computer name or with `localhost` if you have installed the package to your local computer): `http://TargetComputerName/HelloWorldPackage/HelloWorldService.svc`.

To test it with the existing client, just change the endpoint address to the following:

```
<endpoint address=
  "http://TargetComputerName/HelloWorldPackage/HelloWorldService.svc"
```

 Now, when you run this client program, it will use the WCF service hosted within IIS, which we just installed from the package.

Summary

In this chapter, we have published the `HelloWorld` WCF service from Visual Studio to an on-premises computer and to the cloud. We have also created a WCF service package and then installed it to another computer. In the next chapter, we will learn how to debug a WCF service so that you can troubleshoot it if there are any problems.

4

Debugging the HelloWorld WCF Service

In the previous chapters, we built a basic `HelloWorld` WCF service and hosted it in a few different ways. We have also deployed this service to an on-premise machine and to the cloud. In this chapter, we will learn how to debug WCF services.

In this chapter, we will cover the following topics:

- Debugging a WCF service from a client application
- Directly debugging a WCF service
- Attaching the debugger to a running WCF service process
- Debugging a WCF service hosted in the cloud

Debugging a WCF service from a client application

Now that we have a fully working WCF service, let's have a look at the debugging options of this service. We will use our original client, `HelloWorldClient`, to discuss the debugging options; so, in the following sections, whenever you come across terms such as client, the client program, or the client application, refer to `HelloWorldClient`.

The first and the most common scenario is to start a client program in the debug mode and then step into our WCF service. Next, we will try this option to debug the service.

Starting the debugging process

Follow these steps to start the debugging process from the client application:

1. Start Visual Studio as an administrator and open the HelloWorld solution.

2. Change the client program's configuration file to call HelloWorldService hosted within IIS Express. Open the App.config file inside the HelloWorldClient project and set the address of the endpoint to http://localhost:55859/HostExpressServer/HelloWorldService.svc.

> Remember that the port number can be different in your environment. You should change it to the port that IIS Express has assigned to your service.

3. In the **Solution Explorer**, right-click on the **HelloWorldClient** project and select **Set as Startup Project** from the context menu.

4. Open the Program.cs file inside the HelloWorldClient project and set a breakpoint at the following line:

```
var client = new HelloWorldServiceClient();
```

Your screen will look as follows:

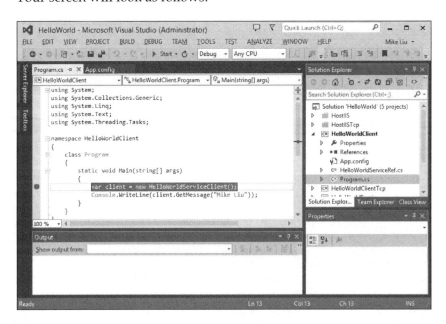

5. Now, press *F5* or select menu options **DEBUG | Start Debugging** to start the debugging process.

Debugging the client application

When we start debugging our application, the cursor stops at the breakpoint line, as you can see in the following **HelloWorld (Debugging)** screenshot. The active line is highlighted, and you can examine the variables just as you can do for any other C# applications:

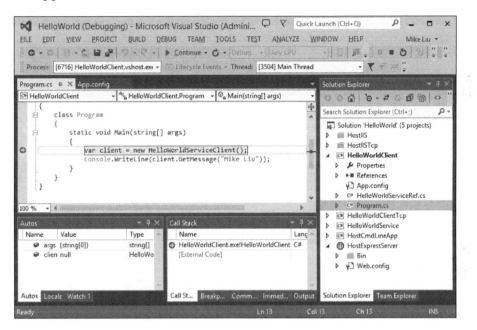

At this point, the channel between the client and the hosting server (HostExpressServer) has not been created. Press *F10* or select menu options **DEBUG | Step Over** to skip over this line. If you don't have the menu options **DEBUG | Step Over**, you might have to reset your development environment settings through the menu options **TOOLS | Import and Export Settings...** (check appropriate options in **Import and Export Settings Wizard**).

Now, the line following the highlighted line in the preceding screenshot should be active and highlighted. At this point, we have a valid client object, which contains all of the information related to the WCF service such as the channel, the endpoint, the members, and the security credentials.

The following screenshot shows the details of the endpoint of the `client` variable:

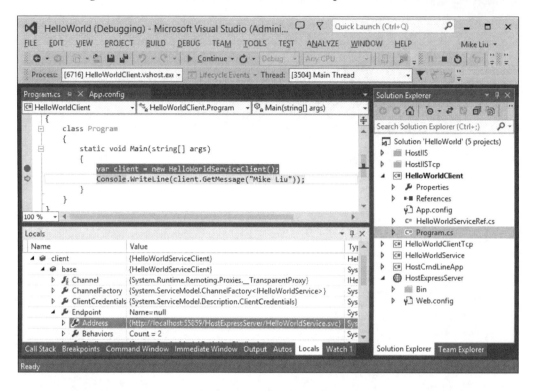

Stepping into the WCF service

Now, press *F11* to step into the service code. The cursor now resides on the opening bracket of the `GetMessage` method of `HelloWorldService`. You can now examine the variables and their values inside `HelloWorldService` just as you would for any other program. Keep pressing *F10* and you should eventually come back to the client program.

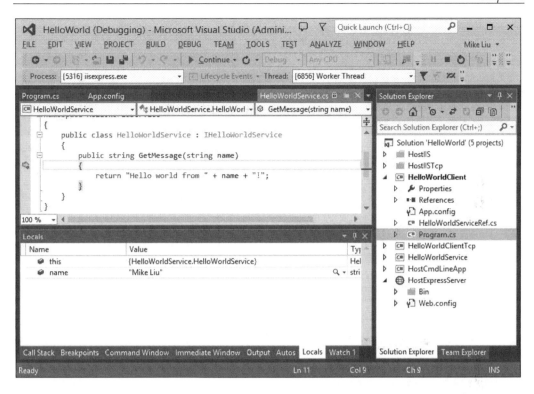

However, if you stay inside the `HelloWorldService` project for too long, when you come back to the `HelloWorldClient` project, you will get an exception which says that it has timed out. This is because, by default, the `HelloWorldClient` will call the `HelloWorldService` and wait for a response for a maximum time of one minute. You can add an attribute, `sendTimeout/receiveTimeout`, to the binding and set it to a higher value in the `App.config` configuration file, depending on your own needs.

You might also have noticed that you don't see the output window of the `HelloWorldClient`. This is because, in the debug mode, once a console application finishes, the console window is closed. You have to add one line at the end of `Program.cs` to wait for a keystroke so that you can look at the output before it closes. You can do this by adding the following line of code:

```
Console.ReadKey();
```

You can step into the service from the client only if TOOLS own the source code of the service and the service is hosted on the same machine as the client program. In certain environments, you might not be able to step inside the service directly from the client application due to some debugging settings of your Visual Studio or IIS Express. In this case, you can use the techniques we will learn in the *Attaching the debugger to a running WCF service process* section, later in this chapter, to debug the service.

Directly debugging the WCF service

In the previous section, we started debugging the client program and then stepped into the service program. Sometimes, we might not want to run the client application in the debug mode. For example, if the client application is a third-party product, we won't have the source code, or the client application might run on a different machine altogether. In such cases, if we need to we can run the service in the debugging mode and debug only the service.

Starting the WCF service in the debugging mode

To start the `HelloWorldService` in the debug mode, first set the `HostExpressServer` as the startup project. Then, open `HelloWorldService.cs` from the `HelloWorldService` project, and set a breakpoint on the first line inside the `GetMessage` method.

Now, press *F5* to start the service in the debugging mode, it will wait for requests. A browser will open, displaying the **403.14** error page. If you go back to the Visual Studio IDE, you will find that a new solution folder, **Script Documents**, has been added to the solution. This folder is the actual content of the web page being displayed in the browser. As its content is dynamically generated, this folder will only be included in the solution when the `HostExpressServer` is being debugged. Whenever you stop the debugging session, this folder will go away automatically.

Starting the client application

Now that we have the WCF service running in the debugging mode, we need to start the client application so that we can step inside the WCF service that is being debugged.

However, first let's remove the breakpoint on the client program so that we can focus on the service itself.

Now, there are two ways to start the `HelloWorldClient` program. The first one is to start it within the same instance of Visual Studio. While leaving the `HelloWorldService` running in the debugging mode, in the **Solution Explorer** of the Visual Studio, right-click on the **HelloWorldClient** project and select **Debug | Start new instance** so that `HelloWorldClient` will also start running in the debugging mode. Immediately, you will step inside the WCF service, stopping on the first line of the `GetMessage` method within `HelloWorldService`. From this point onwards, you can keep debugging the service as you would do for any other program.

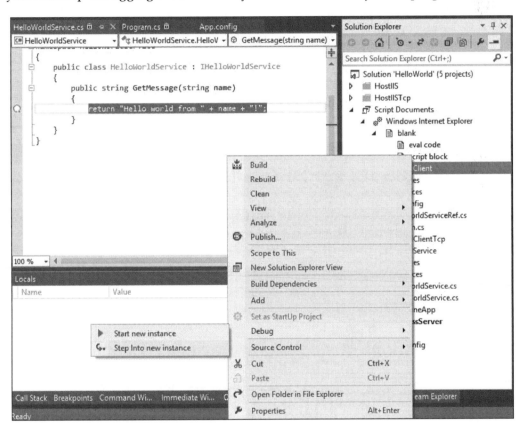

Another way to start `HelloWorldClient` is to start it from Windows Explorer. Go to the `C:\SOAwithWCFandEF\Projects\HelloWorld\HelloWorldClient\bin\Debug` directory and double-click on the `HelloWorldClient.exe` file. You will then get the same result as you did when you started it from within Visual Studio.

Attaching the debugger to a running WCF service process

Another common scenario while debugging is when attaching the debugger to a running WCF service. Suppose HelloWorldService is hosted and running outside Visual Studio, either in IIS or in a managed application such as HostCmdLineApp. In this case, the client application is also running outside of Visual Studio. At a certain point, you might want to start debugging the running WCF service. In this case, we can attach the debugger to the running WCF service process and start debugging it.

> Even if the WCF service is hosted inside Visual Studio, like with the HostExpressServer website, in certain environments, you might still not be able to step inside the service directly from the client application due to some debugging settings of your Visual Studio or IIS Express. In this case, you can use the same technique we will learn here to debug the service, just by attaching to the IIS Express process.

Running the WCF service and client applications in a non-debugging mode

To test this scenario, change the App.config file in the client program project to use the IIS hosting HelloWorldService. This means that we use the following address for the endpoint in the App.config file for the HelloWorldClient project: http://localhost/HelloWorldService/HelloWorldService.svc.

Build the solution and set a breakpoint inside the GetMessage method of the HelloWorldService project. Then, set the HelloWorldClient project as the startup project and run HelloWorldClient in a non-debugging mode by pressing *Ctrl + F5*. You will see the breakpoint that we had previously set within the HelloWorldService is not hit this time. This is because the service is now hosted by IIS and is not available for debugging by this instance of Visual Studio.

Debugging the WCF service hosted in IIS

To debug the service hosted by IIS, we can attach the debugger to the IIS process. However, before we can debug it, we have to enable debugging for the web application. Just open the Web.config file under the HostIIS folder and change the debug value to True.

Now, perform the following steps:

1. Start Visual Studio and select menu options **DEBUG | Attach to Process...**. The **Attach to Process** window should now appear. If you can't see the **DEBUG** menu from Visual Studio, just open any project or create a new empty project.

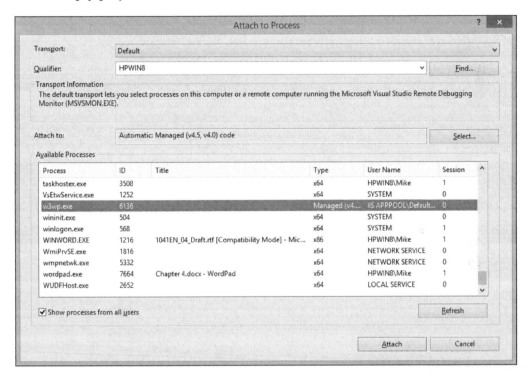

2. Select the **w3wp.exe** process from the list of available processes and click on the **Attach** button. Note that you need to check **Show processes from all users** in order to see **w3wp.exe** in the available processes list. If it is still not there, run `HelloWorldClient` once and hit the **Refresh** button; **w3wp.exe** will appear in the list.

3. Now, you will find the IIS worker process attached to the debugger. Open the `HelloWorldService.cs` file and set a breakpoint if you haven't done so already.

4. Now, run the `HelloWorldClient` program in the non-debugging mode from Windows Explorer or run it in the debugging mode by right-clicking on the **HelloWorldClient** project and selecting the **Debug | Start new instance** option from Visual Studio. You will see that the breakpoint inside the service is now hit.

If you are not able to set a breakpoint inside the HelloWorldService.cs file (or the breakpoint is disabled after you attach a debugger to the w3wp.exe process), make sure you have enabled debugging for the HostIIS application (as we did at the beginning of this section) and the HostIIS\bin folder contains the latest binary files from the HelloWorldService folder.

If you didn't start Visual Studio as an administrator, you will get a dialog window asking you to restart Visual Studio using different credentials. Select **Restart under different credentials** and you will be able to continue.

When you have finished debugging HelloWorldService using this method, you can select menu options **DEBUG | Detach All** or **DEBUG | Stop Debugging** to exit the debugging mode.

You might also have noticed that when you attach to w3wp.exe, IIS Express is also started, even though we have not used it at all at this time. This is because the **Always Start When Debugging** property of HostExpressServer is set to True. You can turn it off if you feel it is annoying.

Debugging a WCF service hosted in the cloud

In previous sections of this chapter, we learned how to debug WCF services, but the services are all hosted on an on-premise computer. Now, in the last section of this chapter, we will learn how to debug the WCF service, HelloWorldCloud, that we have deployed to the cloud in the last chapter. We will enable the debugging of the service, attach a debugger to the service process, and debug it using Visual Studio on our local computer.

Enabling debugging of the service

To debug a cloud service from a remote machine, debugging functionality must be enabled explicitly when the service is deployed to the cloud. When debugging is enabled for a cloud service, required services (msvsmon.exe, for example) will be installed on the virtual machines that run the role instances. As we didn't enable remote debugging when we published the HelloWorld service to the cloud, we have to republish the service with remote debugging enabled.

You can follow these steps to create a new hosting website.

1. Start Visual Studio as an administrator and open the `HelloWorld` solution.

2. From the **Solution Explorer**, right-click on the publishing website **HostBaseServer** and select **Publish Web Site** from the context menu. The **Publish Web** dialog box should appear.

3. Select **HelloWorldCloud (2)** from the profiles drop-down list.

4. Click the **Settings** link from the left-hand side of the dialog box and choose **Debug** from the **Configuration** drop-down list.

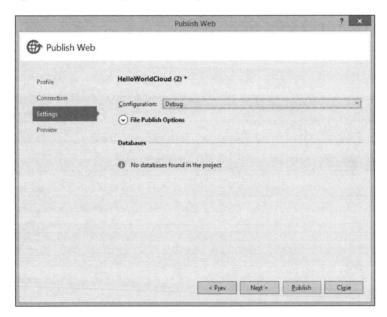

5. Click on the **Publish** button to republish the WCF service to the cloud.

Enabling remote debugging for a cloud service doesn't exhibit degraded performance or incur additional charges to the service. However, you shouldn't use remote debugging on a production service because clients who use the service might be adversely affected.

Attaching to the cloud service process

Now, the service has been redeployed to the cloud with debugging enabled, and we can start debugging it remotely from Visual Studio. First, let's attach debugger to it from Visual Studio.

1. From the **Server Explorer**, expand the node **Windows Azure | Web Sites**. Here, you should see the website you created and deployed the `HelloWorldCloud` service to in *Chapter 3, Deploying the HelloWorld WCF Service*. We use `HelloWorldCloud` as an example here, but you should see your own website:

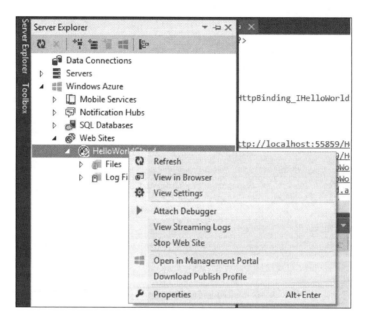

2. You might need to sign in to Azure again if you haven't done so, or you haven't checked the **keep me signed in** flag. If you don't see your website after signing in, you can refresh the **Web Sites** node.

3. Now, right-click on the website and select **Attach Debugger** from the context menu. The service process in the cloud is now attached to the debugger and Visual Studio is changed to be in the debugging mode.

4. Restart the website.

Debugging the service

Now we have attached the Visual Studio debugger to the cloud service, let's start debugging this service.

1. From the **Solution Explorer**, open the `Web.config` file from the `HelloWorldClient` project.

2. Change the endpoint address to be the cloud one.

3. Open the `HelloWorldService.cs` file in the `HelloWorldService` project.

4. Set a breakpoint within the file.

5. Right-click on the **HelloWorldClient** project and select **Debug | Start new instance** to start the client application.

6. Press *F11* when the service is being called.

7. Watch the breakpoint inside the `HelloWorldService` file being hit when the client application runs.

 If you cannot set a breakpoint inside the `HelloWorldService` file, or you cannot step into the service file, you might need to restart the cloud website after you republish it.

Summary

In this chapter, we have hosted the `HelloWorld` WCF service in several different ways and explored different scenarios to debug a WCF service. Now that we have the basic skills for WCF service development, in the next chapter, we will start developing a three-layered WCF service following the best practices of WCF service development.

5
Implementing a Three-layer WCF Service

In the previous chapters, we created a basic WCF service. The WCF service we have created, `HelloWorldService`, has only one method, named `GetMessage`. As this was just an example, we implemented this WCF service in one layer only. Both the service interface and implementation are within one deployable component.

In the following two chapters, we will implement a WCF service, which will be called `LayerNorthwindService`, to reflect a real-world service. In this chapter, we will separate the service interface layer from the business logic layer, and in the following chapter, we will add a data access layer to the service.

Note that the service we will create in the next two chapters is only a simplified version of a real-world WCF service. In a real-world situation, there is no doubt that the WCF service will contain more custom scenarios, business logic, and data constraints. For learning purposes, we will just create a WCF service in three layers, with minimum business logic and some basic functionality. After you have acquired the basic skills to create the framework for a layered WCF service, you can customize the solution according to your own needs.

In this chapter, we will create and test the WCF service by performing the following steps:

- Creating the WCF service project using the built-in Visual Studio WCF service template
- Creating the service operation contracts
- Creating the data contracts

- Adding a **business domain object (BDO)** project
- Adding a business logic layer project
- Calling the business logic layer from the service interface layer
- Testing the service

Why layer a service?

An important aspect of **Service-oriented Architecture (SOA)** design is that service boundaries should be explicit (being technology-neutral or agnostic), which means hiding all the details of the implementation behind the service boundary. This includes not revealing or dictating which particular technology is used.

Furthermore, inside the implementation of a service, the code responsible for the data manipulation should be separated from the code responsible for the business logic. Therefore, in the real world, it is always a good practice to implement a WCF service in three or more layers. The three layers are the service interface layer, the business logic layer, and the data access layer.

- **Service interface layer**: This layer will include the service contracts and operation contracts used to define the service interfaces that will be exposed at the service boundary. Data contracts are also defined to pass data in and out of the service. Fault contracts are defined if any exceptions are expected to be thrown outside the service.

- **Business logic layer**: This layer will apply the actual business logic to the service operations. It will check the preconditions of each operation, perform business activities, and return any necessary results to the interface layer of the service.

- **Data access layer**: This layer will take care of all the tasks needed to access the underlying databases. It will use a specific data adapter to query and update the databases. This layer will handle connections to databases, transaction processing, and concurrency controlling. Neither the service interface layer nor the business logic layer needs to worry about these things.

The service interface layer will be compiled into a separate class assembly and hosted in a service host environment. Only the outside world will know about, and have access to, this layer. Whenever a request is received by the service interface layer on the hosting server, the request will be dispatched to the business logic layer, and the business logic layer will get the actual work done. If any database support is needed by the business logic layer, it will always go through the data access layer.

Creating a new solution and project using the built-in WCF service template

To start with, we will first create a new solution for the layered service and then add a new WCF service project to this solution. This time we will use the built-in Visual Studio WCF template for the new project.

Creating the WCF service project

There are a few built-in WCF service templates within Visual Studio. In this section, we will use the service library template to create our WCF service project. If you are interested in other templates, you can try each one of them yourself and choose the appropriate one for your own developments.

Follow these steps to create the `LayerNorthwind` solution and the project using the service library template:

1. Start Visual Studio, go to **FILE** | **New** | **Project...**, and you will see the **New Project** dialog box. Don't open the `HelloWorld` solution (from the previous chapter) as from this point onwards, we will create a completely new solution and save it in a different location.

2. In the **New Project** window, specify **WCF Service Library** as the project template from **Visual C#** | **WCF**, `LayerNorthwindService` as the (project) name, `C:\SOAwithWCFandEF\Projects\` as the **Location**, and change the solution name from the defaulted **LayerNorthwindService** to `LayerNorthwind`. Make sure that the **Create directory for solution** checkbox is selected.

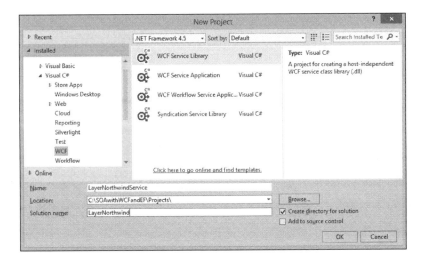

3. Click on the **OK** button, and the solution is created with a WCF project inside it. The project already has an `IService1.cs` file to define a service interface and `Service1.cs` to implement the service. It also has an `App.config` file, which we will cover shortly.

Now we have created the WCF service project. This project actually contains an application containing a WCF service, a hosting application (`WcfSvcHost`), and a WCF Test Client. This means that we don't need to write any other code to host it, and as soon as we have implemented our service, we can use the built-in WCF Test Client to invoke it. This makes it very convenient for WCF development.

Creating the service interface layer

In the previous section, we have created a WCF project using the WCF Service Library template. In this section, we will create the service interface layer contracts.

As two sample files have already been created for us, we will try to reuse them as much as possible. Then, we will start customizing these two files to create the service contracts.

Creating service interfaces

To create the service interfaces, we need to do the following to the `IService1.cs` file:

1. Change the filename from `IService1.cs` to `IProductService.cs`. This will also change the interface name from all related places inside the project.

2. Change the first operation contract definition. Consider the following line:

```
string GetData(int value);
```

Change it to this line:

```
Product GetProduct(int id);
```

3. Change the second operation contract definition. Refer to the following line:

```
CompositeType GetDataUsingDataContract(CompositeType composite);
```

Change it to this line:

```
bool UpdateProduct(Product product, ref string message);
```

With these changes, we have defined two service contracts. The first one will be used to get the product details for a specific product ID, while the second one will be used to update a specific product. However, the product type, which we have used to define these service contracts, is still not defined. We will define it right after this section.

The changed part of the service interface should now look as follows:

```
using System;
using System.Collections.Generic;
using System.Linq;
using System.Runtime.Serialization;
using System.ServiceModel;
using System.Text;

namespace LayerNorthwindService
{
    [ServiceContract]
    public interface IProductService
    {
        [OperationContract]
        Product GetProduct(int id);

        [OperationContract]
        bool UpdateProduct(Product product, ref string message);

        // TODO: Add your service operations here
    }
//Unchanged part omitted
}
```

This is not the whole content of the `IProductService.cs` file. The bottom part of this file should still have the `CompositeType` class, which we will change to our product type in the next section.

Creating data contracts

Another important aspect of the SOA design is that you should not assume that the application supports a complex object model. One part of the service boundary definition is the data contract definition for the complex types that will be passed as operation parameters or return values.

For maximum interoperability and alignment with the SOA principles, you should not pass any .NET-specific types, such as `DataSet` or `Exceptions` across the service boundary, as your service might be called by clients who might not understand the .NET-specific types. You should stick to fairly simple data structure objects, with only primitive properties. You can pass objects that have nested complex types, such as *Customer with an Order collection*. However, you should not make any assumption about the consumer being able to support object-oriented constructs, such as inheritance or base classes for interoperable web services.

In our example, we will create a complex data type to represent a product object. This data contract will have five properties:

* `ProductID`
* `ProductName`
* `QuantityPerUnit`
* `UnitPrice`
* `Discontinued`

These will be used to communicate with the client applications. For example, a supplier may call the web service to update the price of a particular product or to mark a product for discontinuation.

It is preferable to put data contracts in separate files within a separate assembly, but to simplify our example, we will put the data contract in the same file as the service contract. We will have to modify the `IProductService.cs` file, as follows:

1. Open the `IProductService.cs` file if it is not open.
2. Delete the existing `CompositeType` class.
3. Add a new `DataContract` class called `Product`.

The data contract part of the finished service contract file, `IProductService.cs`, should now look as follows:

```
[DataContract]
public class Product
{
        [DataMember]
        public int ProductID { get; set; }
        [DataMember]
        public string ProductName { get; set; }
        [DataMember]
```

```
public string QuantityPerUnit { get; set; }
[DataMember]
public decimal UnitPrice { get; set; }
[DataMember]
public bool Discontinued { get; set; }
}
```

Implementing the service contracts

To implement the two service interfaces that we defined in the previous section, we need to do the following to the Service1.cs file:

1. Change the filename from Service1.cs to ProductService.cs.

2. Delete the GetData and GetDataUsingDataContract methods.

3. Add the following method to get a product (you can also right-click on the IProductService interface, select **Implement Interface** to add the skeleton methods, and then customize the methods):

```
public Product GetProduct(int id)
{
  // TODO: call business logic layer to retrieve product
  var product = new Product();
  product.ProductID = id;
  product.ProductName =
    "fake product name from service layer";
  product.UnitPrice = 10.0m;
  product.QuantityPerUnit = "fake QPU";
  return product;
}
```

 In this method, we created a fake product and returned it to the client. Later, we will remove the hardcoded product from this method and call the business logic to get the real product.

4. Add the following method to update a product:

```
public bool UpdateProduct(Product product,
  ref string message)
{
  var result = true;

  // first check to see if it is a valid price
```

```
if (product.UnitPrice <= 0)
{
  message = "Price cannot be <= 0";
  result = false;
}
// ProductName can't be empty
else if (string.IsNullOrEmpty(product.ProductName))
{
  message = "Product name cannot be empty";
  result = false;
}
// QuantityPerUnit can't be empty
else if (string.IsNullOrEmpty(product.QuantityPerUnit))
{
  message = "Quantity cannot be empty";
  result = false;
}
else
{
  // TODO: call business logic layer to update product
  message = "Product updated successfully";
  result = true;
}

return result;
}
```

In the preceding method, we don't update anything. Instead, it always returns a `true` value if a valid product is passed in. In one of the following sections, we will implement the business logic to update the product and apply some business logic for the update.

Now, we have finished implementing the service interface. The content of the `ProductService.cs` file should look as follows:

```
using System;
using System.Collections.Generic;
using System.Linq;
using System.Runtime.Serialization;
using System.ServiceModel;
using System.Text;

namespace LayerNorthwindService
{
```

```csharp
public class ProductService : IProductService
{
  public Product GetProduct(int id)
  {
    // TODO: call business logic layer to retrieve
    // product
    var product = new Product();
    product.ProductID = id;
    product.ProductName =
      "fake product name from service layer";
    product.UnitPrice = 10.0m;
    product.QuantityPerUnit = "fake QPU";
    return product;
  }

  public bool UpdateProduct(Product product,
  ref string message)
  {
    var result = true;

    // first check to see if it is a valid price
    if (product.UnitPrice <= 0)
    {
      message = "Price cannot be <= 0";
      result = false;
    }
    // ProductName can't be empty
    else if
    (string.IsNullOrEmpty(product.ProductName))
    {
      message = "Product name cannot be empty";
      result = false;
    }
    // QuantityPerUnit can't be empty
    else if
    (string.IsNullOrEmpty(product.QuantityPerUnit))
    {
      message = "Quantity cannot be empty";
      result = false;
    }
    else
    {
```

```
        // TODO: call business logic layer to update
        // product
        message = "Product updated successfully";
        result = true;
    }

    return result;
    }
  }
}
```

Modifying the App.config file

As we have changed the service name, we have to make appropriate changes to the configuration file.

Follow these steps to change the configuration file:

1. Open the App.config file from the **Solution Explorer**.
2. Change the Service1 string in the baseaddress node to ProductService.
3. Change the service address port from the default one to 8080. This setting is done for the client application, which we will create soon.
4. Remove the Design_Time_Addresses/ part from the baseAddress of the service.

The content of the App.config file should now look as follows (all the comments are removed):

```
<?xml version="1.0" encoding="utf-8" ?>
<configuration>

  <appSettings>
    <add key="aspnet:UseTaskFriendlySynchronizationContext"
    value="true" />
  </appSettings>

  <system.web>
    <compilation debug="true" />
  </system.web>
  <system.serviceModel>
    <services>
```

```xml
  <service
  name="LayerNorthwindService.ProductService">
    <endpoint address="" binding="basicHttpBinding"
      contract=
      "LayerNorthwindService.IProductService">
      <identity>
        <dns value="localhost"/>
      </identity>
    </endpoint>
    <endpoint address="mex" binding="mexHttpBinding"
            contract="IMetadataExchange"/>
    <host>
      <baseAddresses>
        <add baseAddress =
        "http://localhost:8080/LayerNorthwindService/
ProductService/" />
      </baseAddresses>
    </host>
  </service>
</services>
<behaviors>
  <serviceBehaviors>
    <behavior>
      <serviceMetadata httpGetEnabled="True"
      httpsGetEnabled="True"/>
      <serviceDebug includeExceptionDetailInFaults="False" />
    </behavior>
  </serviceBehaviors>
</behaviors>
</system.serviceModel>

</configuration>
```

Testing the service using the WCF Test Client

As we are using the WCF Service Library template in this example, we are now ready to test the web service. As we pointed out when creating the project, the service will be hosted in the Visual Studio WCF Service Host environment.

To start the service, press *F5* or *Ctrl + F5*. The WcfSvcHost application will be started, and the WCF Test Client will also start. This is a Visual Studio built-in test client for the WCF Service Library projects.

In order to run the WCF Test Client, you have to log in to your machine as a local administrator. You also have to start Visual Studio as an administrator because we have changed the service port from the default one to 8080, and running Visual Studio as an administrator will automatically register this port.

You will see the **WCF Test Client** page, as shown in the following screenshot:

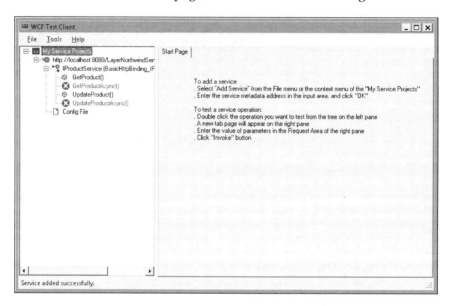

If you get an **Access is denied** error, make sure you run Visual Studio as an administrator. Ignore the errors for the async methods, as they are not supported by WCF Test Client.

Now, from the WCF Test Client window, we can double-click on an operation to test it. First, let's test the GetProduct operation:

1. In the left panel of the client, double-click on the **GetProduct()** operation; the GetProduct request will be shown in the panel on the right-hand side.

2. In the **Request** panel, specify an integer for the product ID and click on the **Invoke** button to let the client call the service. You might get a dialog box that warns you about the security of sending information over the network. Click on the **OK** button to acknowledge this warning (you can check the **In the future, do not show this message** option so that it is not displayed again).

Now, the message **Invoking Service…** will be displayed in the status bar as the client is trying to connect to the server. It might take a while for this initial connection to be made, as several things need to be done in the background. Once the connection has been established, a channel will be created and the client will call the service to perform the requested operation. Once the operation has been completed on the server side, the response package will be sent back to the client, and the WCF Test Client will display this response in the panel at the bottom:

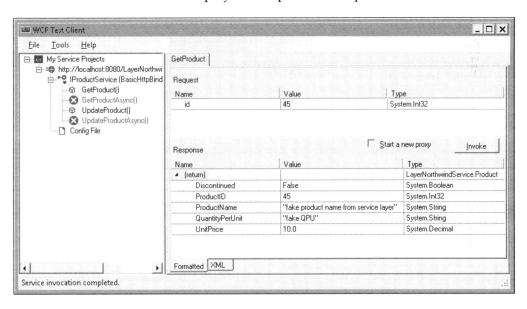

If you start the test client in the debugging mode (by pressing *F5*), you can set a breakpoint at a line inside the `GetProduct` method, in the `LayerNorthwindService.cs` file. Moreover, when the **Invoke** button is clicked, the breakpoint will be hit so that you can debug the service, as we learned earlier.

Note that the response is always the same, no matter what product ID you use to retrieve the product. Specifically, the product name is hardcoded for testing purposes, as shown in the preceding screenshot.

Also, because the product ID is an integer value from the WCF Test Client, you can only enter an integer for it. If a noninteger value is entered, when you click on the **Invoke** button, you will get an error message which warns you that you have entered a value with the wrong type.

Now, let's test the `UpdateProduct` operation:

1. Double-click on the **UpdateProduct()** operation in the left panel, and **UpdateProduct** will be shown in the panel on the right-hand side in a new tab.

2. Select **LayerNorthwindService.Product** for the product dropdown, enter a value for each input parameter, and then click on the **Invoke** button to test it. Depending on the value you enter in the **UnitPrice** column, you will get a **True** or **False** response package back.

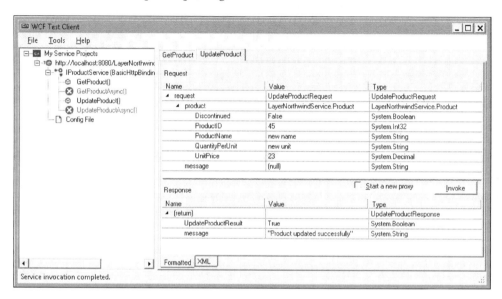

 Click on the arrow key of the product value item to expand the product value so that you can enter values for the attributes of the product input.

The **Request** and **Response** packages are displayed in grids by default, but you have the option to display them in the XML format. Just select the **XML** tab at the bottom of the right-hand side panel, and you will see the XML-formatted **Request** and **Response** packages.

From these XML strings, you can see that they are actually SOAP messages:

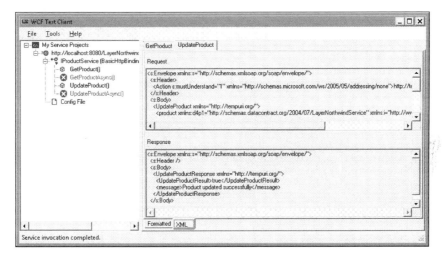

Besides testing operations, you can also take a look at the configuration settings of the web service. Just double-click on **Config File** in the panel on the left-hand side and the configuration file will be displayed in the panel on the right-hand side. This will show you the bindings for the service, the addresses of the service, and the contract for the service, as follows:

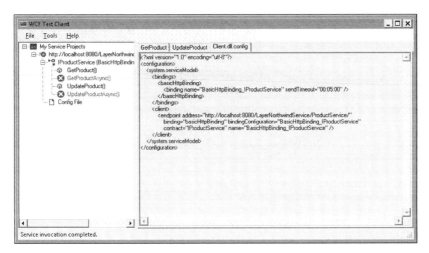

If you are satisfied with the test results, just close the WCF Test Client, and you will go back to the Visual Studio IDE. Note that as soon as you close the client, the WCF Service Host is stopped. This is different from hosting a service inside IIS Express, where IIS Express stays active even after you close the client.

Testing the service using your own client

It is very convenient to test a WCF service using the built-in WCF Test Client, but sometimes, it is desirable to test a WCF service using your own test client. The built-in WCF Test Client is limited to test only simple WCF services. For complex WCF services, for example, a service where the parameter is a more complex object, we have to create our own test client.

To create our own client in order to consume the WCF service, we first need to host the WCF service in a host application. For this purpose, we can use the methods that we learned in the previous chapter to host the WCF service in IIS, IIS Express, or a managed .NET application.

In addition to the previous methods we learned, we can also use the built-in WCF Service Host to host the WCF service. So, we don't need to create a host application, but we just need to create a client. In this section, we will use this hosting method to save us some time.

First, let's find a way to get the metadata for the service. From Visual Studio's built-in WCF Test Client, you cannot examine the **Web Services Description Language (WSDL)** of the service, although the client itself must have used the WSDL to communicate with the service. To see the WSDL outside the WCF Service Test Client, just copy the address of the service from the configuration file and paste it in a web browser. In our example, the address of the service is `http://localhost:8080/LayerNorthwindService/ProductService/`. So, copy and paste this address to a web browser, and we will see the WSDL of the service, just as we have seen many times before.

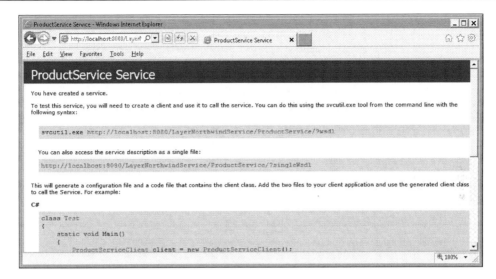

 To get the metadata for the service, the service host application must run. The easiest way to start `LayerNorthwindService` in the WCF Service Host is to start the WCF Test Client and leave it running.

Now that we know how to get the metadata for our service, we can start building the test client. We can leave the host application running and manually generate the proxy classes by using the same method that we used earlier. However, this time, we will let Visual Studio do it for us.

Follow these steps to build your own client to test the WCF service:

1. Add a new **Console Application** project to the `LayerNorthwind` solution. Let's call it `LayerNorthwindClient`.

2. Add a reference to the WCF service. In the Visual Studio Solution Explorer, right-click on the **LayerNorthwindClient** project, select **Add | Service Reference…** from the context menu, and you will see the **Add Service Reference** dialog box.

3. In the **Add Service Reference** dialog box, type the address `http://localhost:8080/LayerNorthwindService/ProductService/` in the **Address** box, and then click on the **Go** button to connect to the service.

4. Also, you can simply click on the **Discover** button (or click on the little arrow next to the **Discover** button and select **Services** from the **Solution Explorer**) to find this service.

In order to connect to or discover a service in the same solution, you don't have to start the host application for the service. The WCF Service Host will automatically start for this purpose. However, if it has not started in advance, it might take a while for the **Add Service Reference** window to download the required metadata information for the service.

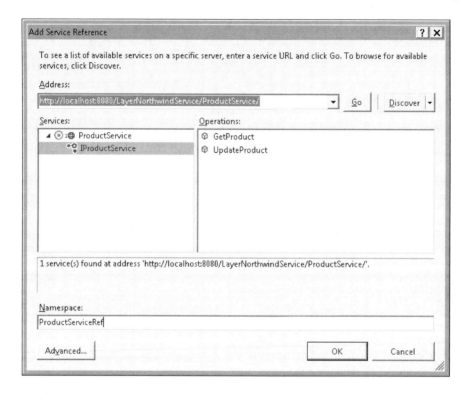

5. The **ProductService** option should now be listed on the left-hand side of the window. You can expand it and select the service contract to view its details.

6. Next, let's change the namespace of this service from `ServiceReference1` to `ProductServiceRef`. This will make the reference meaningful in the code.

7. Now, click on the **OK** button in the **Add Service Reference** dialog box to add the service reference. You will see that a new folder named **ProductServiceRef** is created under **Service References** in the **Solution Explorer** for the **LayerNorthwindClient** project. This folder contains lots of files, including the WSDL file, the service map, and the actual proxy code. If you can't see them, click on **Show All Files** in the **Solution Explorer**.

The `App.config` config file is also modified to include the service details.

At this point, the proxy code to connect to the WCF service has been created and added to the project for us without us having to enter a single line of code. What we need to do next is write just a few lines of code to call the service.

Just as we did earlier, we will modify the `Program.cs` file to call the WCF service:

1. First, open the `Program.cs` file and add the following `using` line to the file:

    ```
    using LayerNorthwindClient.ProductServiceRef;
    ```

2. Then, inside the `Main` method, add the following line of code to create a `client` object:

    ```
    var client = new ProductServiceClient();
    ```

3. Finally, add the following lines of code to the file in order to call the WCF service to get and update a product:

    ```
    var product = client.GetProduct(23);
    Console.WriteLine("product name is " + product.ProductName);
    Console.WriteLine("product price is " + product.UnitPrice.
    ToString());
    product.UnitPrice = 20.0m;
    var message = "";
    var result = client.UpdateProduct(product, ref message);
    Console.WriteLine("Update result is " + result.ToString());
    Console.WriteLine("Update message is " + message);
    Console.ReadLine();
    ```

Now, you can run the client application to test the service. Remember that you need to run Visual Studio as an administrator. Make a note of the following:

*   If you want to start the application in the debugging mode (*F5*), you need to add a `Console.ReadLine();` statement at the end of the program so that you can see the output of the program. Also, remember to set the `LayerNorthwindClient` application as the startup project. The WCF Service Host application will be started automatically before the client is started (but the WCF Test Client won't be started).

- If you want to start the client application in the nondebugging mode (*Ctrl + F5*), you need to start the WCF Service Host application and the WCF Test Client application in advance, as there will be no service for the client to call otherwise. You can start the WCF Service Host application and the WCF Test Client from another Visual Studio IDE instance, or you can set LayerNorthwindService as the startup project, start it in the nondebugging mode (*Ctrl + F5*), and leave it running. Then, you can change LayerNorthwindClient to be the startup project and start it in the nondebugging mode. Also, you can set the solution to start with multiple projects, with LayerNorthwindService as the first project to be run and LayerNorthwindClient as the second project to be run.

- You can also start the WCF service in the debugging mode, then right-click on the client project, and go to **Debug | Start new instance** in order to start the client program in the debugging mode.

 In my environment, I've set the solution to start with multiple projects, so I am sure that the WCF service is always started before the client application, no matter whether it is in the debugging mode or not.

The output of this client program is as shown in the following screenshot:

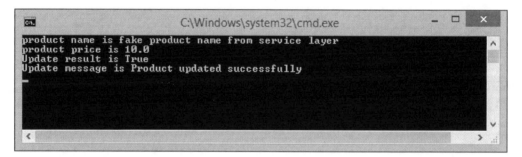

Adding a business logic layer

Until now, the WCF service contained only one layer. In this section, we will add a business logic layer and define some business rules in this layer.

Adding the business domain object project

Before we add the business logic layer, we need to add a project for the business domain objects. The business domain object project will hold definitions such as products, customers, and orders. These domain objects will be used across the business logic layer, the data access layer, and the service layer. They will be very similar to the data contracts that we defined in the previous section but will not be seen outside the service. The product business domain object will have the same properties as the product's contract data, plus some extra properties such as UnitsInStock and ReorderLevel. These properties will be used internally and shared by all the layers of the service. For example, when an order is placed, UnitsInStock should be updated as well. Also, if the updated UnitsInStock is less than ReorderLevel, an event should be raised to trigger the reordering process.

The business domain data objects by themselves do not act as a layer. They are just pure C# classes (also called POCO classes), representing internal data within the service implementations. There is no logic inside these business domain objects. In reality, the business domain object classes can be very different from the data contracts, property names, property types, and data structures.

As with the data contracts, the business domain object classes should be in their own assembly. Therefore, we first need to create a project for them. Just add a new C# class library, LayerNorthwindBDO, to the solution. Then, modify the Class1.cs file, which has been autocreated by Visual Studio, as follows:

1. Rename the Class1.cs file to ProductBDO.cs.

2. Add the following properties to this class:

    ° ProductID
    ° ProductName
    ° QuantityPerUnit
    ° UnitPrice
    ° Discontinued
    ° UnitsInStock
    ° UnitsOnOrder
    ° ReorderLevel

 Five of the preceding properties are also present in the product service data contract. The last three properties are used inside the service implementations. For example, UnitsOnOrder might be used to trigger business logic when discontinuing a product.

The following is the code list of the ProductBDO class:

```csharp
using System;
using System.Collections.Generic;
using System.Linq;
using System.Text;
using System.Threading.Tasks;

namespace LayerNorthwindBDO
{
    public class ProductBDO
    {
        public int ProductID { get; set; }
        public string ProductName { get; set; }
        public string QuantityPerUnit { get; set; }
        public decimal UnitPrice { get; set; }
        public int UnitsInStock { get; set; }
        public int ReorderLevel { get; set; }
        public int UnitsOnOrder { get; set; }
        public bool Discontinued { get; set; }
    }
}
```

Adding the business logic project

Next, let's create the business logic layer project. Again, we just need to add a new C# class library project, LayerNorthwindLogic, to the solution. Then, modify the Class1.cs file as follows:

1. Rename the file from Class1.cs to ProductLogic.cs.

2. Add a reference to the LayerNorthwindBDO project.

Now, we need to add some code to the ProductLogic class:

1. Add the following using line:

   ```csharp
   using LayerNorthwindBDO;
   ```

2. Add the GetProduct method. It should look as follows:

   ```csharp
   public ProductBDO GetProduct(int id)
   {
       // TODO: call data access layer to retrieve product
       var p = new ProductBDO();
       p.ProductID = id;
   ```

```
    p.ProductName =
        "fake product name from business logic layer";
    p.UnitPrice = 20.00m;
    p.QuantityPerUnit = "fake QPU";
    return p;
}
```

In this method, we create a `ProductBDO` object, assign values to some
of its properties, and return the object to the caller. Everything is still
hardcoded so far.

 We hardcode the product name as `fake product name from`
`business logic layer` so that we know that this is a different
product from the one that is returned directly by the service layer.

3. Add the `UpdateProduct` method, as follows:

```
public bool UpdateProduct(ProductBDO product,
    ref string message)
{
    var productInDB =
        GetProduct(product.ProductID);
    // invalid product to update
    if (productInDB == null)
    {
        message = "cannot get product for this ID";
        return false;
    }
    // a product can't be discontinued
    // if there are non-fulfilled orders
    if (product.Discontinued == true
        && productInDB.UnitsOnOrder > 0)
    {
        message = "cannot discontinue this product";
        return false;
    }
    else
    {
        // TODO: call data access layer to update product
        message = "Product updated successfully";
        return true;
    }
}
```

Within this method, we still haven't updated anything in the database, but this time, we added several pieces of logic to the UpdateProduct method. First, we try to retrieve the product to see if it is a valid product to update; if not, we will return false and stop. We also added logic to check whether it is okay to discontinue a product, and if not, we will return false and stop.

4. Add test logic to the GetProduct method.

   As said earlier, we added a check to make sure that a supplier cannot discontinue a product if there are unfulfilled orders for this product. However, at this stage, we cannot truly enforce this logic. The reason behind this is when we check the UnitsOnOrder property of a product, it is always 0 as we haven't assigned a value to it in the GetProduct method.

   For test purposes, we can change the GetProduct method to include the following line of code:

   ```
   if(id > 50) p.UnitsOnOrder = 30;
   ```

   Now, when we test the service, we can select a product with an ID that is greater than 50, and try to update its Discontinued property to see what result we will get.

After you put all of this together, the content of the ProductLogic.cs file should be as follows:

```
using System;
using System.Collections.Generic;
using System.Linq;
using System.Text;
using System.Threading.Tasks;
using LayerNorthwindBDO;

namespace LayerNorthwindLogic
{
    public class ProductLogic
    {
        public ProductBDO GetProduct(int id)
        {
            // TODO: call data access layer to retrieve product
            var p = new ProductBDO();
            p.ProductID = id;
            p.ProductName =
                "fake product name from business logic layer";
            p.UnitPrice = 20.00m;
```

```
            p.QuantityPerUnit = "fake QPU";
            if (id > 50) p.UnitsOnOrder = 30;
            return p;
        }
    public bool UpdateProduct(ProductBDO
        product, ref string message)
        {
            var productInDB =
                GetProduct(product.ProductID);
            // invalid product to update
            if (productInDB == null)
            {
                message = "cannot get product for this ID";
                return false;
            }
            // a product can't be discontinued
            // if there are non-fulfilled orders
            if (product.Discontinued == true
                && productInDB.UnitsOnOrder > 0)
            {
                message = "cannot discontinue this product";
                return false;
            }
            else
            {
                // TODO: call data access layer to update product
                message = "Product updated successfully";
                return true;
            }
        }
    }
}
```

Calling the business logic layer from the service interface layer

We now have the business logic layer ready and can modify the service contracts to call this layer so that we can enforce some business logic.

First, we want to make it very clear that we are going to change the service implementations and not the interfaces. Therefore, we will only change the ProductService.cs file.

We will not touch the IProductService.cs file. All the existing clients (if there are any) that are referencing our service will not notice that we are changing the implementation.

Follow these steps to customize the service interface layer
(the LayerNorthwindService project):

1. From the **Solution Explorer**, right-click on the **LayerNorthwindService**
    project and select **Add | Reference....** Then, add references to the
    LayerNorthwindLogic and **LayerNorthwindBDO** projects.

2. Now, we have added two references. We then add the following two
    using statements to the ProductService.cs file:

    ```
    using LayerNorthwindBDO;
    using LayerNorthwindLogic;
    ```

3. Next, inside the GetProduct method, we can use the following statements
    to get the product from our business logic layer:

    ```
    var productLogic = new ProductLogic();
    var productBDO = productLogic.GetProduct(id);
    ```

4. However, we cannot return this product to the caller because this product is
    of the ProductBDO type, which is not the type that the caller is expecting. The
    caller is expecting a return value of the type Product, which is a data contract
    defined within the service interface (sometimes called a **data transfer object** or
    a **DTO**). We need to translate this ProductBDO object to a ProductDTO object.
    To do this, we add the following new method to the ProductService class:

    ```
    private void TranslateProductBDOToProductDTO(
        ProductBDO productBDO,
        Product product)
    {
        product.ProductID = productBDO.ProductID;
        product.ProductName = productBDO.ProductName;
        product.QuantityPerUnit = productBDO.QuantityPerUnit;
        product.UnitPrice = productBDO.UnitPrice;
        product.Discontinued = productBDO.Discontinued;
    }
    ```

5. Inside the preceding translation method, we copy all the properties from the
    ProductBDO object to the service contract data object, but not the last three
    properties—UnitsInStock, UnitsOnOrder, and ReorderLevel. These three
    properties are used only inside the service implementations. External callers
    cannot see them at all.

6. The `GetProduct` method should now look as follows:

```
public Product GetProduct(int id)
{
    var productLogic = new ProductLogic();
    var productBDO = productLogic.GetProduct(id);
    var product = new Product();
    TranslateProductBDOToProductDTO(productBDO, product);
    return product;
}
```

7. We can modify the `UpdateProduct` method in the same way, making it look as shown in the following code snippet:

```
public bool UpdateProduct(Product product,
    ref string message)
{
    var result = true;

    // first check to see if it is a valid price
    if (product.UnitPrice <= 0)
    {
        message = "Price cannot be <= 0";
        result = false;
    }
    // ProductName can't be empty
    else if (string.IsNullOrEmpty(product.ProductName))
    {
        message = "Product name cannot be empty";
        result = false;
    }
    // QuantityPerUnit can't be empty
    else if
    (string.IsNullOrEmpty(product.QuantityPerUnit))
    {
        message = "Quantity cannot be empty";
        result = false;
    }
    else
    {
        var productLogic = new ProductLogic();
        var productBDO = new ProductBDO();
        TranslateProductDTOToProductBDO(product,
        productBDO);
```

```
                return productLogic.UpdateProduct(productBDO, ref
                message);
            }
            return result;
        }
    }
```

8. Note that we have to create a new method in order to transform a product contract data object into a `ProductBDO` object. During the transformation, we leave the three extra properties unassigned in the `ProductBDO` object because we know that a supplier won't update these properties.

9. Since we have to create a `ProductLogic` variable in both the methods, let's make it a class member:

```
ProductLogic productLogic = new ProductLogic();
```

The final content of the `ProductService.cs` file is as follows:

```
using System;
using System.Collections.Generic;
using System.Linq;
using System.Runtime.Serialization;
using System.ServiceModel;
using System.Text;
using LayerNorthwindBDO;
using LayerNorthwindLogic;

namespace LayerNorthwindService
{
    public class ProductService : IProductService
    {
        ProductLogic productLogic = new ProductLogic();
        public Product GetProduct(int id)
        {
            var productBDO = productLogic.GetProduct(id);
            var product = new Product();
            TranslateProductBDOToProductDTO(productBDO, product);
            return product;
        }

        public bool UpdateProduct(Product product,
            ref string message)
        {
            var result = true;
            // first check to see if it is a valid price
            if (product.UnitPrice <= 0)
            {
                message = "Price cannot be <= 0";
                result = false;
```

```
        }
        // ProductName can't be empty
        else if (string.IsNullOrEmpty(product.ProductName))
        {
            message = "Product name cannot be empty";
            result = false;
        }
        // QuantityPerUnit can't be empty
        else if
        (string.IsNullOrEmpty(product.QuantityPerUnit))
        {
            message = "Quantity cannot be empty";
            result = false;
        }
        else
        {
            var productBDO = new ProductBDO();
            TranslateProductDTOToProductBDO(product,
            productBDO);
            return productLogic.UpdateProduct(
                productBDO, ref message);
        }
        return result;
    }

    private void TranslateProductBDOToProductDTO(
        ProductBDO productBDO,
        Product product)
    {

        product.ProductID = productBDO.ProductID;
        product.ProductName = productBDO.ProductName;
        product.QuantityPerUnit = productBDO.QuantityPerUnit;
        product.UnitPrice = productBDO.UnitPrice;
        product.Discontinued = productBDO.Discontinued;
    }

    private void TranslateProductDTOToProductBDO(
        Product product,
        ProductBDO productBDO)
    {

        productBDO.ProductID = product.ProductID;
        productBDO.ProductName = product.ProductName;
        productBDO.QuantityPerUnit = product.QuantityPerUnit;
        productBDO.UnitPrice = product.UnitPrice;
        productBDO.Discontinued = product.Discontinued;
    }
  }
}
```

Testing the WCF service with a business logic layer

We can now compile and test the new WCF service with a business logic layer. We will use the WCF Test Client to simplify the process:

1. Set the `LayerNorthwindService` project as the startup project.

2. Start the WCF Service Host application and WCF Service Test Client by pressing *F5* or *Ctrl + F5*.

3. In the WCF Service Test Client, double-click on the **GetProduct()** operation to bring up the `GetProduct` test screen.

4. Enter a value of `56` for the `ID` field and then click on the **Invoke** button.

5. You will see that this time, the product is returned from the business logic layer, instead of the service layer. Also, note that the `UnitsOnOrder` property is not displayed as it is not part of the service contract data type. However, we know that a product has a `UnitsOnOrder` property, and we will use this for our next test.

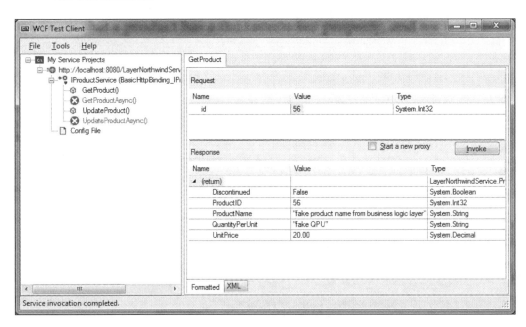

Now, let's try to update a product:

1. In the WCF Service Test Client, double-click on the **UpdateProduct()** operation to bring up the **UpdateProduct** test screen.

2. Enter `-10` as the price and click on the **Invoke** button. You will see that the **Response** result is **False**.

3. Enter a valid price, say `25.6`, a name, and a quantity per unit, and leave the **Discontinued** property set to **False**. Then, click on the **Invoke** button. You will see that the **Response** result is now **True**.

4. Change the **Discontinued** value from **False** to **True** and click on the **Invoke** button again. The **Response** result is still **True**. This is because we didn't change the product ID, and it has been defaulted to `0`. Remember, in our business logic layer in the `GetProduct` operation, for a product with an ID less than or equal to `50`, we didn't set the `UnitsOnOrder` property; thus, it defaults to `0`. In our business logic for the `UpdateProduct` operation, it is OK to set the **Discontinued** property to **True** if `UnitsOnOrder` is less than or equal to `0`.

5. Change the product ID to **51**, leave the **Discontinued** value as **True** and the product price as **25.6**, and click on the **Invoke** button again. This time, you will see that the **Response** result is **False**. This is because the business logic layer has checked the **UnitsOnOrder** and **Discontinued** properties and didn't allow us to make the update.

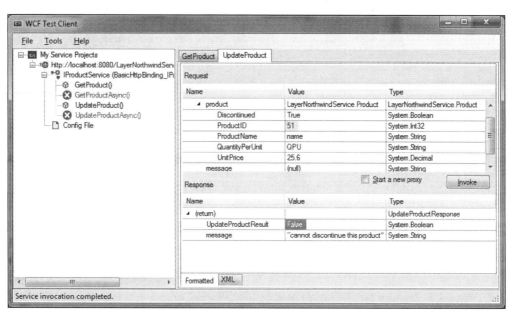

Summary

In this chapter, we created a real-world WCF service that has a service contract layer and a business logic layer. We used the built-in WCF Service Library template to create the service and followed the WCF service development's best practices to separate the service interfaces from the business logic.

In the next chapter, we will add one more layer, the data access layer, to the service and add error handling to the service.

6

Adding Database Support and Exception Handling

In the previous chapter, we created a WCF service with two layers. We didn't add the third layer, that is, the data access layer. Therefore, all of the service operations just returned a fake result from the business logic layer.

In this chapter, we will add the third layer to the WCF service. We will also introduce fault contracts for service error handling.

We will accomplish the following tasks in this chapter:

- Creating the data access layer project
- Calling the data access layer from the business logic layer
- Preparing the Northwind database for the service
- Adding the connection string to the configuration file
- Querying the database using GetProduct
- Testing the GetProduct method
- Updating the database using UpdateProduct
- Testing the UpdateProduct method
- Adding a fault contract to the service
- Throwing a fault contract exception to the client
- Updating the client program to catch the fault exception
- Changing exception options
- Testing the service fault contract

Adding a data access layer

We have two layers, the service interface layer and the business logic layer, in our solution now. We don't have any code to interact with a data store to manipulate the underlying data. As said in the previous chapter, such code should be separated from these two layers, so now we will add one more layer, the data access layer, for this purpose. Within this third layer, we will query a real database to get the product information and update the database for a given product.

Creating the data access layer project

First, we will create the project for the data access layer. As we did for the business logic layer, what we need to do is add a C# class library project named LayerNorthwindDAL (where **DAL** stands for **Data Access Layer**) to the solution. Then, we need to change the default class file to be our **Data Access Object (DAO)** file.

Now, modify the Class1.cs file as follows:

1. Rename it to ProductDAO.cs. This will also rename the class name and all related places in the project.

2. Add a LayerNorthwindBDO reference to the project.

Next, let's modify ProductDAO.cs for our product service:

1. Add the following using statement:

    ```
    using LayerNorthwindBDO;
    ```

2. Add two new methods to the ProductDAO class. The first method is GetProduct, which should be as follows:

    ```
    public ProductBDO GetProduct(int id)
    {
        // TODO: connect to DB to retrieve product
        var p = new ProductBDO();
        p.ProductID = id;
        p.ProductName =
            "fake product name from data access layer";
        p.UnitPrice = 30.00m;
        p.QuantityPerUnit = "fake QPU";
        return p;
    }
    ```

In this method, all the product information is still hardcoded though we have changed the product name to be specific to the data access layer. We will soon modify this method to retrieve the actual product information from a real `Northwind` database.

3. Add the second method, `UpdateProduct`, as shown in the following code snippet:

```
public bool UpdateProduct(ProductBDO product, ref string message)
{
    // TODO: connect to DB to update product
    message = "product updated successfully";
    return true;
}
```

Again, we didn't update any database in this method. We will also modify this method soon to update to the real `Northwind` database.

The content of the `ProductDAO.cs` file should now be as follows:

```
using System;
using System.Collections.Generic;
using System.Linq;
using System.Text;
using System.Threading.Tasks;
using LayerNorthwindBDO;

namespace LayerNorthwindDAL
{
  public class ProductDAO
  {
    public ProductBDO GetProduct(int id)
    {
      // TODO: connect to DB to retrieve product
      var p = new ProductBDO();
      p.ProductID = id;
      p.ProductName =
      "fake product name from data access layer";
      p.UnitPrice = 30.00m;
      p.QuantityPerUnit = "fake QPU";
      return p;
    }
```

```
public bool UpdateProduct(ProductBDO product,
 ref string message)
{
  // TODO: connect to DB to update product
  message = "product updated successfully";
  return true;
}
}
}
```

Calling the data access layer from the business logic layer

Before we modify these two methods to interact with a real database, we will first modify the business logic layer to call them so that we know that the three-layer framework is working:

1. Add a reference of this new layer to the business logic layer project. From **Solution Explorer**, just right-click on the **LayerNorthwindLogic** project item, select **Add | Reference…** from the context menu, select **LayerNorthwindDAL** from **Projects** under the **Solutions** tab, and then click on the **OK** button.

2. Open the `ProductLogic.cs` file under the **LayerNorthwindLogic** project and add a using statement:

    ```
    using LayerNorthwindDAL;
    ```

3. Add a new class member:

    ```
    ProductDAO productDAO = new ProductDAO();
    ```

4. Modify the `GetProduct` method to contain only the following line:

    ```
    return productDAO.GetProduct(id);
    ```

    We will use the data access layer to retrieve the product information. At this point, we will not add any business logic to this method.

5. Modify the last two lines of the `UpdateProduct` method to call the data access layer. The method call should look as follows:

    ```
    return productDAO.UpdateProduct(product, ref message);
    ```

In this method, we replaced the last `return` statement to call the data access layer method, `UpdateProduct`. This means that all of the business logic is still enclosed in the business logic layer and the data access layer should be used only to update the product in the database.

Here is the full content of the `ProductLogic.cs` file:

```csharp
using System;
using System.Collections.Generic;
using System.Linq;
using System.Text;
using System.Threading.Tasks;
using LayerNorthwindBDO;
using LayerNorthwindDAL;

namespace LayerNorthwindLogic
{
  public class ProductLogic
  {
    ProductDAO productDAO = new ProductDAO();
    public ProductBDO GetProduct(int id)
    {
      return productDAO.GetProduct(id);
    }

    public bool UpdateProduct(ProductBDO
    product, ref string message)
    {
      var productInDB =
      GetProduct(product.ProductID);
      // invalid product to update
      if (productInDB == null)
      {
        message = "cannot get product for this ID";
        return false;
      }
      // a product can't be discontinued
      // if there are non-fulfilled orders
      if (product.Discontinued == true
      && productInDB.UnitsOnOrder > 0)
      {
        message = "cannot discontinue this product";
        return false;
      }
      else
      {
        return productDAO.UpdateProduct(product,
        ref message);
      }
    }
  }
}
```

If you run the program and test it using the WCF Test Client, you will get exactly the same result as before, although now it is a three-layer application and you will see a different, but obviously still fake, product name.

Preparing the database

As we have the three-layer framework ready, we will now implement the data access layer to actually communicate with a real database.

In this book, we will use Microsoft's sample `Northwind` database. This database is not installed by default in SQL Server, so we need to install it first (you can use any version of Microsoft SQL Server, but in this book, we will use SQL Server 2014):

1. Download the database package. Just search for `Northwind Sample Databases download` on the Internet or go to `http://www.microsoft.com/download/en/details.aspx?id=23654`.

 This sample database was designed for SQL Server 2000, but it can also be used with more recent versions of SQL Server.

2. Install (extract) the package to `C:\SQL Server 2000 Sample Databases`.

3. Install the `Northwind` database. You can attach the database files to your SQL Server or run the scripts to create the databases. For detailed instructions, you can have a look at the following link: `http://msdn.microsoft.com/en-us/library/8b6y4c7s.aspx`.

Adding the connection string to the configuration file

Now that we have the `Northwind` database installed, we will modify our data access layer to use this actual database. At this point, we will use a raw `SqlClient` adapter to do the database work. We will replace this layer with LINQ to Entities in a later chapter.

Before we start coding, we need to add a connection string to the configuration file. We don't want to hardcode the connection string in our project. Instead, we will set it in the `App.config` file so that it can be changed on the fly.

You can open the `App.config` file under the `LayerNorthwindService` project and add a new configuration node, `connectionStrings`, as a child node of the root configuration node, `configuration`. You can choose Windows integrated security or SQL Server login as the security mode for your connection.

The following code snippet shows my connection string with the integrated security class (note that the add node should be in one line in Visual Studio; we have broken them into three lines just for printing purposes):

```
<connectionStrings>
  <add name ="NorthwindConnectionString"
    connectionString="server=localhost;Integrated
    Security=SSPI;database=Northwind" />
</connectionStrings>
```

Querying the database using GetProduct

As we have added the connection string as a new key to the configuration file, we need to retrieve this key in the DAO class so that we can use it when we want to connect to the database. Follow these steps to get and use this new key from within the DAO class:

1. Add a reference to System.Configuration from the framework to the LayerNorthwindDAL project. We need this reference to read the connection string in the configuration file.

2. Open the ProductDAO.cs file in the LayerNorthwindDAL project and first add the following two using statements:

    ```
    using System.Data.SqlClient;
    using System.Configuration;
    ```

3. Add a new class member to the ProductDAO class:

    ```
    string connectionString = ConfigurationManager.
        ConnectionStrings["NorthwindConnectionString"].
        ConnectionString;
    ```

    We will use this connection string to connect to the Northwind database for both the GetProduct and UpdateProduct methods.

4. Modify the GetProduct method to get the product from the database as follows:

    ```
    public ProductBDO GetProduct(int id)
    {
      ProductBDO p = null;
      using (SqlConnection conn =
      new SqlConnection(connectionString))
      {
        using (SqlCommand cmd = new SqlCommand())
        {
    ```

```
cmd.CommandText =
"select * from Products where ProductID=@id";
cmd.Parameters.AddWithValue("@id", id);
cmd.Connection = conn;
conn.Open();
using (SqlDataReader reader =
cmd.ExecuteReader())
{
  if (reader.HasRows)
  {
    reader.Read();
    p = new ProductBDO();
    p.ProductID = id;
    p.ProductName =
    (string)reader["ProductName"];
    p.QuantityPerUnit =
    (string)reader["QuantityPerUnit"];
    p.UnitPrice =
    (decimal)reader["UnitPrice"];
    p.UnitsInStock =
    (short)reader["UnitsInStock"];
    p.UnitsOnOrder =
    (short)reader["UnitsOnOrder"];
    p.ReorderLevel =
    (short)reader["ReorderLevel"];
    p.Discontinued =
    (bool)reader["Discontinued"];
  }
}
return p;
}
```

In this method, we first create a SQL connection (`SqlConnection`) to the `Northwind` database and then issue a SQL query to get the product details for the given product ID. Remember that we are going to change this ADO.NET code to LINQ to Entities in a later chapter.

Testing the GetProduct method

If you now set `LayerNorthwindService` as the startup project and run the
application, you can get the actual product information from the database,
as seen in the following screenshot:

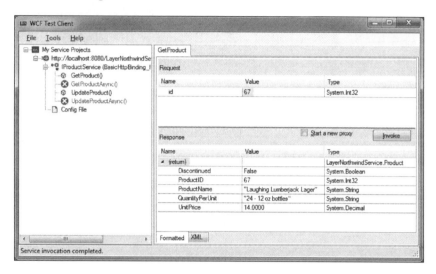

If you get an error screen, it is probably because you have set your connection string
incorrectly. Double-check the new connection string node in your `App.config` file
and try again until you can connect to your database.

If your connection string is correct, double-check the column names to make sure
that they are not misspelled. You might also need to adjust your connection string
depending on the way you are connecting to the database.

Instead of the connection error message, you might see the following error message:

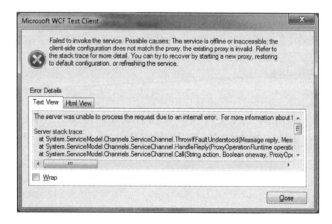

This error will occur when you try to get the product information for a product with a product ID of 0. The error message does not give much detail about what went wrong here because we did not let the server reveal the details of any error. Let's follow the instructions in the error message to change the setting includeExceptionDetailInFaults to True in the App.config file and run it again. Now, you will see that the error detail has changed to **Object reference not set to an instance of an object**.

A little investigation will tell us that there is a bug in our ProductService class. Inside the ProductService.GetProduct method, after we call the business logic layer to get the product detail for an ID, we will get a null product if the ID is not a valid product ID in the database. When we pass this null object to the next method (TranslateProductBDOToProductDTO), we get the error message shown in the preceding screenshot. Actually, this will happen whenever you enter a product ID outside the range of 1 to 77. This is because, in the sample Northwind database, there are only 77 products, with product IDs ranging from 1 to 77. To fix this problem, we can add the following statement inside the GetProduct method in the ProductService class right after the call to the business logic layer:

```
if (productBDO == null)
    throw new Exception("No product found for id " + id);
```

In the ProductService.cs file, the GetProduct method will now be as follows:

```
public Product GetProduct(int id)
{
    var productBDO = productLogic.GetProduct(id);
    if (productBDO == null)
    throw new Exception("No product found for id " + id);
    var product = new Product();
    TranslateProductBDOToProductDTO(productBDO, product);
    return product;
}
```

For now, we will raise an exception if an invalid product ID is entered. Later, we will convert this exception to a FaultContract type so that the caller will be able to catch and process the fault properly.

Now run the application again, and if you enter an invalid product ID, say 0, you will get an error message **No product found for id 0**. This is much clearer than the previous **Object reference not set to an instance of an object** error message.

Updating the database using UpdateProduct

Next, we will modify the UpdateProduct method to update the product record in the database. The UpdateProduct method in the LayerNorthwindDAL project should be modified as follows:

```
public bool UpdateProduct(ProductBDO product,
  ref string message)
{
  message = "product updated successfully";
  var ret = true;
  using (SqlConnection conn =
  new SqlConnection(connectionString))
  {
    var cmdStr = @"UPDATE products
    SET ProductName=@name,
    QuantityPerUnit=@unit,
    UnitPrice=@price,
    Discontinued=@discontinued
    WHERE ProductID=@id";
    using (SqlCommand cmd = new SqlCommand(cmdStr, conn))
    {
      cmd.Parameters.AddWithValue("@name",
      product.ProductName);
      cmd.Parameters.AddWithValue("@unit",
      product.QuantityPerUnit);
      cmd.Parameters.AddWithValue("@price",
      product.UnitPrice);
      cmd.Parameters.AddWithValue("@discontinued",
      product.Discontinued);
      cmd.Parameters.AddWithValue("@id",
      product.ProductID);
      conn.Open();
      if (cmd.ExecuteNonQuery() != 1)
      {
        message = "no product was updated";
        ret = false;
      }
    }
  }
  return ret;
}
```

Inside this method, we have used parameters to specify arguments to the update command. This is a good practice because it will prevent SQL Injection attacks, as the SQL statement is precompiled instead of being dynamically built.

Testing the UpdateProduct method

We can follow these steps to test the `UpdateProduct` method:

1. Start the WCF service by pressing *Ctrl* + *F5* or just *F5*. The WCF Test Client should also start automatically.

2. Double-click on the **UpdateProduct()** operation in the WCF Test Client.

3. Select **LayerNorthwindService.Product** from the product's dropdown, then enter a valid product ID, name, price, and quantity per unit.

4. Click on **Invoke**.

You should get a `True` response. To check this, just go to the **GetProduct()** page, enter the same product ID, click on **Invoke**, and you will see that all of your updates have been saved to the database.

The content of the `ProductDAO.cs` file is now as follows:

```
using System;
using System.Collections.Generic;
using System.Linq;
using System.Text;
using System.Threading.Tasks;
using LayerNorthwindBDO;
using System.Data.SqlClient;
using System.Configuration;

namespace LayerNorthwindDAL
{
  public class ProductDAO
{
  //Note put following three lines in one line in your code
    string connectionString = ConfigurationManager.
    ConnectionStrings["NorthwindConnectionString"].
    ConnectionString;

    public ProductBDO GetProduct(int id)
    {
      ProductBDO p = null;
      using (SqlConnection conn =
      new SqlConnection(connectionString))
      {
        using(SqlCommand cmd = new SqlCommand())
        {
```

```csharp
cmd.CommandText =
"select * from Products where ProductID=@id";
cmd.Parameters.AddWithValue("@id", id);
cmd.Connection = conn;
conn.Open();
using(SqlDataReader reader = cmd.ExecuteReader())
{
  if (reader.HasRows)
  {
    reader.Read();
    p = new ProductBDO();
    p.ProductID = id;
    p.ProductName =
    (string)reader["ProductName"];
    p.QuantityPerUnit =
    (string)reader["QuantityPerUnit"];
    p.UnitPrice =
    (decimal)reader["UnitPrice"];
    p.UnitsInStock =
    (short)reader["UnitsInStock"];
    p.UnitsOnOrder =
    (short)reader["UnitsOnOrder"];
    p.ReorderLevel =
    (short)reader["ReorderLevel"];
    p.Discontinued =
    (bool)reader["Discontinued"];
  }
 }
}
  }
  return p;
}

public bool UpdateProduct(ProductBDO product,
ref string message)
{
  message = "product updated successfully";
  var ret = true;
  using (SqlConnection conn =
  new SqlConnection(connectionString))
  {
    var cmdStr = @"UPDATE products
    SET ProductName=@name,
    QuantityPerUnit=@unit,
    UnitPrice=@price,
```

```
            Discontinued=@discontinued
            WHERE ProductID=@id";
            using(SqlCommand cmd = new SqlCommand(cmdStr, conn))
            {
              cmd.Parameters.AddWithValue("@name",
              product.ProductName);
              cmd.Parameters.AddWithValue("@unit",
              product.QuantityPerUnit);
              cmd.Parameters.AddWithValue("@price",
              product.UnitPrice);
              cmd.Parameters.AddWithValue("@discontinued",
              product.Discontinued);
              cmd.Parameters.AddWithValue("@id",
              product.ProductID);
              conn.Open();
              if (cmd.ExecuteNonQuery() != 1)
              {
                message = "no product is updated";
                ret = false;
              }
            }
          }
        }
        return ret;
      }
    }
  }
```

Adding error handling to the service

In the previous sections, when we were trying to retrieve a product, but the product ID passed in was not a valid one, we just threw an exception. Exceptions are technology-specific and therefore are not suitable for crossing the service boundary of SOA-compliant services. Thus, for WCF services, we should not throw normal exceptions.

What we need are SOAP faults that meet industry standards for seamless interoperability.

The service interface layer operations that might throw fault exceptions must be decorated with one or more `FaultContract` attributes, defining the exact fault exception.

On the other hand, the service consumer should catch specific fault exceptions to be in a position to handle the specified fault exceptions.

Adding a fault contract

We will now wrap the exception in the GetProduct operation with a FaultContract type.

Before we implement our first FaultContract type, we need to modify the App.config file in the LayerNorthwindService project. We will change the includeExceptionDetailInFaults setting back to False so that every unhandled, faultless exception will be a violation. In this way, client applications won't know the details of those exceptions so that the service technology and the hosting environment won't be revealed to them.

 You can set includeExceptionDetailInFaults to True while debugging, as this can be very helpful in diagnosing problems during the development stage. In production, it should always be set to False.

Open the App.config file in the LayerNorthwindService project, change includeExceptionDetailInFaults from True to False, and save it.

Next, we will define a FaultContract type. For simplicity, we will define only one FaultContract type and leave it inside the IProductService.cs file, although in a real system you can have as many fault contracts as you want, and they should also normally be in their own files. The ProductFault fault contract is defined as follows:

```
[DataContract]
public class ProductFault
{
    public ProductFault(string msg)
    {
        FaultMessage = msg;
    }

    [DataMember]
    public string FaultMessage;
}
```

We then decorate the service operations, GetProduct and UpdateProduct, with the following attribute:

```
[FaultContract(typeof(ProductFault))]
```

This is to tell the service consumers that these operations might throw a fault of the type, ProductFault.

The content of IProductService.cs should now be as follows:

```csharp
using System;
using System.Collections.Generic;
using System.Linq;
using System.Runtime.Serialization;
using System.ServiceModel;
using System.Text;

namespace LayerNorthwindService
{
    [ServiceContract]
    public interface IProductService
    {
        [OperationContract]
        [FaultContract(typeof(ProductFault))]
        Product GetProduct(int id);

        [OperationContract]
        [FaultContract(typeof(ProductFault))]
        bool UpdateProduct(Product product, ref string message);
    }

    [DataContract]
    public class Product
    {
        [DataMember]
        public int ProductID;

        [DataMember]
        public string ProductName;

        [DataMember]
        public string QuantityPerUnit;

        [DataMember]
        public decimal UnitPrice;

        [DataMember]
        public bool Discontinued;
    }

    [DataContract]
    public class ProductFault
    {
        public ProductFault(string msg)
        {
            FaultMessage = msg;
        }
```

```
        [DataMember]
        public string FaultMessage;
    }
}
```

Throwing a fault contract exception

Once we have modified the interface, we need to modify the implementation.
Open the `ProductService.cs` file and change `GetProduct` to be as follows:

```
public Product GetProduct(int id)
{
    ProductBDO productBDO = null;
    try
    {
        productBDO = productLogic.GetProduct(id);
    }
    catch (Exception e)
    {
        var msg = e.Message;
        var reason = "GetProduct Exception";
        throw new FaultException<ProductFault>
            (new ProductFault(msg), reason);
    }

    if (productBDO == null)
    {
        var msg =
            string.Format("No product found for id {0}",
            id);
        var reason = "GetProduct Empty Product";
        if (id == 999)
        {
            throw new Exception(msg);
        }
        else
        {
            throw new FaultException<ProductFault>
                (new ProductFault(msg), reason);
        }
    }
    var product = new Product();
    TranslateProductBDOToProductDTO(productBDO, product);
    return product;
}
```

In this modified method, we have wrapped the call to the business logic method, hence to the data access layer method, in a try-catch block. If anything goes wrong when the product is being retrieved from the database, such as the login is invalid, the database server is down, or the network is broken, we will throw a fault exception, so the client will be able to catch the exception and display a proper message to the end user, should they wish to.

We will also throw a `ProductFault` exception if an invalid ID is passed into the `GetProduct` operation. However, we will throw a normal C# exception if the passed ID is `999`. Later, we will use this special ID to compare a normal C# exception with a fault exception.

For the `UpdateProduct` method, we need to do the same thing as with the `GetProduct` method, that is, wrapping the call to the business logic method within a try-catch block. In a sum, consider the following code in the `UpdateProduct` method:

```
return productLogic.UpdateProduct(
    productBDO, ref message);
```

Change the preceding code to look like the following code:

```
try
{
    result = productLogic.UpdateProduct(
        productBDO, ref message);
}
catch (Exception e)
{
    var msg = e.Message;
    var reason = "UpdateProduct Exception";
    throw new FaultException<ProductFault>
        (new ProductFault(msg), reason);
}
```

Now, we build the `LayerNorthwindService` project. After it has been successfully built, we will use the client that we built earlier to test this service. We will examine the fault message and the exception details after a normal exception and a fault exception have been thrown.

Updating the client program to catch the fault exception

Now, let's update the client program so that the fault exception is handled:

1. First, we need to update the service reference because we have changed the contracts for the service. From the `LayerNorthwindClient` project, expand the **Service References** node and right-click on **ProductServiceRef**. Select **Update Service Reference** from the context menu and the **Updating Service Reference** dialog box will pop up. The WCF Service Host will start automatically, and the updated metadata information will be downloaded to the client side. The proxy code will be updated with modified and new service contracts.

2. Then, open `Program.cs` under the `LayerNorthwindClient` project and add the following `using` statement:

   ```
   using System.ServiceModel;
   ```

3. Add the following method to the `Program` class:

   ```
   static void TestException(ProductServiceClient client,
       int id)
   {
       if (id != 999)
           Console.WriteLine("\n\nTest Fault Exception");
       else
           Console.WriteLine("\n\nTest normal Exception");

       try
       {
           var product = client.GetProduct(id);
       }
       catch (TimeoutException ex)
       {
           Console.WriteLine("Timeout exception");
       }
       catch (FaultException<ProductFault> ex)
       {
           Console.WriteLine("ProductFault.");
           Console.WriteLine("\tFault reason: " +
               ex.Reason);
           Console.WriteLine("\tFault message: " +
               ex.Detail.FaultMessage);
       }
       catch (FaultException ex)
       {
           Console.WriteLine("Unknown Fault");
           Console.WriteLine(ex.Message);
   ```

```
        }
        catch (CommunicationException ex)
        {
            Console.WriteLine("Communication exception");
        }
        catch (Exception ex)
        {
            Console.WriteLine("Unknown exception");
        }
    }
}
```

4. Inside this method, we first call `GetProduct` with an ID as the argument. If the ID is an invalid product ID, the service will throw a `ProductFault` exception. So, we have to add the `catch` statement to catch the `ProductFault` exception. We will print the reason and the message of the fault exception. We have also added several other exceptions such as timeout exception, communication exception, and general fault exception so that we can handle every situation. Note that the order of the `catch` statements is very important and should not be changed.

5. If `999` is passed to this method as the ID, the service will throw a normal C# exception instead of a fault exception. As you can see, with this exception we don't have a way to find the reason and details of the exception, so we will just print out the raw exception message.

6. Now, add the following statements to the end of the `Main` function in this class:

```
// FaultException
TestException(client, 0);
// regular C# exception
TestException(client, 999);
```

So, we will first test the `ProductFault` exception and then the regular C# exception.

7. Finally, set the solution to start with the projects, `LayerNorthwindService` and `LayerNorthwindClient` (make sure that the service project is started before the client project).

The full content of `Program.cs` is now as follows:

```
using System;
using System.Collections.Generic;
using System.Linq;
using System.Text;
using System.Threading.Tasks;
using LayerNorthwindClient.ProductServiceRef;
using System.ServiceModel;
```

```csharp
namespace LayerNorthwindClient
{
    class Program
    {
        static void Main(string[] args)
        {
            var client = new ProductServiceClient();
            var product = client.GetProduct(23);
            Console.WriteLine("product name is " +
                product.ProductName);
            Console.WriteLine("product price is " +
                    product.UnitPrice.ToString());
            product.UnitPrice = 20.0m;
            var message = "";
            var result = client.UpdateProduct(product,
                ref message);
            Console.WriteLine("Update result is " +
                            result.ToString());
            Console.WriteLine("Update message is " +
                            message);

            // FaultException
            TestException(client, 0);
            // regular C# exception
            TestException(client, 999);

            Console.WriteLine("Press any key to continue ...");
            Console.ReadLine();
        }

        static void TestException(ProductServiceClient client,
            int id)
        {
            if (id != 999)
                Console.WriteLine("\n\nTest Fault Exception");
            else
                Console.WriteLine("\n\nTest normal Exception");

            try
            {
                var product = client.GetProduct(id);
            }
            catch (TimeoutException ex)
            {
                Console.WriteLine("Timeout exception");
            }
            catch (FaultException<ProductFault> ex)
            {
                Console.WriteLine("ProductFault. ");
                Console.WriteLine("\tFault reason:" +
```

```
            ex.Reason);
        Console.WriteLine("\tFault message:" +
            ex.Detail.FaultMessage);
    }
    catch (FaultException ex)
    {
        Console.WriteLine("Unknown Fault");
        Console.WriteLine(ex.Message);
    }
    catch (CommunicationException ex)
    {
        Console.WriteLine("Communication exception");
    }
    catch (Exception ex)
    {
        Console.WriteLine("Unknown exception");
    }
}
}
}
```

Changing the exception options

We can test the program now. However, if you run the program in the debugging mode, it will break right after the exception is thrown inside the service code, with an error message **An exception of type 'System.ServiceModel.FaultException'1'** **occurred in LayerNorthwindService.dll but was not handled in user code**. Your screen will look like this:

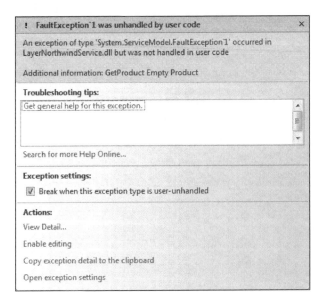

You can press *F5* to continue your testing but this will happen every time when you debug this program. To avoid this, you can first make sure that the debugging option, **Enable Just My Code (TOOLS | Options | Debugging)**, is checked. Then, change the exception option, **System.ServiceModel.FaultException'1 (DEBUG | Exceptions | Common Language Runtime Exceptions | System.ServiceModel)**, to not break when it is **User-unhandled** (uncheck this option). The following is the screenshot to set the exception option:

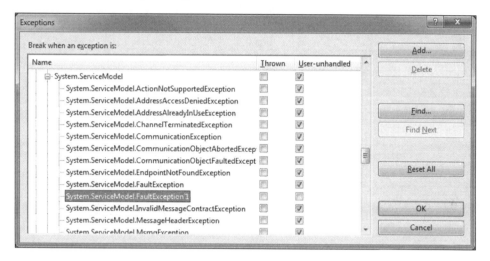

Testing the fault exception

Now, you can run the client program to test the fault exceptions (remember to set `LayerNorthwindService` and `LayerNorthwindClient` to be the startup projects). You will get the output shown in the following screenshot:

As you can see from the output, the client has the full details of the customized fault exception, such as fault reason and fault message. On the other hand, for the regular C# exception, the client does not have the fault details, except the raw fault message, which is a generic error message to all unhandled service faults.

If you turn on the flag, like the generic fault error message suggested, the client will be able to get the exception messages from the service side, but meanwhile, a lot of other details will also be revealed, such as the call stack and language specification of the service. As we said earlier, this is against the SOA principal, and it is not recommended for production.

Summary

In this chapter, we added the third layer, the data access layer, to `LayerNorthwindService`. We have also added exception handling to the service. Now, we have finished implementing the three-layer WCF service, according to the WCF service development best practices.

In the next chapters, we will learn LINQ and Entity Framework and then apply LINQ to Entities to our WCF service.

7
LINQ to Entities – Basic Concepts and Features

In the previous chapters, we learned how to create a three-layer WCF service. In this and the following chapters, we will learn how to use LINQ to query a database, or in other words, how to use LINQ to Entities in C#. After reading these two chapters, we will have a good understanding of LINQ to Entities so that we can rewrite the data access layer of our WCF service with LINQ to Entities to securely and reliably communicate with the underlying database.

In this chapter, we will cover the following topics:

- LINQ to Entities
- Creating a LINQ to Entities test application
- Creating the data model
- Querying and updating a database table
- Viewing generated SQL statements
- Deferred execution
- Deferred loading versus eager loading
- Joining two tables
- Querying a view

In the next chapter, we will cover the advanced concepts and features of LINQ to Entities such as stored procedure support, simultaneous updating, and transaction processing.

LINQ to Entities

LINQ to Entities provides the LINQ support that enables developers to write queries against Entity Framework's conceptual model using Visual Basic or Visual C#. Queries against Entity Framework are represented by command-tree queries, which execute against the object context. LINQ to Entities converts the LINQ queries to the command-tree queries, executes the queries against Entity Framework, and returns objects that can be used by both Entity Framework and LINQ.

LINQ to Entities allows developers to create flexible, strongly typed queries against the conceptual data model, **Entity Data Model (EDM)**, by using the LINQ expressions and standard LINQ query operators.

Creating a LINQ to Entities test application

Now, let's start exploring LINQ to Entities with some examples. We will apply the skills we are going to learn in this chapter and in *Chapter 8, LINQ to Entities – Advanced Concepts and Features*, to the data access layer of our WCF service, so that from the WCF service we can communicate with the database using LINQ to Entities instead of the raw ADO.NET data adapter.

First, we need to create a new project to test LINQ to Entities. Just follow these steps to create this test application:

1. Start Visual Studio, select the menu options **FILE | New | Project...**, and you will see the **New Project** dialog box. Do not open the LayerNorthwind solution (from the previous chapter), as in this chapter we will create a completely new solution and save it in a different location.

2. In the **New Project** window, specify **Visual C# | Console Application** as the project template, TestLINQToEntities as the project name, and C:\SOAwithWCFandEF\Projects\ as the location. Make sure that the **Create directory for solution** checkbox is selected.

3. Click on the **OK** button to create the project.

Creating the data model

To use LINQ to Entities, we need to add a conceptual data model, EDM, to the project. There are two ways to create an EDM: create it from a database or create it manually. Here, we will create the EDM from the Northwind database. We will add two tables and one view from the Northwind database into our project, so that later on we can use them to demonstrate LINQ to Entities.

Installing Entity Framework

To utilize LINQ to Entities, we first need to install Entity Framework to the project. Follow these steps to do this:

1. From the **Solution Explorer**, right-click on the project item and then select **Manage NuGet Packages.....**

2. On the **Manage NuGet Packages** window, select **Online | nuget.org | EntityFramework**.

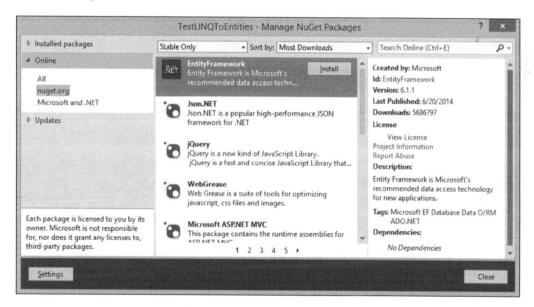

3. Click on the **Install** button to install Entity Framework to the project. This will add three references to the project, change the config file to include nodes for Entity Framework, add a folder called packages for the Entity Framework package, and add a packages.config file for the package to the project.

As you can see, Entity Framework 6.1.1 was installed when this book was written. You might have a newer version to install when you are reading this section.

Adding a LINQ to Entities item to the project

Once Entity Framework is installed to the project, let's add a new item to our test project TestLINQToEntities. The new item added should be the **ADO.NET Entity Data Model** type and named Northwind.edmx, as shown in the following **Add New Item - TestLINQToEntities** dialog window:

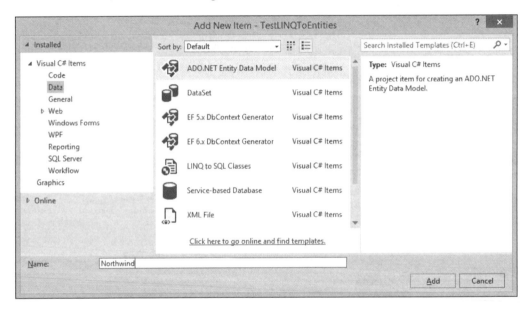

After you click on the **Add** button, the **Entity Data Model Wizard** window will pop up. Follow these steps to finish this wizard:

1. On the **Choose Model Contents** page, select **EF Designer from database**. Later, we will connect to the Northwind database and let Visual Studio generate the conceptual data model for us. If you choose the **Empty EF Designer model** option here, you will have to manually create the data model, which might be applicable in certain circumstances such as the absence of a physical database while you do the modeling. You can even create your physical database from your model later if you have chosen this option and have finished your model.

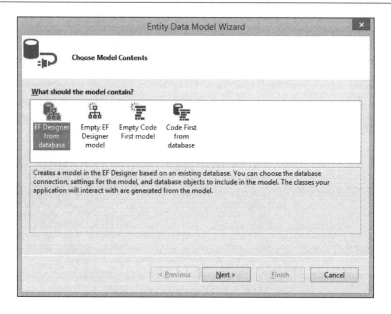

2. Click on the **Next** button in this window. The **Choose Your Data Connection** window should be displayed.

3. As this is our first LINQ to Entities application, there is no existing data connection to choose from, so let's click on the **New Connection...** button. The **Choose Data Source** window should be displayed on the screen.

We will now set up a new data connection with the following steps:

1. Select **Microsoft SQL Server** as the data source and leave **.NET Framework Data Provider for SQL Server** as the data provider. Click on the **Continue** button to close this window.

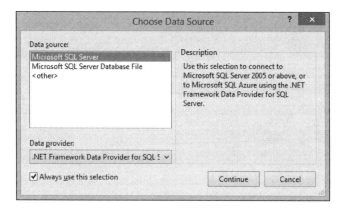

2. Now the **Connection Properties** window should pop up on your screen. In this window, enter your database server name as **Server name** or `localhost` if the database is on your local machine.

3. Then, specify the login details to your database.

4. Click on the **Test Connection** button to test your database connection settings. You should get the **Test connection succeeded** message. If not, modify your server name or login details and make sure that your SQL Server service is started.

5. Now, select **Northwind** as the database name. If you don't see **Northwind** in the database list, you need to install it to your SQL Server (refer to the previous chapter for installation details). Now, the **Connection Properties** window should appear as shown in the following screenshot:

6. Click on the **OK** button in the **Connection Properties** window to go back to the **Entity Data Model Wizard** window. The **Choose Your Data Connection** page in the **Entity Data Model Wizard** window should now look as shown in the following screenshot:

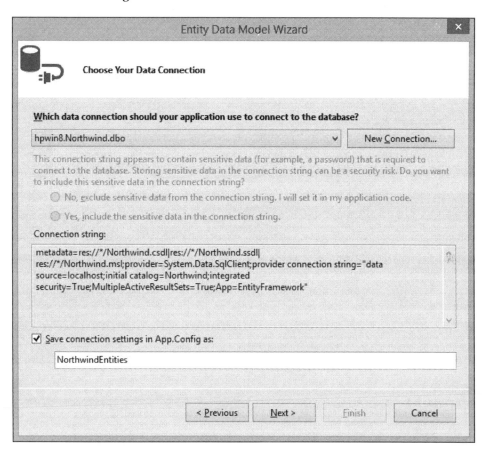

7. Click on the **Next** button on this window to go to the next page.

8. On the **Choose Your Database Objects and Settings** page, select the tables **Products** and **Categories**, the **Current Product List** view, and then click on the **Finish** button:

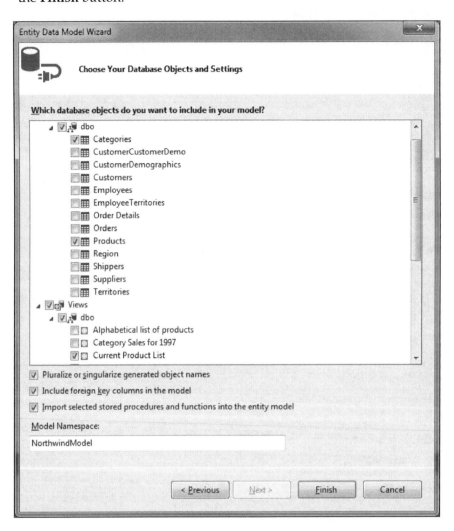

After you click on the **Finish** button, you might get a security warning dialog box. This is because Visual Studio will now run a custom template to generate the **Plain Old CLR/C# Object (POCO)**, which means that classes for your data model are just made up strictly of data properties rather than functionality and that they are not tied to Entity Framework in any way. Just click on **OK** to dismiss this dialog box (you can check the **Do not show this message again** checkbox to dismiss it forever).

At this point, the Visual Studio LINQ to Entities designer should be open, as shown in the following screenshot:

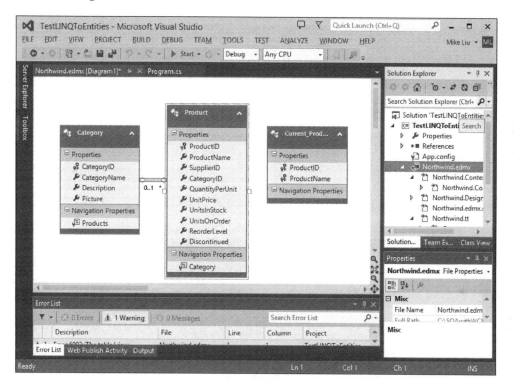

The generated LINQ to Entities classes

If you browse in the **Solution Explorer**, you will find that the following classes have been generated for the project:

```
public partial class NorthwindEntities : DbContext
public partial class Product
public partial class Category
public partial class Current_Product_List
```

The NorthwindEntities class, which is under the Northwind.Context.cs file, is the main conduit through which we'll query entities from the database as well as apply changes back to it. It contains three properties of the DbSet<> type, one for each table/view that we will be working with. It inherits from the DbContext class, which represents the main entry point for the LINQ to Entities framework.

The next two classes, `Product` and `Category`, are for the two tables that we are interested in. They are all POCO classes with a few properties. Note that `Product` has a navigation property called `Category`, and `Category` has a collection property called `Products`. We can use these properties to get the category of a product or the product list of a category.

The last class, `Current_Product_List`, is for the view. This is a simple class with only two property members.

 These four classes are generated through the T4 template system and should not be manually altered in any way. If any of them is modified, the changes will be overwritten when the files are regenerated. If you do need to customize them, you can modify the template or put your changes in a partial class.

Querying and updating a database table

Now that we have the entity classes created, we will use them to interact with the database. We will first work with the `Products` table to query and update records as well as to insert and delete records.

We will put our code in the `Program.cs` file. To make it easier to maintain, we will create a method, `TestTables`, put the code inside this method, and then call this method from the `Main` method.

Querying records

First, we will query the database to get some products. To query a database by using LINQ to Entities, we first need to construct a `DbContext` object as follows:

```
var NWEntities = new NorthwindEntities();
```

We can then use the LINQ query syntax to retrieve records from the database using the following code:

```
IEnumerable<Product> beverages = from p in NWEntities.Products
                where p.Category.CategoryName == "Beverages"
                orderby p.ProductName
                select p;
```

The preceding code will retrieve all of the products in the `Beverages` category sorted by the product name.

You can use the following statement to print out the total number of beverage products in the Northwind database:

```
Console.WriteLine("There are {0} Beverages", beverages.Count());
```

After we have finished working with this context object, we need to dispose of it as follows:

```
NWEntities.Dispose();
```

As a best practice, we should wrap all the preceding code in a using statement, so the code will be as follows:

```
using (var NWEntities = new NorthwindEntities())
{
// retrieve all Beverages products
IEnumerable<Product> beverages =
        from p in NWEntities.Products
        where p.Category.CategoryName == "Beverages"
        orderby p.ProductName
        select p;
Console.WriteLine("There are {0} Beverages",
        beverages.Count());
}
```

Updating records

We can update any of the products that we have just retrieved from the database as follows:

```
// update a product
var bev1 = beverages.ElementAtOrDefault(10);
if (bev1 != null)
{
var newPrice = (decimal)bev1.UnitPrice + 10.00m;
Console.WriteLine("The price of {0} is {1}. Update to {2}",
                    bev1.ProductName, bev1.UnitPrice, newPrice);
bev1.UnitPrice = newPrice;
// submit the change to database
NWEntities.SaveChanges();
}
```

We used the `ElementAtOrDefault` method, not the `ElementAt` method, just in case there was no `Beverages` product at element number 10 (`ElementAt` will throw an exception if the index is out of range while `ElementAtOrDefault` will return the default value of the list type, which is `null` in this example). We know that there are 12 beverage products in the sample database, so we increased the eleventh product's price by `10.00` and called `NWEntities.SaveChanges()` to update the record in the database. After you run the program, if you query the database, you will find that the eleventh beverage's price is increased by 10.00.

Inserting records

We can also create a new product and then insert this new product into the database by using the following code:

```
// add a product
var newProduct = new Product {ProductName="new test product" };
NWEntities.Products.Add(newProduct);
NWEntities.SaveChanges();
Console.WriteLine("Added a new product with name
                  'new test product'");
```

Deleting records

To delete a product, we first need to retrieve it from the database and then call the `Remove` method, as shown in the following code snippet:

```
// delete a product
var productsToDelete =
                from p in NWEntities.Products
                where p.ProductName == "new test product"
                select p;
if (productsToDelete.Count() > 0)
{
        foreach (var p in productsToDelete)
        {
            NWEntities.Products.Remove(p);
            Console.WriteLine("Deleted product {0}", p.ProductID);
        }
        NWEntities.SaveChanges();
}
```

You can also use the following statement to delete a product, say p, from the database:

```
NWEntities.Entry(p).State = EntityState.Deleted;
```

Running the program

The following is the content of the `Program.cs` file now:

```csharp
using System;
using System.Collections.Generic;
using System.Linq;
using System.Text;
using System.Threading.Tasks;

namespace TestLINQToEntities
{
  class Program
  {

    static void Main(string[] args)
    {
      // CRUD operations on tables
      TestTables();

      Console.WriteLine("Press any key to continue ...");
      Console.ReadKey();
    }

    static void TestTables()
    {
      using(NorthwindEntities NWEntities =
        new NorthwindEntities())
      {

        // retrieve all Beverages
        IEnumerable<Product> beverages =
          from p in NWEntities.Products
          where p.Category.CategoryName == "Beverages"
          orderby p.ProductName
          select p;
```

```
Console.WriteLine("There are {0} Beverages",
  beverages.Count());

// update one product
var bev1 = beverages.ElementAtOrDefault(10);
if (bev1 != null)
{
  var newPrice = (decimal)bev1.UnitPrice + 10.00m;
  Console.WriteLine("The price of {0} is {1}. Update
  to {2}",
  bev1.ProductName, bev1.UnitPrice, newPrice);
  bev1.UnitPrice = newPrice;
}

// submit the change to database
NWEntities.SaveChanges();

// insert a product
var newProduct = new Product { ProductName =
  "new test product" };
NWEntities.Products.Add(newProduct);
NWEntities.SaveChanges();

Console.WriteLine("Added a new product");

// delete a product
var productsToDelete =
  from p in NWEntities.Products
where p.ProductName == "new test product"
  select p;
if (productsToDelete.Count() > 0)
{
  foreach (var p in productsToDelete)
  {
    NWEntities.Products.Remove(p);
    Console.WriteLine("Deleted product {0}",
    p.ProductID);
  }
  NWEntities.SaveChanges();
}
}
}
}
}
```

If you run the program now, the output will be as shown in the following screenshot:

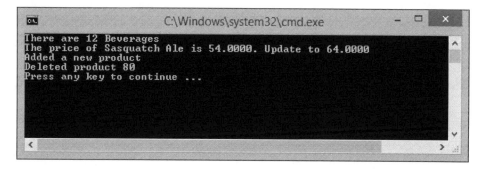

Viewing the generated SQL statements

You might wonder which SQL statements are used by LINQ to Entities to interact with the databases. In this section, we will use two ways to view the generated SQL statements used by LINQ to Entities queries. The first one is to use the ToString method and the second one is to use SQL Profiler.

Viewing the SQL statements using ToString

First, let's write a new test method to contain one LINQ to Entities query:

```
static void ViewGeneratedSQL()
{
    using(var NWEntities =
        new NorthwindEntities())
    {

        var beverages =
            from p in NWEntities.Products
            where p.Category.CategoryName == "Beverages"
            orderby p.ProductName
            select p;
    }
}
```

Now, we can print out the SQL statement of the LINQ to Entities query using the following statement:

```
// view SQL using ToString method
Console.WriteLine("The SQL statement is:" +
    beverages.ToString());
```

 In Entity Framework 4 or earlier, if you apply `.ToString()` to a LINQ to Entities query variable, you will get the type of the variable, which is `System.Data.Objects.ObjectQuery`.

The `Program.cs` file should now be as follows:

```
using System;
using System.Collections.Generic;
using System.Linq;
using System.Text;
using System.Threading.Tasks;

namespace TestLINQToEntities
{
    class Program
    {
        static void Main(string[] args)
        {
            // CRUD operations on tables
            //TestTables();

            ViewGeneratedSQL();

            Console.WriteLine("Press any key to continue ...");
            Console.ReadKey();
        }

        static void TestTables()
        {
            // the body of this method is omitted to save space
        }

        static void ViewGeneratedSQL()
        {
            using(var NWEntities =
                new NorthwindEntities())
            {
```

```
var beverages =
    from p in NWEntities.Products
    where p.Category.CategoryName == "Beverages"
    orderby p.ProductName
    select p;

// view SQL using ToString method
Console.WriteLine("The SQL statement is:\n" +
    beverages.ToString());
        }
    }
}
}
```

Run this program and you will see the output as shown in the following screenshot:

Viewing the SQL statements using SQL Profiler

With the `ToString` method, we can view the generated SQL statements for some LINQ to Entities expressions, but not all of them. For example, when we add a new product to the database, or when we execute a stored procedure in the database, there is no `IQueryable` object for us to use to view the generated SQL statements. In this case, we can use SQL Profiler to view the SQL statements.

SQL Server Profiler is a tool from Microsoft that can be used to create and manage traces and analyze and replay trace results. With SQL Profiler, you can capture any and all events that are happening to a database engine in real time, including the SQL statements that are being executed at that moment.

To view the SQL statements for LINQ to Entities queries by using SQL Profiler, we need to run some LINQ to Entities queries. So, we will keep this in mind for now and try this in the next section while we are learning about another important feature of LINQ to Entities, that is, deferred execution.

Deferred execution

One important thing to remember when working with LINQ to Entities is the deferred execution of LINQ.

Standard query operators differ in the timing of their execution depending on whether they return an aggregation value or a sequence of values. Those methods that return an aggregation value (for example, Average and Sum) execute immediately. Methods that return a sequence defer the query execution and return an enumerable object. These methods do not consume the target data until the query object is enumerated. This is known as **deferred execution**.

Checking deferred execution with SQL Profiler

To test the deferred execution of LINQ to Entities, let's first add the following method to our Program.cs file:

```
static void TestDeferredExecution()
{
    using(var NWEntities =
       new NorthwindEntities())
    {
    // SQL is not yet executed
    var beverages =
        from p in NWEntities.Products
        where p.Category.CategoryName == "Beverages"
        orderby p.ProductName
        select p;

    // SQL is executed on this statement
    Console.WriteLine("There are {0} Beverages",
        beverages.Count());
    }
}
```

Call the preceding method from the `Main` method of the program and comment out the calls to the two previous test methods (`TestTables` and `ViewGeneratedSQL`). Then, perform the following steps:

1. Open Profiler (`All Programs\Microsoft SQL Server\Performance Tools\SQL Server Profiler`).

2. Start a new trace on the `Northwind` database engine. You can refer to MSDN's SQL Server Profiler documentation to learn how to start a new trace on a database engine.

3. Go back to Visual Studio and set a break point on the first line of the `TestDeferredExecution` method.

4. Press *F5* to start debugging the program.

The program is now running and the cursor should be stopped on the first line of the method. Press *F10* to move to the next line of code and press *F10* again to step over the following line of code:

```
var beverages =
    from p in NWEntities.Products
    where p.Category.CategoryName == "Beverages"
    orderby p.ProductName
        select p;
```

Switch to Profiler and you will find that there is nothing in there.

However, when you press *F10* in Visual Studio and when the following statement is executed, you will see (in Profiler) that a query has been executed in the database:

```
Console.WriteLine("There are {0} Beverages", beverages.Count());
```

The query executed in the database is as follows:

```
SELECT
[GroupBy1].[A1] AS [C1]
FROM ( SELECT
  COUNT(1) AS [A1]
  FROM   [dbo].[Products] AS [Extent1]
  INNER JOIN [dbo].[Categories] AS [Extent2] ON
  [Extent1].[CategoryID] = [Extent2].[CategoryID]
  WHERE N'Beverages' = [Extent2].[CategoryName]
)  AS [GroupBy1]
```

The **SQL Server Profiler** window should look as shown in the following screenshot:

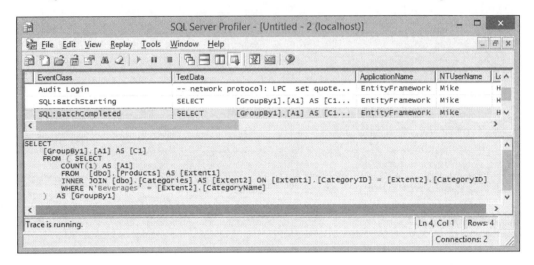

From Profiler, we know that, under the hood, LINQ actually first created a subquery to get the total beverage products' count, and then got this count from the subquery result. It also used an inner join to get the categories of products.

Deferred execution for aggregation methods

If the query expression returns an aggregation value, the query will be executed as soon as it is defined. For example, we can add the following statement to our test deferred execution method to get the average price of all products:

```
// SQL is executed on this statement
var averagePrice = (from p in NWEntities.Products
                    select p.UnitPrice).Average();
Console.WriteLine("The average price is {0}", averagePrice);
```

Start SQL Profiler and then press *F5* to start debugging the program. When the cursor is stopped on the line to print out the average price (in the **SQL Server Profiler** window), we see that a query has been executed to get the average price, and when the printing statement is being executed, no further query is executed in the database.

The **SQL Server Profiler** window is shown in the following screenshot:

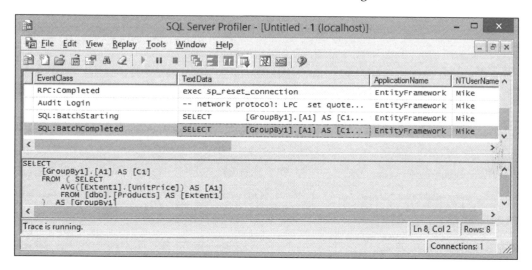

Deferred execution for aggregation methods within sequence expressions

However, just because a query is using one of the aggregation methods such as sum, average, or count, this doesn't mean that the query will be executed as soon as it is defined. If the query result is a sequence, the execution will still be deferred. The following is an example of this kind of query:

```
// SQL is not executed even though there is a singleton method
var cheapestProductsByCategory =
  from p in NWEntities.Products
  group p by p.CategoryID into g
  select new
  {
    CategoryID = g.Key,
     CheapestProduct =
          (from p2 in g
           where p2.UnitPrice == g.Min(p3 => p3.UnitPrice)
           select p2).FirstOrDefault()
  };
Console.WriteLine("Cheapest products by category:");
// SQL is executed on this statement
foreach (var p in cheapestProductsByCategory)
{
```

```
    if (p.CategoryID == null || p.CheapestProduct == null)
        continue;
    Console.WriteLine("category {0}: product name: {1} price: {2}",
                      p.CategoryID, p.CheapestProduct.ProductName,
                      p.CheapestProduct.UnitPrice);
}
```

Start SQL Profiler and then press *F5* to start debugging the program. When the cursor is stopped at the beginning of the `foreach` line, in Profiler we don't see the query statement to get the minimum price for any product. When we press *F10* again, the cursor is stopped on the `cheapestProductsByCategory` variable, in the `foreach` line of code, but we still don't see the query statement to get the cheapest products.

Then, after we press *F10* twice, the cursor is stopped on the `var p` keyword in the `foreach` line of code, and this time in Profiler, we see that the query is executed.

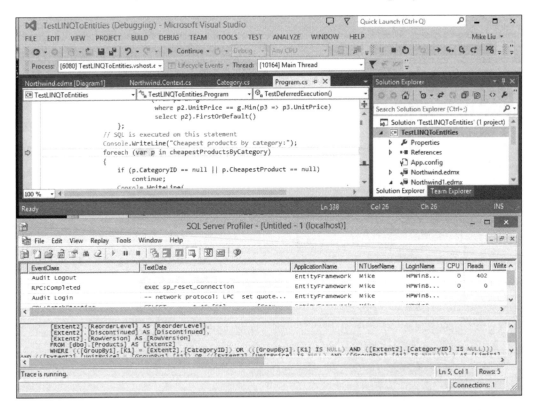

The actual SQL statements for this LINQ to Entities expression are as follows:

```
SELECT
1 AS [C1],
[GroupBy1].[K1] AS [CategoryID],
[Limit1].[ProductID] AS [ProductID],
[Limit1].[ProductName] AS [ProductName],
[Limit1].[SupplierID] AS [SupplierID],
[Limit1].[CategoryID] AS [CategoryID1],
[Limit1].[QuantityPerUnit] AS [QuantityPerUnit],
[Limit1].[UnitPrice] AS [UnitPrice],
[Limit1].[UnitsInStock] AS [UnitsInStock],
[Limit1].[UnitsOnOrder] AS [UnitsOnOrder],
[Limit1].[ReorderLevel] AS [ReorderLevel],
[Limit1].[Discontinued] AS [Discontinued]
FROM   (SELECT
  [Extent1].[CategoryID] AS [K1],
  MIN([Extent1].[UnitPrice]) AS [A1]
  FROM [dbo].[Products] AS [Extent1]
  GROUP BY [Extent1].[CategoryID] ) AS [GroupBy1]
OUTER APPLY  (SELECT TOP (1)
  [Extent2].[ProductID] AS [ProductID],
  [Extent2].[ProductName] AS [ProductName],
  [Extent2].[SupplierID] AS [SupplierID],
  [Extent2].[CategoryID] AS [CategoryID],
  [Extent2].[QuantityPerUnit] AS [QuantityPerUnit],
  [Extent2].[UnitPrice] AS [UnitPrice],
  [Extent2].[UnitsInStock] AS [UnitsInStock],
  [Extent2].[UnitsOnOrder] AS [UnitsOnOrder],
  [Extent2].[ReorderLevel] AS [ReorderLevel],
  [Extent2].[Discontinued] AS [Discontinued]
  FROM [dbo].[Products] AS [Extent2]
  WHERE ((([GroupBy1].[K1] = [Extent2].[CategoryID]) OR ((([GroupBy1].
[K1] IS NULL) AND ([Extent2].[CategoryID] IS NULL))) AND ((([Extent2].
[UnitPrice] = [GroupBy1].[A1]) OR ((([Extent2].[UnitPrice] IS NULL) AND
([GroupBy1].[A1] IS NULL)))) ) AS [Limit1]
```

From this output, you can see that when the cheapestProductsByCategory variable is accessed, it first calculates the minimum price for each category. Then, for each category it returns the first product with that price. In a real application, you probably wouldn't want to write such a complex query in your code. Instead, you might want to put it in a stored procedure, which we will discuss in the next chapter.

The test method is as follows:

```
static void TestDeferredExecution()
{
  using(var NWEntities =
      new NorthwindEntities())
  {
  // SQL is not executed
  var beverages =
    from p in NWEntities.Products
    where p.Category.CategoryName == "Beverages"
    orderby p.ProductName
    select p;

  // SQL is executed on this statement
  Console.WriteLine("There are {0} Beverages",
       beverages.Count());

  // SQL is executed on this statement
  var averagePrice = (from p in NWEntities.Products
                      select p.UnitPrice).Average();
  Console.WriteLine("The average price is {0}", averagePrice);

  // SQL is not executed even there is a singleton method
  var cheapestProductsByCategory =
      from p in NWEntities.Products
      group p by p.CategoryID into g
      select new
    {
      CategoryID = g.Key,
      CheapestProduct =
          (from p2 in g
          where p2.UnitPrice == g.Min(p3 => p3.UnitPrice)
          select p2).FirstOrDefault()
    };
  // SQL is executed on this statement
  Console.WriteLine("Cheapest products by category:");
  foreach (var p in cheapestProductsByCategory)
  {
    if (p.CategoryID == null || p.CheapestProduct == null)
      continue;
    Console.WriteLine(
```

```
                "category {0}: product name: {1} price: {2}",
                p.CategoryID, p.CheapestProduct.ProductName,
                p.CheapestProduct.UnitPrice);
        }
    }
}
```

If you comment out all other test methods (`TestTables` and `ViewGeneratedSQL`) and run the program, you should get an output similar to the one shown in the following screenshot:

Deferred execution – lazy loading versus eager loading

In one of the preceding examples, we retrieved the category name of a product using the following expression:

```
p.Category.CategoryName == "Beverages"
```

Even though there is no field called `categoryname` in the `Products` table, we can still get the category name of a product because there is an association between the `Products` and `Category` tables. In the **Northwind.edmx** design pane, click on the line that connects the **Products** and **Categories** tables and you will see all of the properties of the association. Note that its `Referential Constraint` property is `Category.CategoryID -> Product.CategoryID`, meaning that `category ID` is the key field to link these two tables.

Because of this association, we can retrieve the category for each product and also retrieve products for each category.

Lazy loading by default

Even with an association, the associated data is not loaded when the query is executed. For example, suppose we use the following test method to retrieve all of the categories and then access the products for each category:

```
static void TestAssociation()
{
using (var NWEntities = new NorthwindEntities())
  {
     var categories = from c in NWEntities.Categories select c;
     foreach (var category in categories)
     {
       Console.WriteLine("There are {0} products in category {1}",
       category.Products.Count(), category.CategoryName);
     }
  }
}
```

Start SQL Profiler and then press *F5* to start debugging the program. When the cursor is stopped on the `foreach` line (after you press *F10* three times to move the cursor to the `var category` keyword), in Profiler we see the following SQL statement:

```
SELECT
[Extent1].[CategoryID] AS [CategoryID],
[Extent1].[CategoryName] AS [CategoryName],
[Extent1].[Description] AS [Description],
[Extent1].[Picture] AS [Picture]
FROM [dbo].[Categories] AS [Extent1]
```

When you press *F10* to execute the printout line, in Profiler we see the following SQL statement:

```
exec sp_executesql N'SELECT
[Extent1].[ProductID] AS [ProductID],
[Extent1].[ProductName] AS [ProductName],
[Extent1].[SupplierID] AS [SupplierID],
[Extent1].[CategoryID] AS [CategoryID],
[Extent1].[QuantityPerUnit] AS [QuantityPerUnit],
[Extent1].[UnitPrice] AS [UnitPrice],
[Extent1].[UnitsInStock] AS [UnitsInStock],
[Extent1].[UnitsOnOrder] AS [UnitsOnOrder],
[Extent1].[ReorderLevel] AS [ReorderLevel],
```

```
[Extent1].[Discontinued] AS [Discontinued]
FROM [dbo].[Products] AS [Extent1]
WHERE [Extent1].[CategoryID] = @EntityKeyValue1',N'@EntityKeyValue1
int',@EntityKeyValue1=1
```

From these SQL statements, we know that Entity Framework first goes to the database to query all of the categories. Then, for each category, when we need to get the total count of products, it goes to the database again to query all of the products for that category. Because there are eight categories in the database, it goes to the database nine times in total (including the first one to retrieve all categories).

This is because, by default, lazy loading is set to `true`, meaning that the loading of all associated data (children) is deferred until the data is needed.

Eager loading with the Include method

To change the behavior seen in the preceding section, we can use the `Include` method to tell `DbContext` to automatically load the specified children during the initial query:

```
static void TestEagerLoading()
{
    using(var NWEntities = new NorthwindEntities())
    {
     // eager loading products of categories
     var categories = from c
                        in NWEntities.Categories.Include(c=>c.Products)
                        select c;
     foreach (var category in categories)
     {
         Console.WriteLine("There are {0} products in category {1}",
             category.Products.Count(), category.CategoryName);
     }
    }
}
```

Inside this test method, when constructing the LINQ to Entities query, we added an `Include` clause to tell the framework to load all products when loading the categories.

To use `Include` with a lambda expression, you need to add the following `using` statement to the class:

```
using System.Data.Entity;
```

To test it, start SQL Profiler and then press *F5* to start debugging the program. When the cursor is stopped on the `foreach` line (at the `var category` keyword), in Profiler you will see the following SQL statement:

```
SELECT
[Project1].[CategoryID] AS [CategoryID],
[Project1].[CategoryName] AS [CategoryName],
[Project1].[Description] AS [Description],
[Project1].[Picture] AS [Picture],
[Project1].[C1] AS [C1],
[Project1].[ProductID] AS [ProductID],
[Project1].[ProductName] AS [ProductName],
[Project1].[SupplierID] AS [SupplierID],
[Project1].[CategoryID1] AS [CategoryID1],
[Project1].[QuantityPerUnit] AS [QuantityPerUnit],
[Project1].[UnitPrice] AS [UnitPrice],
[Project1].[UnitsInStock] AS [UnitsInStock],
[Project1].[UnitsOnOrder] AS [UnitsOnOrder],
[Project1].[ReorderLevel] AS [ReorderLevel],
[Project1].[Discontinued] AS [Discontinued]
FROM ( SELECT
   [Extent1].[CategoryID] AS [CategoryID],
   [Extent1].[CategoryName] AS [CategoryName],
   [Extent1].[Description] AS [Description],
   [Extent1].[Picture] AS [Picture],
   [Extent2].[ProductID] AS [ProductID],
   [Extent2].[ProductName] AS [ProductName],
   [Extent2].[SupplierID] AS [SupplierID],
   [Extent2].[CategoryID] AS [CategoryID1],
   [Extent2].[QuantityPerUnit] AS [QuantityPerUnit],
   [Extent2].[UnitPrice] AS [UnitPrice],
   [Extent2].[UnitsInStock] AS [UnitsInStock],
   [Extent2].[UnitsOnOrder] AS [UnitsOnOrder],
   [Extent2].[ReorderLevel] AS [ReorderLevel],
   [Extent2].[Discontinued] AS [Discontinued],
```

```
    CASE WHEN ([Extent2].[ProductID] IS NULL) THEN CAST(NULL AS int)
ELSE 1 END AS [C1]
   FROM   [dbo].[Categories] AS [Extent1]
   LEFT OUTER JOIN [dbo].[Products] AS [Extent2] ON [Extent1].
[CategoryID] = [Extent2].[CategoryID]
)  AS [Project1]
ORDER BY [Project1].[CategoryID] ASC, [Project1].[C1] ASC
```

As you can see from the preceding SQL statement, all products for all categories are loaded during the first query.

Comparing lazy loading and eager loading

As you have learned in the previous sections, lazy loading and eager loading are two very different options for the loading-related objects. With lazy loading, the first query will return only the main objects, and every time a related object is needed, another query has to be executed. Each query will have a smaller payload, but there will be multiple queries to the database. With eager loading, the first query will return all objects, including any related objects. When a related object is needed, it will be retrieved right from the object model, not from the database. There will be only one database trip, but the payload will be larger. You should weigh the pros and cons of each option and choose one appropriately.

Joining two tables

Although an association is a kind of join in LINQ, we can also explicitly join two tables using the `Join` keyword, as shown in the following code snippet:

```
static void TestJoin()
{
    using(var NWEntities = new NorthwindEntities())
    {
    var categoryProducts =
        from c in NWEntities.Categories
        join p in NWEntities.Products
        on c.CategoryID equals p.CategoryID
        into productsByCategory
        select new {
            c.CategoryName,
            productCount = productsByCategory.Count()
        };
```

```
        foreach (var cp in categoryProducts)
        {
          Console.WriteLine("There are {0} products in category
          {1}",
                cp.productCount, cp.CategoryName);
        }
      }
    }
```

This was not so useful in the previous example because the `Products` and `Categories` tables are associated with a foreign key relationship. If there is no foreign key association between two tables, or if we have not added the associations between these two tables, this will be particularly useful.

From the following SQL statement, we can see that only one query is executed to get the results:

```
SELECT
[Extent1].[CategoryID] AS [CategoryID],
[Extent1].[CategoryName] AS [CategoryName],
(SELECT
   COUNT(1) AS [A1]
   FROM [dbo].[Products] AS [Extent2]
   WHERE [Extent1].[CategoryID] = [Extent2].[CategoryID]) AS [C1]
FROM [dbo].[Categories] AS [Extent1]
```

In addition to joining two tables, you can also:

- Join three or more tables
- Join a table to itself
- Create left, right, and full outer joins
- Join using composite keys

Querying a view

Querying a view is the same as querying a table (the view needs to have a unique key). For example, you can query the view "current product lists" as follows:

```
static void TestView()
{
   using(var NWEntities = new NorthwindEntities())
   {
   var currentProducts = from p
```

```
                    in NWEntities.Current_Product_Lists
                    select p;
    foreach (var p in currentProducts)
      {
          Console.WriteLine("Product ID: {0} Product Name: {1}",
              p.ProductID, p.ProductName);
      }
    }
  }
```

This will get and print all of the current products using the view.

Summary

In this chapter, we learned the basic concepts and features of LINQ to Entities. We learned how to query a database with LINQ to Entities, update a database with LINQ to Entities, and we also learned how to change loading behaviors with LINQ to Entities.

In the next chapter, we will cover the advanced concepts and features of LINQ to Entities such as stored procedure support, simultaneous updating, and transaction processing.

8

LINQ to Entities – Advanced Concepts and Features

In the previous chapter, we learned some basic concepts and features of LINQ to Entities such as querying and updating database tables and views and changing loading behaviors using the `Include` method.

In this chapter, we will learn some advanced features of LINQ to Entities such as stored procedure support, concurrency control, and transactional processing. After this chapter, we will rewrite the data access layer of our WCF service to utilize the LINQ to Entities technology.

In this chapter, we will cover the following topics:

- Calling a stored procedure
- Concurrency control
- Transaction support

Calling a stored procedure

Calling a stored procedure is different from querying a table or a view because a stored procedure can't be called without the proper preparation. A function import has to be added for the stored procedure and its result set has to be mapped. The modeling of a stored procedure is also different from modeling a table or a view. In the following sections, we will learn how to call a simple stored procedure, map the returned result of a stored procedure to an entity class, and create a new entity for the result set.

We will reuse the same application that we used in the previous chapter and add more methods to the program.

Mapping a stored procedure to a new entity class

First, we will try to call a simple stored procedure. In the sample database, there is a stored procedure called `Ten Most Expensive Products`. We will call this stored procedure to get the top ten most expensive products.

Adding a stored procedure to the model

Before we can call a stored procedure, we need to add it to the Entity Framework model. Perform the following steps:

1. Open the `Northwind.edmx` designer.

2. Right-click on an empty space on the designer surface and select **Update Model from Database…**:

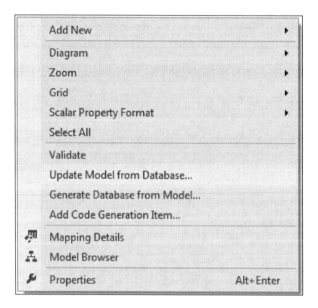

3. From the **Update Wizard** window, on the **Choose Your Database Objects and Settings** page, make sure that the **Add** tab is selected. Then, expand the **dbo** node under **Stored Procedures and Functions** and check **Ten Most Expensive Products**.

4. Make sure that the **Import selected stored procedures and functions into the entity model** option is checked.

5. Click on the **Finish** button.

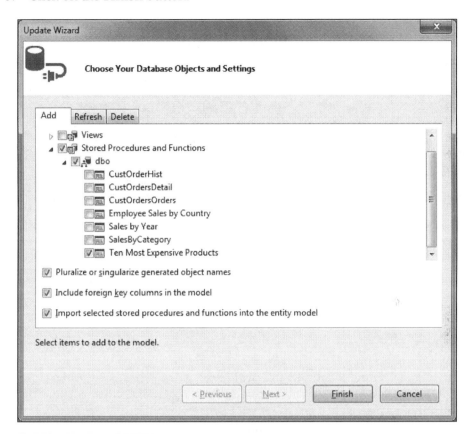

After you save the `Northwind.edmx` diagram, it will add the `Ten_Most_Expensive _Products` method to the `NorthwindEntities` class and add a new class, `Ten_Most _Expensive_Products_Result`, as the result data type of the stored procedure.

Querying a stored procedure

Now, from `Program.cs`, we can call this stored procedure as follows:

```
var tenProducts = from p in
    NWEntities.Ten_Most_Expensive_Products()
    select p;
foreach (var p in tenProducts)
{
    Console.WriteLine("Product Name: {0}, Price: {1}",
    p.TenMostExpensiveProducts, p.UnitPrice);
}
```

The SQL statement is pretty straightforward, as follows:

```
exec [dbo].[Ten Most Expensive Products]
```

The output will look like the one shown in the following screenshot:

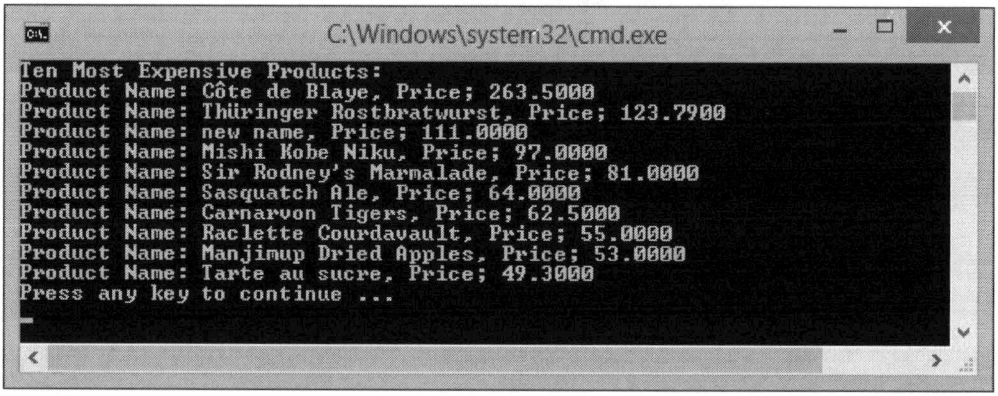

Mapping a stored procedure to an existing entity class

In the preceding example, LINQ to Entities created a new type for the return result of the stored procedure. It actually just added the word, `Result`, after the stored procedure name to create the name of the return data type. If we know that the return result is a kind of entity, we can tell LINQ to Entities to use that specific entity as the return type, instead of creating a new type.

For example, let's create a stored procedure as follows:

```
Create PROCEDURE [dbo].[GetProduct]
    (
    @ProductID int
    )
AS
    SET NOCOUNT ON
    Select * from Products where ProductID = @ProductID
```

You can create this stored procedure in Microsoft SQL Server Management Studio or by right-clicking on the **Stored Procedures** node in the **Server Explorer** of Visual Studio and selecting **Data Connections | Northwind.dbo | Add New Stored Procedure** from the context menu.

After the stored procedure has been created, follow these steps to add it to the entity data model and import a new function:

1. Open the `Northwind.edmx` designer.

2. Right-click on an empty space on the designer surface and select **Update Model from Database…**.

3. From the **Update Wizard** window, on the **Choose Your Database Objects and Settings** page, make sure that the **Add** tab is selected. Then, expand the **dbo** node under **Stored Procedures and Functions** and check **GetProduct**.

4. This time, make sure that the **Import selected stored procedures and functions into the entity model** option is not checked.

5. Click on the **Finish** button.

As we didn't check the **Import selected stored procedures and functions into the entity model** option, the stored procedure has not been imported in the entity model for us. The reason is that we don't want to create a new result type for this stored procedure; instead, we will map this stored procedure to an existing entity, as described in the following steps:

1. On the designer surface, right-click on an empty space and select **Add New** from the context menu and then select **Function Import…**.

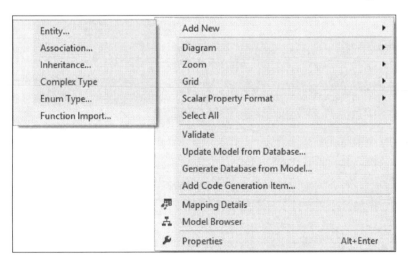

2. In the **Add Function Import** window, type in `GetProduct` in the **Function Import Name** field and select **GetProduct** as the stored procedure name from the drop-down list.

3. Select **Entities** as **Returns a Collection Of** and choose **Product** as the entity from the drop-down list.

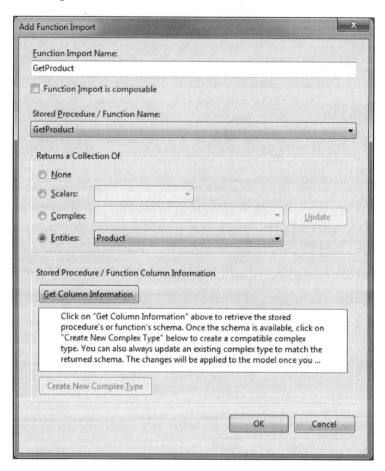

4. Click on the **OK** button.
5. Click on the **Save** button to save the model so that the new function for the new stored procedure can be created in the context class.
6. Now LINQ to Entities will use the `Product` class as the return type of this stored procedure.

To call this method, you can write a statement as follows:

```
var getProduct = NWEntities.GetProduct(1).FirstOrDefault();
```

The complete method for the stored procedure should be as follows:

```
static void TestStoredProcedure()
```

```
    {
    using(var NWEntities = new NorthwindEntities())
      {
        IEnumerable<Ten_Most_Expensive_Products_Result> tenProducts =
                from p
                in NWEntities.Ten_Most_Expensive_Products()
                select p;
        Console.WriteLine("Ten Most Expensive Products:");
        foreach (Ten_Most_Expensive_Products_Result p in tenProducts)
        {
          Console.WriteLine("Product Name: {0}, Price; {1}",
                  p.TenMostExpensiveProducts, p.UnitPrice);
        }

        // map a stored procedure to an entity class
      var getProduct = NWEntities.GetProduct(1).FirstOrDefault();
      Console.WriteLine("\nProduct name for product 1: {0}",
        getProduct.ProductName);
      }
    }
```

If you run the program, you should have an output, as shown in the
following screenshot:

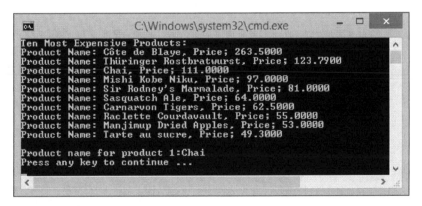

Interestingly, you can add another function for the same stored procedure but with
a different function name (GetProduct1), and for the new function, you can check
the **Complex** radio button to create a new type (GetProduct1_Result) for the result
of the stored procedure, instead of using the Product class. LINQ to Entities will
automatically create a new class for the return type.

The generated return type class, GetProduct1_Result, is almost identical to the Product class.

A big difference between the GetProduct and GetProduct1 methods is that the product you retrieved using GetProduct is managed by DbContext. Any changes you made to it will be committed back to the database if you call SaveChanges() later. However, the product you retrieved using GetProduct1 is not managed by DbContext and thus won't be committed back to the database if you call SaveChanges() later.

Handling simultaneous (concurrent) updates

If two users are updating the same record at the same time, a conflict will occur. There are normally three different ways to handle this conflict. The first method is to let the last update win, so no controlling mechanism is needed. The second one is to use a pessimistic lock, in which case, before updating a record, a user will first lock the record and then process and update the record. At the same time, all other users will have to wait for the lock to be released in order to start the updating process.

The third and most common mechanism in an enterprise product is the optimistic locking mechanism. A record is not locked for update when the data is retrieved, but when the application is ready to commit the changes, it will first check to see whether any other user has updated the same record since that data was retrieved. If nobody else has changed the same record, the update will be committed. If any other user has changed the same record, the update will fail and the user has to decide what to do with the conflict. Some possible options include overwriting the previous changes, discarding their own changes, or refreshing the record, and then reapplying (merging) the changes.

LINQ to Entities supports optimistic concurrency control in two ways. Next, we will learn both of them.

Detecting conflicts using a data column

The first way to detect conflicts is to use a regular data column. We can use the Concurrency Mode property for this purpose.

The Concurrency Mode property

During the designing stage, the **Concurrency Mode** property can be set for a data column to be one of the following two values: **Fixed** and **None (default)**.

For a data column, there are three values to remember:

- The original value before update
- The current value to be updated to
- The database value when the change is submitted

For example, consider the case where you fetch a product record from the database with a `UnitPrice` of `25.00` and update it to `26.00`. After you fetch this product, but before you submit your changes back to the database, somebody else has updated this product's price to `27.00`. In this example, the original value of the price is `25.00`, the current value to be updated to is `26.00`, and the database value when the change is submitted is `27.00`.

When the change is submitted to the database, the original and database values are compared. If they are different, a conflict is detected.

Now, let's look at these two settings. The first setting of the `Concurrency Mode` property is `Fixed`, which means that the column will be used for conflict detection. Whenever this column is being changed, its current and database values will be checked to see whether it has been updated by other users. If it has been, a conflict will be raised.

The second setting, `None`, means that the column will not be used for conflict checking. When a change is submitted to the database, the application will not check the status of this column. Therefore, even if this column has been updated by other users, it won't raise an error. This is the default setting of this property. So, by default, no column will be used for conflict detection.

Adding another entity data model

To test the concurrency of Entity Framework, we need to add a second entity data model to the project for the same database. The reason is that with Entity Framework, each database record has a unique entity key within the entity data model. All entity instances of the same database record will share the same entity key in the data model even if the entities are created within different object contexts.

To understand why this will stop us from testing the concurrency support of Entity Framework, let's first list the steps that we will perform to test the concurrency control.

By performing the following steps, we will test the concurrency control of Entity Framework:

1. Retrieve a product from the database.
2. Update its price in memory.
3. Retrieve the same product from the database.
4. Update its price in memory again.
5. Submit the changes made in step 4 to the database.
6. Submit the changes made in step 2 to the database.

With the concurrency control, the commit in step 6 should fail because the product price has been changed in the database after it has been retrieved. However, if we use the same entity data model, the product that is retrieved in step 1 will be cached. So, in step 3, the product object from the cache will be returned. Thus, the update in step 4 will be based on the update in step 2. The commit to the database in step 5 will actually contain both changes in step 2 and step 4. Therefore, the commit to the database in step 6 will not fail because it really has nothing to change in the database.

That's why we need to add another entity data model to the project, so we can have two independent entity objects pointing to the same record in the database. The following are the steps to add this new entity data model:

1. From the **Solution Explorer**, right-click on the **TestLINQToEntities** project and select **Add | New Item**.
2. Select **Visual C# Items | ADO.NET Entity Data Model** as the template and change the item name to **Northwind1.edmx**.
3. Select **EF Designer from database** as **Model Contents**.
4. Select the existing **Northwind** connection as **Data Connection** and keep the default entity name as **NorthwindEntities1**.
5. Choose the **Products** table as **Database Objects** and keep the default model namespace as **NorthwindModel1**.
6. Click on the **Finish** button to add the model to the project.
7. In the Northwind1.edmx designer, select the **Product** entity.
8. Change **Entity Set Name** to **Product1s**.
9. Change entity's **Name** to **Product1**.
10. Save the model.

Steps 8 and 9 are essential because there is already a public class with the name of `Product` in our project. If you leave it unchanged and try to build/run the solution, you will find that your `Northwind1.designer.cs` file is empty because the designer can't generate it due to the name conflicts. In this case, you need to delete the new entity data model and re-add it to generate the new entity model designer file.

11. Open the original entity data model, **NorthwindEntities**.
12. Move the `Product` entity to a slightly different location on the designer.
13. Save the original entity data model, **NorthwindEntities**.

When you save the new entity data model, your original `Product` class might disappear because Visual Studio thinks you are going to move the **Product** entity from the old model to this new model, even though we have renamed it to **Product1**. This is why we re-save the original model to regenerate the `Product` class.

Writing the test code

Now that we have a new entity data model added to the project, we can write the following code to test the concurrency control of Entity Framework:

```
using(var NWEntities = new NorthwindEntities())
{
    // first user
    Console.WriteLine("First User ...");
    var product = (from p in NWEntities.Products
                    where p.ProductID == 2
                    select p).First();
    Console.WriteLine("Original price: {0}", product.UnitPrice);
    product.UnitPrice += 1.0m;
    Console.WriteLine("Current price to update: {0}",
                    product.UnitPrice);
    // process more products

    // second user
    Console.WriteLine("\nSecond User ...");
    using(var NWEntities1 = new NorthwindEntities1())
    {
        var product1 = (from p in NWEntities1.Product1s
                        where p.ProductID == 2
                        select p).First();
```

```
        Console.WriteLine("Original price: {0}",
                          product1.UnitPrice);
        product1.UnitPrice += 2.0m;
        Console.WriteLine("Current price to update: {0}",
                          product1.UnitPrice);
        NWEntities1.SaveChanges();
        Console.WriteLine("Price update submitted to database");
    }
    // first user is ready to submit changes
    Console.WriteLine("\nFirst User ...");
    NWEntities.SaveChanges();
    Console.WriteLine("Price update submitted to database");
}
```

In this example, we will first retrieve product 2 and increase its price by 1.0. Then, we will simulate another user to retrieve the same product and increase its price by 2.0. The second user will submit the changes first with no error. When the first user tries to submit the changes and the price has already been changed by the second user, the update will still be saved to the database without any problem. This is because, by default, the concurrency control is not turned on, so the later change will always overwrite the previous change.

Testing the conflicts

Now run the program. You will get an output, as shown in the following screenshot:

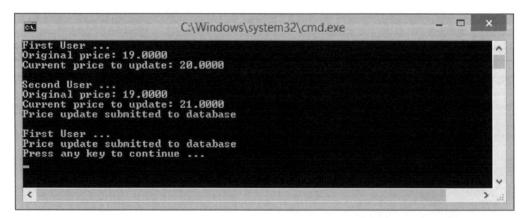

From this screenshot, we know both updates have been submitted to the database without any problem. If you query the database, you will find that the price of product 2 is now 20, not 21, because the first user's update overwrote the second user's update.

Turning on concurrency verification

Now, open `Northwind.edmx`, click on the **UnitPrice** member of the **Product** entity, and change its **Concurrency Mode** property to **Fixed**, as shown in the following screenshot:

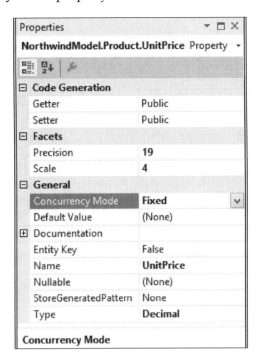

Make sure that you open the `Northwind.edmx` model, not the new `Northwind1.edmx` model, because the second user within the new `Northwind1.edmx` model will submit to the database first, meaning that there will be no conflict for this update.

Run the program again. You will see an exception this time because the `price` column is now used for conflict detection. If you query the database, you will find the price for product 2 is now 22 because it hasn't been overwritten by the first user's update, which would have updated its price to 21 if it hadn't failed due to the concurrent conflict.

> If you look at the autogenerated SQL statement for this update through SQL Profiler, you will find that another `where` clause is added to the SQL statement and that Entity Framework just watches the number of records affected.

The output is as shown in the following screenshot:

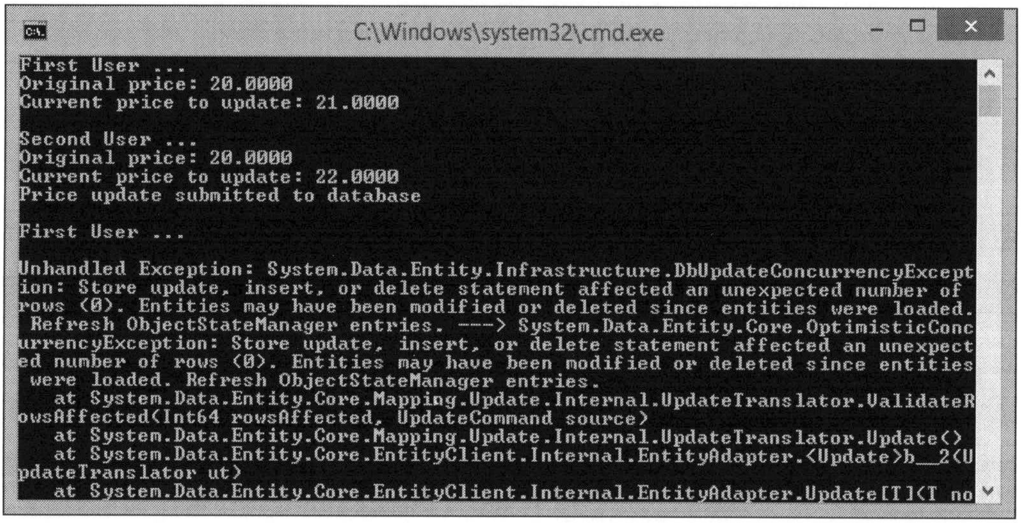

To resolve this conflict, we can add an exception handling block around the first user's update.

First, you need to add a `using` statement to the `Program.cs` file for the concurrency exception type:

```
using System.Data.Entity.Infrastructure;
```

Then, change the saving part as shown in the following code snippet:

```
// first user is ready to submit changes
Console.WriteLine("\nFirst User ...");
try
{
    NWEntities.SaveChanges();
    Console.WriteLine("Price update submitted to database");
}
catch (DbUpdateConcurrencyException e)
{
    Console.WriteLine("Conflicts detected. Refreshing ...");
    var entry = e.Entries.Single();
    entry.OriginalValues.SetValues(entry.GetDatabaseValues());

    NWEntities.SaveChanges();
    Console.WriteLine("Price update submitted to database after
refresh");
}
```

Here, we are just forcing to let the first user win, but in a real-world situation, you might want to give users a warning; let them refresh and then redo the changes, or merge the changes in your code.

The complete method should be as follows:

```
static void TestSimultaneousChanges()
{
  using(var NWEntities = new NorthwindEntities())
  {
    // first user
    Console.WriteLine("First User ...");
    var product = (from p in NWEntities.Products
                    where p.ProductID == 2
                    select p).First();
    Console.WriteLine("Original price: {0}", product.UnitPrice);
    product.UnitPrice += 1.0m;
    Console.WriteLine("Current price to update: {0}",
                    product.UnitPrice);
    // process more products


    // second user
    Console.WriteLine("\nSecond User ...");
    using(var NWEntities1 = new NorthwindEntities1())
    {
        var product1 = (from p in NWEntities1.Product1s
                          where p.ProductID == 2
                          select p).First();
        Console.WriteLine("Original price: {0}",
        product1.UnitPrice);
        product1.UnitPrice += 2.0m;
        Console.WriteLine("Current price to update: {0}",
                          product1.UnitPrice);
        NWEntities1.SaveChanges();
        Console.WriteLine("Price update submitted to database");
    }
    // first user is ready to submit changes
    Console.WriteLine("\nFirst User ...");
    try
    {
        NWEntities.SaveChanges();
        Console.WriteLine("Price update submitted to database");
    }
    catch (DbUpdateConcurrencyException e)
    {
```

```
Console.WriteLine("Conflicts detected. Refreshing ...");

var entry = e.Entries.Single();
entry.OriginalValues.SetValues(entry.GetDatabaseValues());
NWEntities.SaveChanges();
Console.WriteLine("Price update submitted to database
after refresh");
        }
    }
}
```

Run the program now and you will get an output, as shown in the following screenshot:

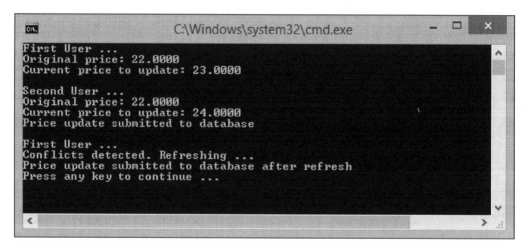

From this output, we know that the first user's update failed due to the concurrency conflict. However, after the refresh, it won the conflict; so, the final price in the database should be 23, which means that the second user's update has been overwritten by the first user's update.

With this mechanism, only the involved column is protected for concurrent updates. All other columns can still be updated by multiple users or processes without causing conflicts. For example, if you change the previous code to update the UnitsInStock property, you won't get a concurrency exception because the Concurrency Mode property of UnitsInStock is not set to Fixed and the concurrency setting of UnitPrice doesn't check the UnitsInStock column in the database.

Detecting conflicts using a version column

The second and more efficient way to provide conflict control is to use a version column in a table. If you add a column `RowVersion` of the `timestamp` type in a table and when you add this table to the entity model, the `RowVersion` column will be marked as a concurrency control version property.

Version numbers are updated every time the associated row is updated. Before the update, if there is a column of the `timestamp` type, LINQ to Entities will first check this column to make sure that the record has not been updated by any of the other users. This column will also be synchronized at the same time as the data row is updated. The new values are visible after `SaveChanges` finishes.

Adding a version column

Now, let's try this in the `Products` table. First, we need to add a new column called **RowVersion**, which is of the **timestamp** type. You can add it within SQL Server Management Studio, as shown in the following screenshot:

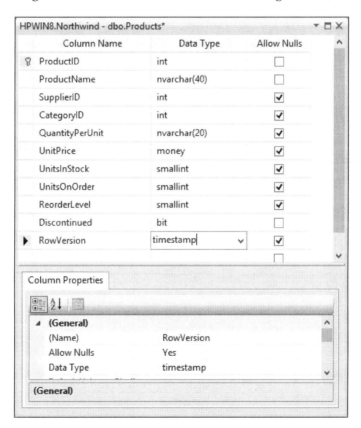

Modeling the Products table with a version column

After saving the changes, we need to refresh our data model to see these changes in the data model. Follow these steps to refresh the model:

1. From Visual Studio, open the `Northwind.edmx` entity designer, right-click on an empty space, and select **Update Model from Database....** Click on the **Refresh** tab and you will see **Products** in the refresh list.

2. Click on the **Finish** button and save the model.

Now, a new property, `RowVersion`, has been added to the `Northwind.edmx` data model. However, its **Concurrency Mode** property is set to **None** now, so you need to change it to **Fixed**. Note that its **StoreGeneratedPattern** value is set to **Computed**, which is to make sure this property will be refreshed every time after an update. The following screenshot displays the **Concurrency Mode** and **StoreGeneratedPattern** properties of the new `RowVersion` entity property:

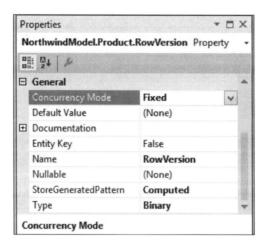

Writing the test code

We can write similar code to test this new version-controlling mechanism:

```
static void TestVersionControl()
{
    using(var NWEntities = new NorthwindEntities())
    {
        // first user
        Console.WriteLine("First User ...");
        var product = (from p in NWEntities.Products
```

```
                    where p.ProductID == 3
                    select p).First();
    Console.WriteLine("Original unit in stock: {0}",
    product.UnitsInStock);
    product.UnitsInStock += 1;
    Console.WriteLine("Current unit in stock to update: {0}",
        product.UnitsInStock);
    // process more products

    // second user
    Console.WriteLine("\nSecond User ...");
    using(var NWEntities1 = new NorthwindEntities1())
    {
      var product1 = (from p in NWEntities1.Product1s
                        where p.ProductID == 3
                        select p).First();
      Console.WriteLine("Original unit in stock: {0}",
        product1.UnitsInStock);
      product1.UnitsInStock += 2;
      Console.WriteLine("Current unit in stock to update: {0}",
          product1.UnitsInStock);
      NWEntities1.SaveChanges();
      Console.WriteLine("update submitted to database");
    }

    // first user is ready to submit changes
    Console.WriteLine("\nFirst User ...");
    try
    {
      NWEntities.SaveChanges();
    }
    catch (DbUpdateConcurrencyException e)
    {
      Console.WriteLine("Conflicts detected. Refreshing ...");
      var entry = e.Entries.Single();
      entry.OriginalValues.SetValues(entry.GetDatabaseValues());
      NWEntities.SaveChanges();
      Console.WriteLine("update submitted to database after
      refresh");
    }
  }
}
```

Testing the conflicts

This time, we tried to update `UnitsInStock` for product 3. From the output, we can see a conflict was detected again when the first user submitted changes to the database, but this time, the versioning is controlled by a version column, not by the unit in the stock column itself:

```
C:\Windows\system32\cmd.exe                              _  □  ×

First User ...
Original unit in stock: 13
Current unit in stock to update: 14

Second User ...
Original unit in stock: 13
Current unit in stock to update: 15
update submitted to database

First User ...
Conflicts detected. Refreshing ...
update submitted to database after refresh
Press any key to continue ...
```

Transaction support

In the previous section, we learned that simultaneous changes by different users can be handled by using a version column or the **Concurrency Mode** property. Sometimes, the same user might have made several changes and some of the changes might not succeed. In this case, we need a way to control the behavior of the overall update result. This is handled by transaction support.

LINQ to Entities uses the same transaction mechanism as ADO.NET, that is, it uses implicit or explicit transactions.

Implicit transactions

By default, LINQ to Entities uses an implicit transaction for each `SaveChanges` call. All updates between two `SaveChanges` calls are wrapped within one transaction.

For example, in the following code, we are trying to update two products. The second update will fail due to a constraint. However, as the first update is in a separate transaction, it has been saved to the database and it will stay in the database:

```
static void TestImplicitTransaction()
{
  using(var NWEntities = new NorthwindEntities())
  {
    var prod1 = (from p in NWEntities.Products
                  where p.ProductID == 4
                  select p).First();
    var prod2 = (from p in NWEntities.Products
                  where p.ProductID == 5
                  select p).First();
    prod1.UnitPrice += 1;
    // update will be saved to database
    NWEntities.SaveChanges();
    Console.WriteLine("First update saved to database");

    prod2.UnitPrice = -5;
    // update will fail because UnitPrice can't be < 0
    // but previous update stays in database
    try
    {
        NWEntities.SaveChanges();
        Console.WriteLine("Second update saved to database");
    }
    catch (Exception)
    {
        Console.WriteLine("Second update not saved to database");
    }
  }
}
```

The output will look as shown in the following screenshot:

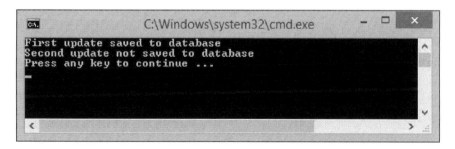

Explicit transactions

In addition to implicit transactions, you can also define a transaction scope to explicitly control the update behavior. All updates within a transaction scope will be within a single transaction. Thus, they will all either succeed or fail.

For example, in the following code snippet, we first start a transaction scope. Then, within this transaction scope, we update one product and submit the change to the database. However, at this point, the update has not really been committed because the transaction scope is still not closed. We then try to update another product, which fails due to the same constraint as in the previous example. The final result is that neither of these two products are updated in the database:

```csharp
static void TestExplicitTransaction()
{
  using(var NWEntities = new NorthwindEntities())
  {
    using (var ts = new TransactionScope())
    {
      try
      {
        var prod1 = (from p in NWEntities.Products
                      where p.ProductID == 4
                      select p).First();
        prod1.UnitPrice += 1;
        NWEntities.SaveChanges();
        Console.WriteLine("First update saved to database, but not
        committed.");
        // now let's try to update another product
        var prod2 = (from p in NWEntities.Products
                      where p.ProductID == 5
                      select p).First();
        // update will fail because UnitPrice can't be < 0
        prod2.UnitPrice = -5;
        NWEntities.SaveChanges();
        ts.Complete();
      }
      catch (Exception e)
      {
        // both updates will fail because they are within one
        // transaction
```

```
        Console.WriteLine("Exception caught. Rollback the first
        update.");
      }
    }
  }
}
```

Note that `TransactionScope` is in the .NET assembly `System.Transactions`. Therefore, first you need to add a reference to `System.Transactions` and then add the following `using` statement to the `Program.cs` file:

```
using System.Transactions;
```

 As best practice, you should always call `Complete()` within a transaction scope to commit the transaction, even if there are only select statements within the scope. If you want to roll back the transaction, there is no specific rollback method, but rather you just don't call `Complete()` and let the scope get disposed.

The output of the program is shown in the following screenshot:

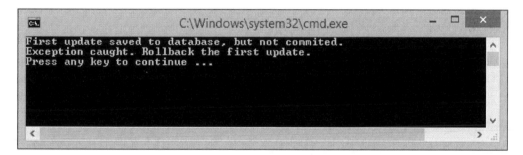

If you start the program in the debugging mode, after the first `SaveChanges` is called, you can go to SQL Server Management Studio and query the price of product 4 by using the following statement:

```
select UnitPrice from products (nolock) where productID = 4
```

The `nolock` hint is equivalent to `READUNCOMMITTED` and it is used to retrieve uncommitted data. With this hint, you can see that its price has been increased by the first change. Then, after the second `SaveChanges` is called, an exception is thrown and the transaction scope is closed. At this point, if you run the preceding query again, you will see that the price of product 4 is rolled back to its original value.

After the first call to the SaveChanges method, you shouldn't use the following statement to query the price value of the product:

```
select UnitPrice from products where productID = 4
```

If you do so, you will not get back a result. Instead, you will be waiting forever as it is waiting for the transaction to be committed.

This also brings up a big trade-off of using explicit/distributed transactions: deadlocks. We will cover more about distributed transactions in *Chapter 10, Distributed Transaction Support of WCF.*

Summary

In this chapter, we learned advanced features of LINQ to Entities, how to use stored procedures, transaction support, and concurrency control for LINQ to Entities. At this point, you should have a good understanding of LINQ to Entities.

In the next chapter, we will apply these skills to the data access layer of our WCF service to connect to databases securely and reliably with LINQ to Entities.

9
Applying LINQ to Entities to a WCF Service

Now that we have learned all of the features related to LINQ and LINQ to Entities, we will use them in the data access layer of a WCF service. We will create a new WCF service very similar to the one we created in the previous chapters, but in this service, we will use LINQ to Entities to connect to the Northwind database to retrieve and update a product.

In this chapter, we will cover the following topics:

- Creating a test solution
- Modeling the Northwind database in the LINQ to Entities designer
- Adding the business domain object project
- Implementing the data access layer using LINQ to Entities
- Adding the business logic layer
- Adding the service interface layer
- Implementing the test client
- Testing the get and update operations of the WCF service
- Testing concurrent updates with LINQ to Entities

Creating the LINQNorthwind solution

The first thing we need to do is create a test solution. In this chapter, we will start from the data access layer. Perform the following steps:

1. Start Visual Studio.
2. Create a new class library project, NorthwindDAL, with solution name LINQNorthwind (make sure that the **Create directory for solution** option is checked to specify the solution name).
3. Change the Class1.cs file to ProductDAO.cs. This will also change the class name and all related places in the project.

Now, you should have a new solution with the empty data access layer class. Next, we will add a model to this layer and create the business logic layer and the service interface layer.

Installing Entity Framework

Just as we did in the last chapter, we first need to install Entity Framework into the project, as in this project, we will use LINQ to Entities to connect to the database. Follow these steps to do this:

1. From the **Solution Explorer**, right-click on the project item, then select **Manage NuGet Packages...**.
2. On the **Manage NuGet Packages** window, select **Online | nuget.org | Entity Framework**.
3. Click on the **Install** button to install Entity Framework in the project.

Modeling the Northwind database

In the previous section, we created the LINQNorthwind solution. Next, we will apply LINQ to Entities to this new solution.

For the data access layer, we will use LINQ to Entities instead of the raw ADO.NET data adapters. As you will see in the next section, we will use one LINQ statement to retrieve product information from the database, and the update LINQ statements will handle the concurrency control for us easily and reliably.

As you might recall, to use LINQ to Entities in the data access layer of our WCF service, we first need to add an entity data model to the project. The following steps are very similar to those described in *Chapter 8, LINQ to Entities – Advanced Concepts and Features*. You can refer to that chapter for more information and screenshots if necessary.

1. In the **Solution Explorer**, right-click on the project item, **NorthwindDAL**, select menu options **Add | New Item...**, and then choose **Visual C# Items | ADO.NET Entity Data Model** as **Template** and enter Northwind.edmx as the name.

2. Select **EF Designer from database**, choose the existing **Northwind** connection and add the Products table to the model.

3. Click on the **Finish** button to add the model to the project.

4. The new column, **RowVersion**, should be in the **Product** entity as we added it in the previous chapter. If it is not there, add it to the database table with a type of **timestamp** and refresh the entity data model from the database (you can look at the *Modeling the Products table with a version column* section in *Chapter 8, LINQ to Entities – Advanced Concepts and Features*, for more details on how to refresh an entity model from a database).

5. In the EMD designer, select the **RowVersion** property of the **Product** entity and change its **Concurrency Mode** from **None** to **Fixed**. Note that its **StoreGeneratedPattern** should remain as **Computed**. You can refer to the *Turning on concurrency verification* section in *Chapter 8, LINQ to Entities – Advanced Concepts and Features*, for a screenshot.

Just as in the previous chapter, this will generate a file called Northwind.Context. cs, which contains the Db context for the Northwind database. Another file called Product.cs is also generated, which contains the Product entity class. You need to save the data model in order to see these two files in the **Solution Explorer**.

> In Visual Studio's **Solution Explorer**, the Northwind.Context.cs file is under the template file, Northwind.Context.tt, and Product.cs is under Northwind.tt. However, in Windows Explorer, both the C# files and template files are within the project folder and they are at the same level.

Creating the business domain object project

In *Chapter 5*, *Implementing a Three-layer WCF Service*, we created a **business domain object** (**BDO**) project to hold the intermediate data between the data access objects and the service interface objects. In this section, we will also add such a project to the solution for the same purpose.

1. In the **Solution Explorer**, right-click on the **LINQNorthwind** solution.

2. Select **Add | New Project...** to add a new class library project named `NorthwindBDO`.

3. Rename the `Class1.cs` file to `ProductBDO.cs`. This will also change the class name and all related files in the project.

4. Add the following properties to this class:

   ◦ `ProductID`

   ◦ `ProductName`

   ◦ `QuantityPerUnit`

   ◦ `UnitPrice`

   ◦ `Discontinued`

   ◦ `UnitsInStock`

   ◦ `UnitsOnOrder`

   ◦ `ReorderLevel`

   ◦ `RowVersion`

The following is the code list of the `ProductBDO` class:

```
using System;
using System.Collections.Generic;
using System.Linq;
using System.Text;
using System.Threading.Tasks;

namespace NorthwindBDO
{
    public class ProductBDO
    {
        public int ProductID { get; set; }
```

```
        public string ProductName { get; set; }
        public string QuantityPerUnit { get; set; }
        public decimal UnitPrice { get; set; }
        public int UnitsInStock { get; set; }
        public int ReorderLevel { get; set; }
        public int UnitsOnOrder { get; set; }
        public bool Discontinued { get; set; }
        public byte[] RowVersion { get; set; }
    }
}
```

As noted earlier, in this chapter, we will use BDO to hold the intermediate data between the data access objects and the data contract objects. Besides this approach, there are some other ways to pass data back and forth between the data access layer and the service interface layer, and two of them are listed as follows:

- The first one is to expose the Entity Framework context objects from the data access layer up to the service interface layer. In this way, both the service interface layer and the business logic layer can interact directly with Entity Framework. This approach is not recommended as it goes against the best practice of service layering, as we have discussed in *Chapter 5, Implementing a Three-layer WCF Service*.

- Another approach is to use self-tracking entities. Self-tracking entities are entities that know how to track their own changes regardless of which tier those changes are made on. You can expose self-tracking entities from the data access layer to the business logic layer and then to the service interface layer and even share the entities with the clients. As self-tracking entities are independent of the entity context, you don't need to expose the entity context objects. The problem with this approach is that you have to share the binary files with all the clients, and thus, it is the least interoperable approach for a WCF service. Now, this approach is not recommended by Microsoft, so we will not discuss it in this book.

Using LINQ to Entities in the data access layer

Next, we will modify the data access layer to use LINQ to Entities to retrieve and update products. We will first create GetProduct to retrieve a product from the database and then create UpdateProduct to update a product in the database.

Adding a reference to the BDO project

Now that we have the BDO project in the solution, we need to modify the data access layer project to reference it.

1. In the **Solution Explorer**, right-click on the **NorthwindDAL** project.
2. Select **Add | Reference...**.
3. Select the **NorthwindBDO** project from the **Projects** tab under **Solution**.
4. Click on the **OK** button to add the reference to the project.

Creating GetProduct in the data access layer

We can now create the GetProduct method in the data access layer's class, ProductDAO, to use LINQ to Entities to retrieve a product from the database. Just as we did in the previous chapter, we will first create an entity DbContext object and then use LINQ to Entities to get the product from the DbContext object. The product we get from DbContext will be a conceptual entity model object. However, we don't want to pass this product object back to the upper-level layer because we don't want to tightly couple the business logic layer with the data access layer. Therefore, we will convert this entity model product object to a ProductBDO object and then pass this ProductBDO object back to the upper-level layers.

To create the GetProduct method, first add the following using statement to the ProductDAO class:

```
using NorthwindBDO;
```

Then, add the following GetProduct method to the ProductDAO class:

```
public ProductBDO GetProduct(int id)
{
    ProductBDO productBDO = null;
    using (var NWEntities = new NorthwindEntities())
    {
        var product = (from p in NWEntities.Products
                         where p.ProductID == id
                         select p).FirstOrDefault();
        if (product != null)
            productBDO = new ProductBDO()
            {
                ProductID = product.ProductID,
                ProductName = product.ProductName,
```

```
                 QuantityPerUnit = product.QuantityPerUnit,
                 UnitPrice = (decimal)product.UnitPrice,
                 UnitsInStock = (int)product.UnitsInStock,
                 ReorderLevel = (int)product.ReorderLevel,
                 UnitsOnOrder = (int)product.UnitsOnOrder,
                 Discontinued = product.Discontinued,
                 RowVersion = product.RowVersion
            };
    }
    return productBDO;
}
```

You will recall from *Chapter 5, Implementing a Three-layer WCF Service*, that within the `GetProduct` method, we had to create an ADO.NET connection, create an ADO.NET command object with that connection, specify the command text, connect to the `Northwind` database, and send the SQL statement to the database for execution. After the result was returned from the database, we had to loop through the `DataReader` and cast the columns to our entity object one by one.

With LINQ to Entities, we only construct one LINQ to Entities statement and everything else is handled by LINQ to Entities. Not only do we need to write less code, but now the statement is also strongly typed. We won't have a runtime error such as **invalid query syntax** or **invalid column name**. Also, a SQL Injection attack is no longer an issue, as LINQ to Entities will also take care of this when translating LINQ expressions to the underlying SQL statements.

 There might be a performance impact in some cases, since LINQ to Entities uses autogenerated queries, which are not always optimized. If this happens to you, you can always plug in your own SQL queries.

Creating UpdateProduct in the data access layer

In the previous section, we created the `GetProduct` method in the data access layer using LINQ to Entities instead of ADO.NET. Now, in this section, we will create the `UpdateProduct` method using LINQ to Entities instead of ADO.NET.

The code for the `UpdateProduct` method in the data access layer class, `ProductDAO`, will be as follows:

```
public bool UpdateProduct(
    ref ProductBDO productBDO,
    ref string message)
{
    message = "product updated successfully";
    var ret = true;

    using (var NWEntities = new NorthwindEntities())
    {
        var productID = productBDO.ProductID;
        Product productInDB =
                (from p
                in NWEntities.Products
                where p.ProductID == productID
                select p).FirstOrDefault();
        // check product
        if (productInDB == null)
        {
            throw new Exception("No product with ID " +
                                productBDO.ProductID);
        }

        // update product
        productInDB.ProductName = productBDO.ProductName;
        productInDB.QuantityPerUnit = productBDO.QuantityPerUnit;
        productInDB.UnitPrice = productBDO.UnitPrice;
        productInDB.Discontinued = productBDO.Discontinued;
        productInDB.RowVersion = productBDO.RowVersion;

        NWEntities.Products.Attach(productInDB);
        NWEntities.Entry(productInDB).State =
            System.Data.Entity.EntityState.Modified;
        var num = NWEntities.SaveChanges();

        productBDO.RowVersion = productInDB.RowVersion;

        if (num != 1)
        {
            ret = false;
            message = "no product is updated";
        }
    }
    return ret;
}
```

Within this method, we first get the product from the database, making sure that the product ID is a valid value in the database. Then, we apply the changes from the entered object to the object we have just retrieved from the database and submit the changes back to the database. Let's go through a few notes about this method:

1. You have to save `productID` in a new variable and then use it in the LINQ query. Otherwise, you will get an error that says **Cannot use ref or out parameter 'productBDO' inside an anonymous method, lambda expression, or query expression**.

2. If `Attach` is not called, `RowVersion` (from the database, not from the client) will be used when submitting to the database, even though you have updated its value before submitting to the database. An update will always succeed, but without concurrency control.

3. If the object state is not set to `Modified`, Entity Framework will not honor your changes to the entity object and you will not be able to save any of the changes to the database.

 If you don't want to use the `ref` parameters, you can define a class for the return result and encapsulate all the `ref` parameters inside this class.

Creating the business logic layer

Now, let's create the business logic layer. The steps here are very similar to the steps in *Chapter 5, Implementing a Three-layer WCF Service*, so you can refer to that chapter for more details:

1. Right-click on the solution item and select **Add | New Project...**. Add a class library project with the name `NorthwindLogic`.

2. Add a project reference to `NorthwindDAL` and `NorthwindBDO` to this new project.

3. Rename the `Class1.cs` file to `ProductLogic.cs`. This will also change the class name and all related places in the project.

4. Add the following two `using` statements to the `ProductLogic.cs` class file:

    ```
    using NorthwindDAL;
    using NorthwindBDO;
    ```

5. Add the following class member variable to the `ProductLogic` class:

    ```
    ProductDAO productDAO = new ProductDAO();
    ```

6. Add the following new method, Get Product, to the ProductLogic class:

```
public ProductBDO GetProduct(int id)
{
    return productDAO.GetProduct(id);
}
```

7. Add the following new method, UpdateProduct, to the ProductLogic class:

```
public bool UpdateProduct(
  ref ProductBDO productBDO,
  ref string message)
{
    var productInDB =
        GetProduct(productBDO.ProductID);
    // invalid product to update
    if (productInDB == null)
    {
        message = "cannot get product for this ID";
        return false;
    }
    // a product cannot be discontinued
    // if there are non-fulfilled orders
    if (productBDO.Discontinued == true
        && productInDB.UnitsOnOrder > 0)
    {
        message = "cannot discontinue this product";
        return false;
    }
    else
    {
        return productDAO.UpdateProduct(ref productBDO,
            ref message);
    }
}
```

Build the solution. We now have only one more step to go, that is, adding the service interface layer.

Creating the service interface layer

The last step is to create the service interface layer. Again, the steps here are very similar to the steps in *Chapter 5, Implementing a Three-layer WCF Service*, so you can refer to this chapter for more details.

1. Right-click on the solution item and select **Add | New Project....** Add a **WCF Service Library** project with the name NorthwindService.

2. Add a project reference to NorthwindLogic and NorthwindBDO to this new service interface project.

3. Right-click on the project item NorthwindService, select **Manage NuGet Packages...** and then install Entity Framework.

4. Change the service interface file, IService1.cs, as follows:

    1. Change its filename from IService1.cs to IProductService.cs. This will also change the interface name and all related places in the project.

    2. Remove the original two service operations and add the following two new operations:

       ```
       [OperationContract]
       [FaultContract(typeof(ProductFault))]
       Product GetProduct(int id);


       [OperationContract]
       [FaultContract(typeof(ProductFault))]
       bool UpdateProduct(ref Product product, ref string message);
       ```

    3. Remove the original CompositeType and add the following data contract classes:

       ```
       [DataContract]
       public class Product
       {
           [DataMember]
           public int ProductID { get; set; }
           [DataMember]
           public string ProductName { get; set; }
           [DataMember]
           public string QuantityPerUnit { get; set; }
           [DataMember]
           public decimal UnitPrice { get; set; }
           [DataMember]
       ```

```
        public bool Discontinued { get; set; }
        [DataMember]
        public byte[] RowVersion { get; set; }
    }


    [DataContract]
    public class ProductFault
    {
        public ProductFault(string msg)
        {
            FaultMessage = msg;
        }


        [DataMember]
        public string FaultMessage;
    }
```

The following is the content of the IProductService.cs file now:

```
using System;
using System.Collections.Generic;
using System.Linq;
using System.Runtime.Serialization;
using System.ServiceModel;
using System.Text;

namespace NorthwindService
{
    [ServiceContract]
    public interface IProductService
    {
        [OperationContract]
        [FaultContract(typeof(ProductFault))]
        Product GetProduct(int id);

        [OperationContract]
        [FaultContract(typeof(ProductFault))]
        bool UpdateProduct(ref Product product,
            ref string message);
    }

    [DataContract]
    public class Product
    {
```

```
    [DataMember]
    public int ProductID { get; set; }
    [DataMember]
    public string ProductName { get; set; }
    [DataMember]
    public string QuantityPerUnit { get; set; }
    [DataMember]
    public decimal UnitPrice { get; set; }
    [DataMember]
    public bool Discontinued { get; set; }
    [DataMember]
    public byte[] RowVersion { get; set; }
}
[DataContract]
public class ProductFault
{
    public ProductFault(string msg)
    {
        FaultMessage = msg;
    }

    [DataMember]
    public string FaultMessage;
}
}
```

5. Change the service implementation file, Service1.cs, as follows:

   1. Change its filename from Service1.cs to ProductService.cs. This will also change the class name and all related places in the project.

   2. Add the following two using statements to the ProductService.cs file:

      ```
      using NorthwindLogic;
      using NorthwindBDO;
      ```

   3. Add the following class member variable:

      ```
      ProductLogic productLogic = new ProductLogic();
      ```

   4. Remove the original two GetProduct and UpdateProduct methods and add the following two methods:

      ```
      public Product GetProduct(int id)
      {
      ```

```
        ProductBDO productBDO = null;
        try
        {
            productBDO = productLogic.GetProduct(id);
        }
        catch (Exception e)
        {
            var msg = e.Message;
            var reason = "GetProduct Exception";
            throw new FaultException<ProductFault>
                (new ProductFault(msg), reason);
        }

        if (productBDO == null)
        {
            var msg =
                string.Format("No product found for id {0}",
                id);
            var reason = "GetProduct Empty Product";
            throw new FaultException<ProductFault>
                (new ProductFault(msg), reason);
        }
        var product = new Product();
        TranslateProductBDOToProductDTO(productBDO, product);
        return product;
    }

    public bool UpdateProduct(ref Product product,
        ref string message)
    {
        var result = true;

        // first check to see if it is a valid price
        if (product.UnitPrice <= 0)
        {
            message = "Price cannot be <= 0";
            result = false;
        }
        // ProductName can't be empty
        else if (string.IsNullOrEmpty(product.ProductName))
        {
            message = "Product name cannot be empty";
            result = false;
        }
```

```
      // QuantityPerUnit can't be empty
      else if
      (string.IsNullOrEmpty(product.QuantityPerUnit))
      {
          message = "Quantity cannot be empty";
          result = false;
      }
      else
      {
          try
          {
              var productBDO = new ProductBDO();
              TranslateProductDTOToProductBDO(product,
              productBDO);
              result = productLogic.UpdateProduct(
                  ref productBDO, ref message);
               product.RowVersion =
                          productBDO.RowVersion;
          }
          catch (Exception e)
          {
              var msg = e.Message;
              throw new FaultException<ProductFault>
                  (new ProductFault(msg), msg);
          }
      }
      return result;
  }
```

6. As we have to translate the data contract objects to the business domain objects, we need to add the following two methods:

```
private void TranslateProductBDOToProductDTO(
    ProductBDO productBDO,
    Product product)
{
    product.ProductID = productBDO.ProductID;
    product.ProductName = productBDO.ProductName;
    product.QuantityPerUnit = productBDO.QuantityPerUnit;
    product.UnitPrice = productBDO.UnitPrice;
    product.Discontinued = productBDO.Discontinued;
    product.RowVersion = productBDO.RowVersion;
}
```

```
private void TranslateProductDTOToProductBDO(
    Product product,
    ProductBDO productBDO)
{
    productBDO.ProductID = product.ProductID;
    productBDO.ProductName = product.ProductName;
    productBDO.QuantityPerUnit = product.QuantityPerUnit;
    productBDO.UnitPrice = product.UnitPrice;
    productBDO.Discontinued = product.Discontinued;
    productBDO.RowVersion = product.RowVersion;
}
```

7. Change the config file, `App.config`, as follows:

    1. Change `Service1` to `ProductService`.

    2. Remove the word, `Design_Time_Addresses/`.

    3. Change the port to `8080`.

    4. Now, `BaseAddress` should be as follows:

        `http://localhost:8080/NorthwindService/ProductService/`

    5. Copy the connection string from the `App.config` file in
        the `NorthwindDAL` project to the `App.config` file in the
        `NorthwindService` project, after the `configSections` node:

        ```
        <connectionStrings>
          <add name="NorthwindEntities"
        connectionString="metadata=res://*/Northwind.csdl|res://*/
        Northwind.ssdl|res://*/Northwind.msl;provider=System.
        Data.SqlClient;provider connection string=&quot;data
        source=localhost;initial catalog=Northwind;integrated securi
        ty=True;MultipleActiveResultSets=True;App=EntityFramework&qu
        ot;" providerName="System.Data.EntityClient" />
        </connectionStrings>
        ```

You should leave the original connection string untouched in the
`App.config` file in the data access layer project. This connection
string is used by the entity model designer at design time. It is
not used at all during runtime, but if you remove it, whenever
you open the entity model designer in Visual Studio, you will be
prompted to specify a connection to your database.

Now, build the solution and there should be no errors.

Testing the service with the WCF Test Client

Now, we can run the program to test the `GetProduct` and `UpdateProduct` operations with the WCF Test Client.

 You might need to run Visual Studio as an administrator to start the WCF Test Client. You can refer to *Chapter 2, Hosting the HelloWorld WCF Service*, for more details on how to set up your WCF development environment.

First, set `NorthwindService` as the startup project and then press *Ctrl + F5* to start the WCF Test Client. Double-click on the **GetProduct** operation, enter a valid product ID, and click on the **Invoke** button. The detailed product information should be retrieved and displayed on the screen, as shown in the following screenshot:

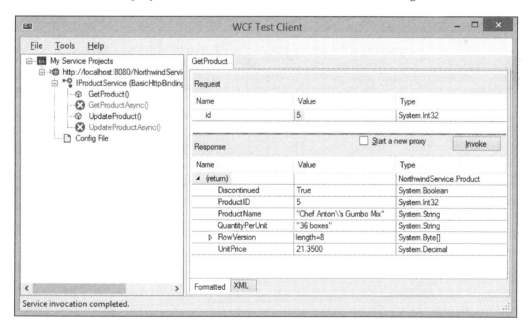

 You might get an error that says **No connection string named 'NorthwindEntities' could be found in the application config file**. This means you forgot to copy the connection string from the DAL project to the service project.

If you get an error that says **Schema specified is not valid. Errors: Northwind. ssdl(2,2) : error 0152: No Entity Framework provider found for the ADO.NET provider**, it means that you forgot to install Entity Framework to the service project.

Now, double-click on the **UpdateProduct** operation, enter a valid product ID, and specify a name, price, quantity per unit, and then click on **Invoke**.

This time, you will get an exception as shown, in the following screenshot:

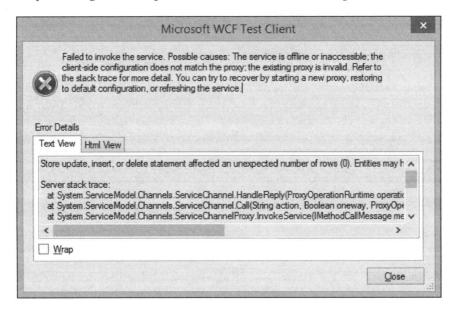

From this screenshot, we can see that the update failed. The error details actually tell us that it is a concurrency error. This is because, using the WCF Test Client, we can't enter a row version as it is not a simple data type parameter. Thus, we didn't succeed in the original RowVersion for the object to be updated, and when updating the object in the database, Entity Framework thinks that this product has been updated by some other users.

Testing concurrency with our own client

From an earlier section, we know that with WCF Test Client we cannot test the UpdateProduct method, nor can we test the concurrency support of the WCF service, because with WCF Test Client, we cannot update products. To test the concurrency support of Entity Framework, we have to use our own test client.

Hosting the WCF service in IIS

The WCF service is now hosted within the WCF Service Host. To test it with our own test client, we will have to start WCF Service Host before we run our own test client. To make things easier, in this section, we will first decouple our WCF service from Visual Studio. We will host it in IIS.

You can follow these steps to host this WCF service in IIS (refer to the *Hosting the service in IIS using the HTTP protocol* section in *Chapter 2, Hosting the HelloWorld WCF Service*).

1. In the **Solution Explorer**, under the **NorthwindService** project, copy the `App.config` file to `Web.config`.

2. Within the `Web.config` file, add the following node as a child node of the service model node, `system.serviceModel`:

```
<serviceHostingEnvironment >
  <serviceActivations>
    <add factory="System.ServiceModel.
    Activation.ServiceHostFactory"
      relativeAddress="./ProductService.svc"
      service="NorthwindService.ProductService"/>
  </serviceActivations>
</serviceHostingEnvironment>
```

3. Remove the following lines from the `Web.config` file:

```
<host>
  <baseAddresses>
    <add baseAddress="http://localhost:8080/
           NorthwindService/ProductService/" />
  </baseAddresses>
</host>
```

4. Now, open IIS Manager, add a new application pool, `NorthwindAppPool`. Make sure that it is a .NET 4.0 application pool, as shown in the following screenshot:

5. After the new application pool is created, select this application pool, go to **Advanced Settings | Process Model | Identity**, click on the **...** button, select **Custom Account**, and then click on the **Set** button. The **Set Credentials** dialog window should pop up on your screen.

6. Change the identity of this new application pool to a user that has appropriate access to the Northwind database. The service that is going to be created in the next step will use this identity to access the Northwind database (the default application pool identity for the new application pool, **ApplicationPoolIdentity**, does not have access to the Northwind database.).

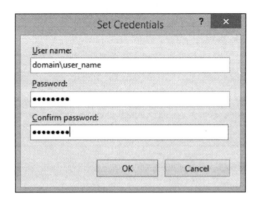

7. Now, in IIS Manager, add a new application, LINQNorthwindService, and set its physical path to C:\SOAwithWCFandEF\Projects\LINQNorthwind\NorthwindService. Choose the newly created application pool as this service's application pool.

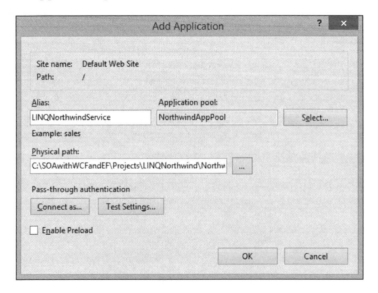

8. Within Visual Studio, in the **Solution Explorer**, right-click on the **NorthwindService** project item, select **Properties**, then click on the **Build Events** tab, and enter the following code to the **Post-build event command line** box:

```
copy .\*.* ..\
```

With this post-build event command line, whenever NorthwindService is rebuilt, the service binary files will be copied to the C:\SOAwithWCFandEF\ Projects\LINQNorthwind\NorthwindService\bin directory so that the service hosted in IIS will always be up to date.

9. Within Visual Studio, in the **Solution Explorer**, right-click on the **NorthwindService** project item and select **Rebuild**.

The steps here are very similar to the steps in *Chapter 2, Hosting the HelloWorld WCF Service*. You can refer to that chapter for more details, such as how to install IIS and enable WCF support within IIS.

Now, you have finished setting up the service to be hosted in IIS. Open Internet Explorer, go to the following address, and you should see the ProductService description in the browser, http://localhost/LINQNorthwindService/ ProductService.svc.

If you get an error that says **Cannot read configuration file due to insufficient permissions**, you should give identity of the new app pool read access to the NorthwindService folder.

Creating the test client

In this section, we will create a WinForm client to get the product details and update the price of a product.

Follow these steps to create the test client:

1. In the **Solution Explorer**, right-click on the solution item, and select **Add | New Project...**.

2. Select **Visual C# | Windows Forms Application** as the template and change the name to LINQNorthwindClient. Click on the **OK** button to add the new project.

3. On the form designer, add the following five controls:
   - ° A label named **lblProductID** with the text, **Product ID**
   - ° A textbox named **txtProductID**
   - ° A button named **btnGetProduct** with the text, **&Get Product Details**
   - ° A label named **lblProductDetails** with the text, **Product Details**
   - ° A textbox named **txtProductDetails** with the **Multiline** property set to **True**

The layout of the form is as shown in the following screenshot:

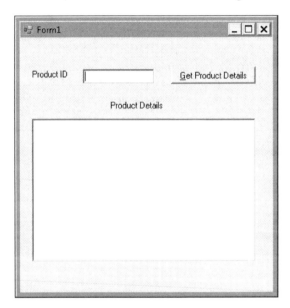

4. In the **Solution Explorer**, right-click on the **LINQNorthwindClient** project and select **Add | Service Reference...**.

5. On the **Add Service Reference** window, enter this address:
   `http://localhost/LINQNorthwindService/ProductService.svc.`

6. Change **Namespace** from **ServiceReference1** to **ProductServiceRef** and click on the **OK** button.

The **Add Service Reference** window should appear, as shown in the following screenshot:

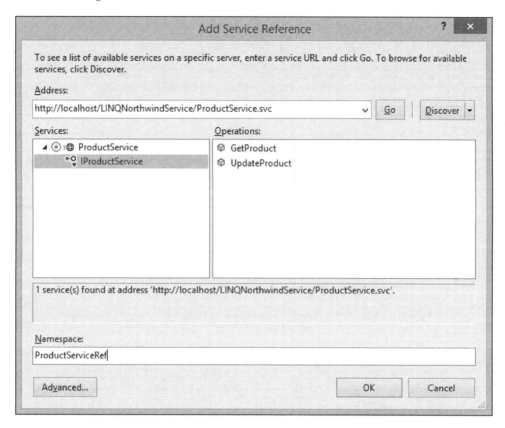

Implementing the GetProduct functionality

Now that we have the test client created, we will customize the client application to test the new WCF service.

First, we need to customize the test client to call the WCF service to get a product from the database so that we can test the GetProduct operation with LINQ to Entities.

We will call a WCF service through the proxy, so let's add the following using statements to the form class in the Form1.cs file:

```
using LINQNorthwindClient.ProductServiceRef;
using System.ServiceModel;
```

Then, in the Forms Designer, double-click on the **btnGetProduct** button and add an event handler for this button, as follows:

```
private void btnGetProduct_Click(object sender, EventArgs e)
{
    var client = new ProductServiceClient();
    string result = "";

    try
    {
        var productID = Int32.Parse(txtProductID.Text);
        var product = client.GetProduct(productID);

        var sb = new StringBuilder();
        sb.Append("ProductID:" +
            product.ProductID.ToString() + "\r\n");
        sb.Append("ProductName:" +
            product.ProductName + "\r\n");
        sb.Append("QuantityPerUnit:" +
            product.QuantityPerUnit + "\r\n");
        sb.Append("UnitPrice:" +
            product.UnitPrice.ToString() + "\r\n");
        sb.Append("Discontinued:" +
            product.Discontinued.ToString() + "\r\n");
        sb.Append("RowVersion:");
        foreach (var x in product.RowVersion.AsEnumerable())
        {
            sb.Append(x.ToString());
            sb.Append(" ");
        }
        result = sb.ToString();
    }
    catch (TimeoutException ex)
    {
        result = "The service operation timed out. " +
            ex.Message;
    }
    catch (FaultException<ProductFault> ex)
    {
        result = "ProductFault returned: " +
            ex.Detail.FaultMessage;
    }
    catch (FaultException ex)
    {
        result = "Unknown Fault: " +
            ex.ToString();
    }
    catch (CommunicationException ex)
    {
        result = "There was a communication problem. " +
```

```
                    ex.Message + ex.StackTrace;
    }
    catch (Exception ex)
    {
        result = "Other exception: " +
            ex.Message + ex.StackTrace;
    }

    txtProductDetails.Text = result;
}
```

Implementing the UpdateProduct functionality

Next, we need to modify the client program to call the UpdateProduct operation of the web service. This method is particularly important to us because we will use it to test the concurrent update control of LINQ to Entities.

First, we need to add some more controls to the form. We will modify the form UI as follows:

1. Open the Form1.cs file from the LINQNorthwindClient project.
2. Add a label named **lblNewPrice** with the text, **New Price**.
3. Add a textbox named **txtNewPrice**.
4. Add a button named **btnUpdatePrice** with the text, **&Update Price**.
5. Add a label named **lblUpdateResult** with the text, **Update Result**.
6. Add a textbox control named **txtUpdateResult** with the **Multiline** property set to **True** and **Scrollbars** set to **Both**.

The form should now appear as shown in the following screenshot:

Now, double-click on the **Update Price** button and add the following event handler method for this button:

```
private void btnUpdatePrice_Click(object sender, EventArgs e)
{
    var result = "";

    if (product != null)
    {
        try
        {
            // update its price
            product.UnitPrice =
                Decimal.Parse(txtNewPrice.Text);
            var client = new ProductServiceClient();
            var sb = new StringBuilder();
            var message = "";
            sb.Append("Price updated to ");
            sb.Append(txtNewPrice.Text);
            sb.Append("\r\n");
            sb.Append("Update result:");
            sb.Append(client.UpdateProduct(ref product,
                    ref message).ToString());
            sb.Append("\r\n");
            sb.Append("Update message: ");
            sb.Append(message);
            sb.Append("\r\n");
            sb.Append("New RowVersion:");
            foreach (var x in product.RowVersion.AsEnumerable())
            {
                sb.Append(x.ToString());
                sb.Append(" ");
            }
            result = sb.ToString();
        }
        catch (TimeoutException ex)
        {
            result = "The service operation timed out. " +
                    ex.Message;
        }
        catch (FaultException<ProductFault> ex)
        {
            result = "ProductFault returned: " +
                    ex.Detail.FaultMessage;
        }
        catch (FaultException ex)
        {
            result = "Unknown Fault: " +
                    ex.ToString();
        }
```

```
        catch (CommunicationException ex)
        {
            result = "There was a communication problem. " +
                     ex.Message + ex.StackTrace;
        }
        catch (Exception ex)
        {
            result = "Other exception: " +
                     ex.Message + ex.StackTrace;
        }
    }
    else
    {
        result = "Get product details first";
    }

    txtUpdateResult.Text = result;
}
```

Note that inside the **Update Price** button's event handler listed previously, we don't get the product from the database first. Instead, we reuse the same product object from the `btnGetProduct_Click` method, which means that we will update whatever product we get when we click on the **Get Product Details** button. In order to do this, we need to move the `product` variable outside the private method, `btnGetProduct_Click`, to be a class variable as follows:

```
Product product;
```

Inside the `btnGetProduct_Click` method, we need not define another variable, `product`, but we can now use the class member `product`. Now, the first few lines of code for the `Form1` class should be as follows:

```
public partial class Form1 : Form
{
    Product product;

    public Form1()
    {
        InitializeComponent();
    }

    private void btnGetProductDetail_Click
        (object sender, EventArgs e)
    {
        var client = new ProductServiceClient();
        var result = "";
        try
```

```
        {
            var productID =
                    Int32.Parse(txtProductID.Text);
            product = client.GetProduct(productID);
            // More code to follow
```

As you can see, we didn't do anything specific with the concurrent update control of the update, but later in the *Testing concurrent updates manually* section within this chapter, we will learn how LINQ to Entities inside the WCF service handles this for us. As done in the previous chapters, we will also capture all kinds of exceptions and display appropriate messages for them.

Testing the GetProduct and UpdateProduct operations

We can build and run the program to test the `GetProduct` and `UpdateProduct` operations now. Make the `LINQNorthwindClient` project the startup project and start it.

1. On the client form (UI), enter `10` as the product ID in the **Product ID** textbox, and click on the **Get Product Details** button to get the product details. Note that **UnitPrice** is now **31.0000**, as shown in the following screenshot (the price and row version might be different in your database):

2. Now, enter 32 as the product price in the **New Price** textbox and click on the **Update Price** button to update its price. **Update result** should be **True**. Note that **RowVersion** has been changed and displayed as **New RowVersion**:

3. To verify the new price, click on the **Get Product Details** button again to get the product details for this product and you will see that **UnitPrice** has been updated to **32.0000**.

Testing concurrent updates manually

We can also test concurrent updates by using the client application, `LINQNorthwindClient`.

In this section, we will start two clients (let's call them Client A and Client B) and update the same product from these two clients at the same time. We will create a conflict between the updates from these two clients so that we can test whether this conflict is properly handled by LINQ to Entities.

The test sequence will be as follows:

1. Client A starts.
2. Client B starts.
3. Client A reads the product information.
4. Client B reads the same product information.
5. Client B updates the product successfully.
6. Client A tries to update the product but fails.

The last step is where the conflict occurs as the product has been updated in between the read and update operations by Client A.

The steps to deal with this situation are as follows:

1. Stop the client application if it is still running in the debugging mode.

2. Start the client application in the non-debugging mode by pressing *Ctrl + F5*. We will refer to this client as Client A.

3. In the Client A application, enter 11 in the **Product ID** textbox and click on the **Get Product Details** button to get the product's details. Note that **UnitPrice** is **21.0000**.

4. Start another client application in the non-debugging mode by pressing *Ctrl + F5*. We will refer to this client as Client B.

5. In the Client B application, enter 11 in the **Product ID** textbox and click on the **Get Product Details** button to get the product's details. Note that **UnitPrice** is still **21.0000**. Client B's form window should be identical to Client A's form window.

6. In Client B's form, enter 22 as the product price in the **New Price** textbox and click on the **Update Price** button to update its price.

7. Client B's update is committed to the database and the **Update result** value is **True**. The price of this product has now been updated to **22** and **RowVersion** has been updated to a new value.

8. In the Client B application, click on the **Get Product Details** button to get the product details to verify the update. Note that **UnitPrice** is now **22.0000**.

9. On Client A's form, enter 23 as the product price in the **New Price** textbox and click on the **Update Price** button to update its price.

10. Client A's update fails with an error message, **Entities may have been modified or deleted since entities were loaded**.

11. In the Client B application, click on the **Get Product Details** button again to get the product's details. You will see that **UnitPrice** is still **22.0000** and **RowVersion** is not changed, which means that Client A's update didn't get committed to the database.

The following screenshot is for Client B. You can see **Update result** is **True** and the price after the update is 22:

The following screenshot is for Client A. You can see that the price before the update is **21.0000** and the update fails with an error message. This error message is caught as an unknown fault from the client side because we didn't handle the concurrency exception in our service:

From the preceding test, we know that the concurrent update is controlled by LINQ to Entities. An optimistic locking mechanism is enforced and one client's update won't overwrite another client's update. The client that has a conflict will be notified by a fault message.

> Concurrent update locking is applied at the record level in the database. If two clients try to update different records in the database, they will not interfere with each other. For example, if you repeat the previous steps to update product 10 in one client and product 11 in another client, there will be no problem at all.

Testing concurrent updates automatically

In the previous section, we tested the concurrent update control of LINQ to Entities, but as you can see, the timing of the update is fully controlled by our input. We know exactly when the conflict will happen. In a real production environment, a conflict may happen at any time, with no indication as to when and how it will happen. In this section, we will simulate a situation such that a conflict happens randomly. We will add a new functionality to update one product 100 times and let two clients compete with each other until one of the updates fails.

For this test, we will put the actual updates in a background worker thread so that the main UI thread won't be blocked:

1. Open the `Form1.cs` file from the `LINQNorthwindClient` project.

2. Add a new class member to the `form` class for the worker thread, as follows:

   ```
   BackgroundWorker bw;
   ```

3. Go to the `Form1.cs` design mode.

4. Add another button called **btnAutoUpdate** with the text, **&Auto Update**.

5. Add the following click event handler for this new button:

   ```
   private void btnAutoUpdate_Click
       (object sender, EventArgs e)
   {
       if (product != null)
       {
           btnAutoUpdate.Text = "Updating Price ...";
           btnAutoUpdate.Enabled = false;

           bw = new BackgroundWorker();
           bw.WorkerReportsProgress = true;
           bw.DoWork += AutoUpdatePrice;
           bw.ProgressChanged += PriceChanged;
   ```

```
      bw.RunWorkerCompleted += AutoUpdateEnd;
      bw.RunWorkerAsync();
   }
   else
   {
      txtUpdateResult.Text = "Get product details first";
   }
}
```

6. Add the following methods to track the status of the updates, as the updates might take a while:

```
private void AutoUpdateEnd
    (object sender, RunWorkerCompletedEventArgs e)
{
    btnAutoUpdate.Text = "&Auto Update";
    btnAutoUpdate.Enabled = true;
}

private void PriceChanged
    (object sender, ProgressChangedEventArgs e)
{
    txtUpdateResult.Text = e.UserState.ToString();
    // Scroll to end of textbox
    txtUpdateResult.SelectionStart =
    txtUpdateResult.TextLength-4;
    txtUpdateResult.ScrollToCaret();
}
```

7. Finally, add the following method to do the actual update:

```
private void AutoUpdatePrice
    (object sender, DoWorkEventArgs e)
{
    var client = new ProductServiceClient();
    var result = "";
    try
    {
      // update its price
      for (int i = 0; i < 100; i++)
      {
            // refresh the product first
            product = client.GetProduct(product.ProductID);
            // update its price
            product.UnitPrice += 1.0m;

            var sb = new StringBuilder();
            var message = "";
            sb.Append("Price updated to ");
            sb.Append(product.UnitPrice.ToString());
```

```
                sb.Append("\r\n");
                sb.Append("Update result:");
                bool updateResult = client.UpdateProduct(
                        ref product, ref message);
                sb.Append(updateResult.ToString());
                sb.Append("\r\n");
                sb.Append("Update message: ");
                sb.Append(message);
                sb.Append("\r\n");
                sb.Append("New RowVersion:");
                foreach (var x in
                product.RowVersion.AsEnumerable())
                {
                    sb.Append(x.ToString());
                    sb.Append(" ");
                }
                sb.Append("\r\n");

                sb.Append("Price updated ");
                sb.Append((i + 1).ToString());
                sb.Append(" times\r\n\r\n");

                result += sb.ToString();

                // report progress
                bw.ReportProgress(i+1, result);

                // sleep a while
                var random = new Random();
                var randomNumber = random.Next(0, 1000);
                System.Threading.Thread.Sleep(randomNumber);
            }
        }
        catch (TimeoutException ex)
        {
            result += "The service operation timed out. " +
                    ex.Message;
        }
        catch (FaultException<ProductFault> ex)
        {
            result += "ProductFault returned: " +
                    ex.Detail.FaultMessage;
        }
        catch (FaultException ex)
        {
            result += "Unknown Fault: " +
                    ex.ToString();
        }
        catch (CommunicationException ex)
        {
```

```
        result += "There was a communication problem. " +
                ex.Message + ex.StackTrace;
    }
    catch (Exception ex)
    {
        result += "Other exception: " +
                ex.Message + ex.StackTrace;
    }

    // report progress
    bw.ReportProgress(100, result);
}
```

The concept here is that once the **btnAutoUpdate** button is clicked, it will keep updating the price of the selected product 100 times, with a price increase of `1.00` in each iteration. If two clients—again let's call them Client A and Client B—are running, and this button is clicked for both the clients, one of the updates will fail as the other client will also be updating the same record.

The sequence of the updates will be as follows:

1. Client A reads the product's details, updates the product, and commits the changes back to the database.

2. Client A sleeps for a while, then repeats the preceding step.

3. Client B reads the product's details, updates the same product, and commits the changes back to the database.

4. Client B sleeps for a while, then repeats the preceding step.

5. At some point, these two sets of processes will cross; so the following events will happen:

    1. Client A reads the product's details.

    2. Client A processes the product in memory.

    3. Client B reads the product's details.

    4. Client A finishes processing and commits the changes back to the database.

    5. Client B finishes processing and tries to commit the changes back to the database.

    6. Client B's update fails because it finds that the product has been updated while it was still processing the product.

    7. Client B stops.

    8. Client A keeps updating the product until it has done so 100 times.

Now, follow these steps to finish this test:

1. Start the client program twice in the non-debugging mode by pressing *Ctrl + F5*. Two clients should be up and running.

2. For each client, enter 3 in the **Product ID** textbox and click on **Get Product Details** to get the product details. Both clients should display the price as **10.0000**.

3. Click on the **Auto Update** button on each client.

You will see that one of the clients fails while the other one keeps updating the database for 100 times.

The following screenshot shows the results in the successful client. As you can see, the initial price of the product was **10.0000**, and after the updates, this price has been changed to a new one. From the source code, we know that this client only updates the price 100 times with an increase of 1.00 each time. The new price now is not 110.00, because another client has updated this product a few more times:

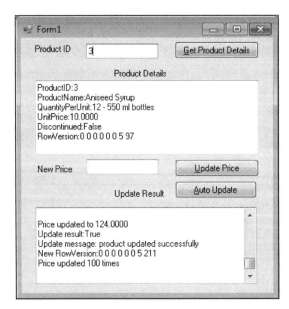

The following screenshot shows the results in the failed client. As you can see, the initial price of the product was **10.000**. After updating the price a few times, when this client tries to update the price again, it fails with the error message, **Entities may have been modified or deleted since entities were loaded**:

 However, if you enter two different product IDs in each client, both client updates will be successful until all 100 updates have been made. This again proves that locking is applied on a record level of the database.

Summary

In this chapter, we used LINQ to Entities to communicate with the database in the data access layer, rather than using the raw ADO.NET APIs. We have used only one LINQ statement to retrieve product information from the database, and as you have seen, the updates with LINQ to Entities prove to be much easier than with the raw ADO.NET data adapters. Now, WCF and LINQ are combined together for our services, so we can take advantage of both technologies.

In the next chapter, we will explore transaction support of WCF with LINQ to Entities so that we can write transactional WCF services.

10
Distributed Transaction
Support of WCF

In the previous chapters, we created a WCF service using LINQ to Entities in the data access layer. Now, we will apply settings to make the service participate in distributed client transactions. Client applications will control the transaction scope and decide whether a service should commit or roll back its transaction.

In this chapter, we will first verify that the Northwind WCF service, which we built in the previous chapter, does not support distributed transaction processing. We will then learn how to enhance this WCF service to support distributed transaction processing and how to configure all related computers to enable the distributed transaction support. To demonstrate this, we will propagate a transaction from the client to the WCF service and verify that all sequential calls to the WCF service are within one single distributed transaction. We will also explore the multiple database support of the WCF service and discuss how to configure **Microsoft Distributed Transaction Coordinator (MSDTC)** and the firewall for the distributed WCF service.

We will cover the following topics in this chapter:

- Creating the DistNorthwind solution
- Hosting the WCF service in IIS
- Testing the transaction behavior of the existing WCF service
- Enabling distributed transaction support
- Understanding the distributed transaction support of a WCF service
- Testing the distributed transaction support of the new WCF service
- Trade-offs of distributed transactions

Creating the DistNorthwind solution

In this chapter, we will create a new solution based on the LINQNorthwind solution. We will copy all of the source code from the LINQNorthwind directory to a new directory and then customize it to suit our needs.

Follow these steps to create the new solution:

1. Create a new directory named DistNorthwind under the existing C:\SOAwithWCFandEF\Projects\ directory.

2. Copy all the files under the C:\SOAwithWCFandEF\Projects\ LINQNorthwind directory to the C:\SOAwithWCFandEF\Projects\ DistNorthwind directory.

3. Remove the LINQNorthwindClient folder. We will create a new client for this solution.

4. Change the solution file's name from LINQNorthwind.sln to DistNorthwind.sln.

Now, we have the file structures ready for the new solution. Here, we will reuse the old service to demonstrate how to enable transactions for the existing WCF service.

First, we need to make sure that this old service still works in the new solution, and we also need to make a small change to the service implementation so that we can test transaction support along with it. Once we have the service up and running, we will create a new client to test this new service using the following steps:

1. Start Visual Studio and open the C:\SOAwithWCFandEF\Projects\ DistNorthwind\DistNorthwind.sln solution.

2. Click on the **OK** button to close the **projects were not loaded correctly** warning dialog.

3. From the **Solution Explorer**, remove the LINQNorthwindClient project.

4. Open the ProductService.cs file under the NorthwindService project in this new solution and remove the condition check for a negative price in the UpdateProduct method. Later, we will try and update a product's price to be negative in order to test the distributed transaction support of WCF.

If this check is not removed, when we try to update a price to be negative later in this chapter, the operation will stop at this validation check. It won't be able to reach the data access layer where LINQ to Entities will be used and the remote database will get involved, which is the key part in a distributed transaction support test.

The following screenshot shows the final structure of the new solution, `DistNorthwind`:

Now, we have finished creating the solution. If you build the solution now, you should not see any errors. You can set the service project as the startup project, run the program, and the output should be the same as seen in the *Testing the service with the WCF Test Client* section in *Chapter 9, Applying LINQ to Entities to a WCF Service.*

Hosting the WCF service in IIS

In the previous chapter, we hosted `NorthwindService` in IIS. Since we will change the service settings in this chapter to support distributed transaction, we need to create a different IIS application for the service.

Just open IIS manager, add a new `DistNorthwindService` application, and set its physical path to `C:\SOAwithWCFandEF\Projects\DistNorthwind\NorthwindService`. Choose the application pool, `NorthwindAppPool`, which was created in the last chapter, as this service's application pool.

Now, you have finished setting up the service to be hosted in IIS. Open Internet Explorer, go to `http://localhost/DistNorthwindService/ProductService.svc`, and you should see the `ProductService` description in the browser.

Testing the transaction behavior of the existing WCF service

Before learning how to enhance this WCF service to support distributed transactions, we will confirm whether the existing WCF service supports distributed transactions.

To do so, we will first create a **Windows Presentation Foundation** (**WPF**) client to call the same service twice in one method. We will make the first service call succeed and the second service call fail. After the two service calls, we will verify that the update in the first service call will be committed to the database, even though the second service call fails, which means that the WCF service does not support distributed transactions.

We will then wrap the two service calls in one transaction scope and redo the test. Again, we will verify that the update in the first service call will still be committed to the database, which means the WCF service does not support distributed transactions even if both the service calls are within the scope of one transaction.

Going one step further, we will add a second database support to the WCF service and modify the client to update both databases in one method. We will then verify that the update in the first service call will still be committed to the database, which means the WCF service does not support distributed transactions with multiple databases.

Now, let's start the test step by step.

Creating a client to call the WCF service sequentially

The first scenario that we will test is where within one method of the client application, two service calls will be made and one of them fails. We then check whether the update in the successful service call has been committed to the database. If it has been committed, it will mean that the two service calls are not within a single atomic transaction and will indicate that the WCF service does not support distributed transactions.

You can follow these steps to create a WPF client for this test case:

1. In the **Solution Explorer**, right-click on the solution item and select **Add | New Project...** from the context menu.
2. Click on **Visual C#** and then select **WPF Application** as the template.

3. Enter `DistNorthwindWPF` as **Name**.

4. Click on the **OK** button to create the new client project.

Now, the new test client should have been created and added to the solution. Follow these steps to customize this client so that we can call `ProductService` twice within one method and test the distributed transaction support of this WCF service:

1. On WPF's `MainWindow` designer surface, add the following controls (you can double-click on the **MainWindow.xaml** item to open this window, and make sure you are in the design mode, not the XAML mode):

   ○ A label with **Content Product ID**

   ○ Two textboxes named **txtProductID1** and **txtProductID2**

   ○ A button named **btnGetProduct** with the content **Get Product Details**

   ○ A separator to separate the preceding controls from the following controls

   ○ Two labels with the content **Product1 Details** and **Product2 Details**

   ○ Two textboxes named **txtProduct1Details** and **txtProduct2Details**, with their **AcceptsReturn** properties as **checked**, **VerticalScrollbarVisibility** set to **Auto**, and **IsReadOnly** set to **checked**

   ○ A separator to separate the preceding controls from the following controls

   ○ A label with the content **New Price**

   ○ Two textboxes named **txtNewPrice1** and **txtNewPrice2**

   ○ A button named **btnUpdatePrice** with the content **Update Price**

   ○ A separator to separate the preceding controls from the following controls

   ○ Two labels with the content **Update1 Results** and **Update2 Results**

   ○ Two textboxes named **txtUpdate1Results** and **txtUpdate2Results** with the **AcceptsReturn** property as **checked**, **VerticalScrollbarVisibility** set to **Auto**, and **IsReadOnly** as **checked**

Your **MainWindow** design surface should be as shown in the following screenshot:

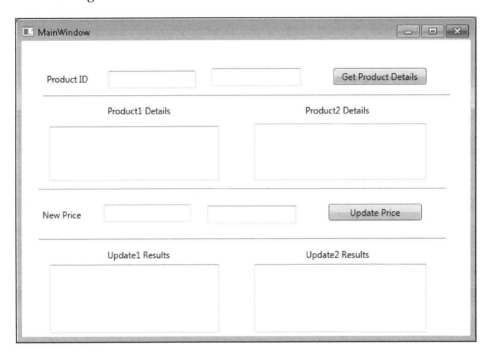

2. In the **Solution Explorer**, right-click on the **DistNorthwindWPF** project item, select **Add | Service Reference...**, and add a service reference of the product service to the project. The namespace of this service reference should be ProductServiceProxy, and the URL of the product service should be http://localhost/DistNorthwindService/ProductService.svc.

 If you get an error saying **An error (Details) occurred while attempting to find service and the error details are... Metadata contains a reference that cannot be resolved**, you might need to give your IIS identity proper access rights to access your C:\Windows\Temp directory.

3. On the MainWindow.xaml designer surface, double-click on the **Get Product Details** button to create an event handler for this button.

4. In the MainWindow.xaml.cs file, add the following using statement:

    ```
    using DistNorthwindWPF.ProductServiceProxy;
    ```

5. Again, in the `MainWindow.xaml.cs` file, add the following two class members:

```
Product product1, product2;
```

6. Now, add the following method to the `MainWindow.xaml.cs` file:

```
private string GetProduct(TextBox txtProductID,
                          ref Product product)
{
    var result = "";

    try
    {
        var productID = Int32.Parse(txtProductID.Text);
        var client = new ProductServiceClient();
        product = client.GetProduct(productID);

        var sb = new StringBuilder();
        sb.Append("ProductID:" +
            product.ProductID.ToString() + "\n");
        sb.Append("ProductName:" +
            product.ProductName + "\n");
        sb.Append("UnitPrice:" +
            product.UnitPrice.ToString() + "\n");
        sb.Append("RowVersion:");
        foreach (var x in
        product.RowVersion.AsEnumerable())
        {
            sb.Append(x.ToString());
            sb.Append(" ");
        }
        result = sb.ToString();
    }
    catch (Exception ex)
    {
        result = "Exception: " + ex.Message.ToString();
    }

    return result;
}
```

This method will call the product service to retrieve a product from the database, format the product details to a string, and return the string. This string will be displayed on the screen. The product object will also be returned so that later on, we can reuse this object to update the price of the product.

7. Inside the event handler of the **Get Product Details** button, add the following two lines of code to get and display the product details:

```
txtProduct1Details.Text = GetProduct(txtProductID1, ref product1);
txtProduct2Details.Text = GetProduct(txtProductID2, ref product2);
```

Now, we have finished adding code to retrieve products from the database through the Product WCF service. Set `DistNorthwindWPF` as the startup project, press *Ctrl + F5* to start the client, enter 30 and 31 as the product IDs, and then click on the **Get Product Details** button. You should get a window as shown in the following screenshot:

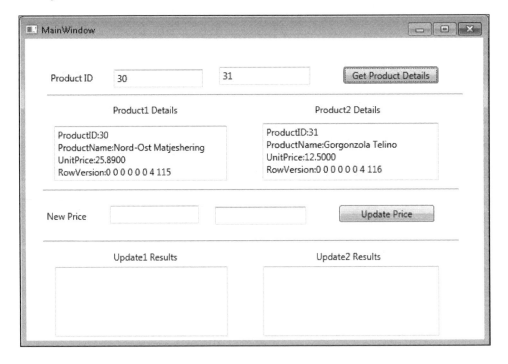

From the preceding screenshot, we can see that the price of the product 30 is now **25.8900**, and the price of the product 31 is now **12.5000**. Next, we will write code to update the prices of these two products to test the distributed transaction support of the WCF service.

To update the prices of these two products, follow these steps to add the code to the project:

1. On the `MainWindow.xaml` design surface, double-click on the **Update Price** button to add an event handler for this button.

2. Add the following method to the `MainWindow.xaml.cs` file:

```
private string UpdatePrice(
  TextBox txtNewPrice,
  ref Product product,
  ref bool updateResult)
{
  var result = "";
  var message = "";

  try
  {
    product.UnitPrice =
        Decimal.Parse(txtNewPrice.Text);

    var client =
      new ProductServiceClient();
    updateResult =
      client.UpdateProduct(ref product, ref message);
    var sb = new StringBuilder();

    if (updateResult == true)
    {
      sb.Append("Price updated to ");
      sb.Append(txtNewPrice.Text.ToString());
      sb.Append("\n");
      sb.Append("Update result:");
      sb.Append(updateResult.ToString());
      sb.Append("\n");
      sb.Append("Update message:");
      sb.Append(message);
      sb.Append("\n");
      sb.Append("New RowVersion:");
    }
    else
    {
      sb.Append("Price not updated to ");
      sb.Append(txtNewPrice.Text.ToString());
      sb.Append("\n");
      sb.Append("Update result:");
      sb.Append(updateResult.ToString());
      sb.Append("\n");
```

```
        sb.Append("Update message:");
        sb.Append(message);
        sb.Append("\n");
        sb.Append("Old RowVersion:");
    }
    foreach (var x in product.RowVersion.AsEnumerable())
    {
        sb.Append(x.ToString());
        sb.Append(" ");
    }

    result = sb.ToString();
    }
    catch (Exception ex)
    {
        result = "Exception: " + ex.Message;
    }

    return result;
}
```

This method will call the product service to update the price of a product in the database. The update result will be formatted and returned so that later on, we can display it. The updated product object with the new row version will also be returned so that later on, we can update the price of the same product repeatedly.

3. Inside the event handler of the **Update Price** button, add the following code to update the products' prices:

```
if (product1 == null)
{
    txtUpdate1Results.Text = "Get product details first";
}
else if (product2 == null)
{
    txtUpdate2Results.Text = "Get product details first";
}
else
{
    bool update1Result = false, update2Result = false;

    txtUpdate1Results.Text = UpdatePrice(
        txtNewPrice1, ref product1, ref update1Result);
    txtUpdate2Results.Text = UpdatePrice(
        txtNewPrice2, ref product2, ref update2Result);
}
```

Testing the sequential calls to the WCF service

Now, let's run the program to test the distributed transaction support of the WCF service. We will first update two products with two valid prices to make sure that our code works with normal use cases. Then, we will update one product with a valid price and another with an invalid price. We will verify that the update with the valid price has been committed to the database, regardless of the failure of the other update.

Let's follow these steps to perform the test:

1. Press *Ctrl + F5* to start the program.

2. Enter 30 and 31 as the product IDs in the top two textboxes and click on the **Get Product Details** button to retrieve the two products. Note that the prices for these two products are **25.89** and **12.5**, respectively.

3. Enter 26.89 and 13.5 as the new prices in the **New Price** textboxes and click on the **Update Price** button to update the values for these two products. The update results are **True** for both the updates, as shown in the following screenshot:

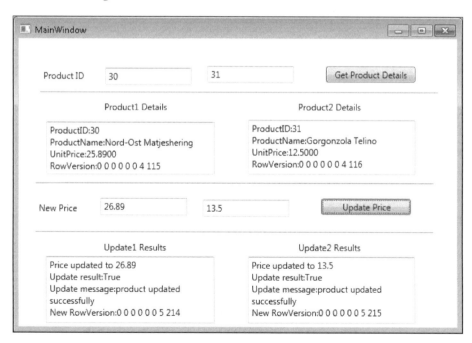

4. Now, enter 27.89 and -14.5 as the new prices in the **New Price** textboxes and click on the **Update Price** button to update the values for these two products. This time, the update result for product 30 is still **True**, but for the second update, the result is **False**. Click on the **Get Product Details** button again to refresh the product prices so that we can verify the update results, as shown in the following screenshot:

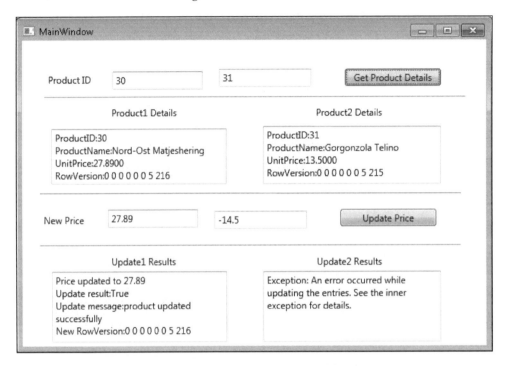

We know that the second service call should fail; so, the second update should not be committed to the database. From the test result, we know that this is true (the second product's price did not change). However, from the test result, we also know that the first update in the first service call has been committed to the database (the first product's price has changed). This means that the first call to the service is not rolled back even when a subsequent service call fails. Therefore, each service call is in a separate standalone transaction. In other words, two sequential service calls are not within one distributed transaction.

Wrapping the WCF service calls in one transaction scope

This test is not a complete distributed transaction test. On the client side, we didn't explicitly wrap the two updates in one transaction scope. We should test to see what will happen if we put the two updates within one transaction scope.

Follow these steps to wrap the two service calls in one transaction scope:

1. Add a reference to `System.Transactions` in the client project.

2. Add a `using` statement to the `MainWindow.xaml.cs` file, as follows:

   ```
   using System.Transactions;
   ```

3. Add a `using` statement to put both the updates within one transaction scope. Now, the click event handler for the **Update Price** button should be as follows:

   ```
   if (product1 == null)
   {
     txtUpdate1Results.Text = "Get product details first";
   }
   else if (product2 == null)
   {
     txtUpdate2Results.Text = "Get product details first";
   }
   else
   {
     bool update1Result = false, update2Result = false;

     using (var ts = new TransactionScope())
     {
       txtUpdate1Results.Text = UpdatePrice(
       txtNewPrice1, ref product1, ref update1Result);
       txtUpdate2Results.Text = UpdatePrice(
       txtNewPrice2, ref product2, ref update2Result);
       if (update1Result == true && update2Result == true)
           ts.Complete();
     }
   }
   ```

Run the client program again, still using 30 and 31 as the product IDs, and enter 28.89 and -14.5 as the new prices. You will find that even though we have wrapped both the updates within one transaction scope, the first update is still committed to the database—it is not rolled back even though the transaction scope is not completed—and requests all the participating parties to roll back. After the updates, the price of the product 30 will change to 28.89 and the price of the product 31 will remain 13.5.

At this point, we have proved that the WCF service does not support distributed transactions with multiple sequential service calls. Irrespective of whether the two sequential calls to the service have been wrapped in one transaction scope or not, each service call is treated as a standalone separate transaction and it does not participate in any distributed transactions.

Testing the multiple database support of the WCF service

In the previous sections, we tried to call the WCF service sequentially to update records in the same database. We have proved that this WCF service does not support distributed transactions. In this section, we will do one more test to add a new WCF service—DistNorthwindRemoteService—in order to update records in another database on another computer. We will call the UpdateProduct operation in this new service, together with the original UpdateProduct operation from the old service and then check whether the two updates to the two databases will be within one distributed transaction or not.

This new service is very important for our distributed transaction support test because the distributed transaction coordinator will only be activated if more than two servers are involved in the same transaction. For test purposes, we cannot just update two databases on the same SQL Server even though a transaction within a single SQL Server that spans two or more databases is actually a distributed transaction. This is because SQL Server manages the distributed transactions internally, but for the user, it operates as a local transaction.

Configuring a remote database on a remote machine

To test the multiple database support, we first need to install a database on another machine and configure this machine properly. Going forward, we will call this machine as the remote machine or remote server and call the previous development machine as the local machine or local server.

Follow these steps to configure this remote machine:

1. Install a fresh `Northwind` database for SQL Server on the remote machine. Add a new `RowVersion` column to the `Products` table in this remote `Northwind` database.

2. Make sure that **Allow remote connections to this server** is enabled for this remote database. In the following section, we will create a new WCF service to connect to in order to get product details and update the product information in this remote database; so, this option needs to be enabled. You can open SQL Server Management Studio, go to **Properties** of the database server, and verify this in the **Connections** tab of the **Server Properties** window.

> **Allow remote connections to this server** is a property of the database server, not of the `Northwind` database.

3. Enable TCP on the remote SQL database server. You can open **Sql Server Configuration Manager**, expand the **SQL Server Network Configuration** node, select **Protocols for MSSQLSERVER**, and then enable the **TCP/IP** protocol, as follows:

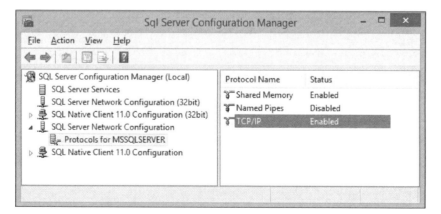

4. Allow the SQL Server process through firewall if the firewall is turned on on the remote machine. To enable the SQL Server port in firewall, open the **Allow a program through Windows Firewall** window, find the **SQL Server Windows NT** program and make sure it is enabled for your network:

 If SQL Server is not in the list, click on the **Add another app...** button and then browse to and add the SQL Server process to the list. The process file should be located in a folder such as `C:\Program Files\Microsoft SQL Server\MSSQL12.MSSQLSERVER\MSSQL\Binn\sqlservr.exe`.

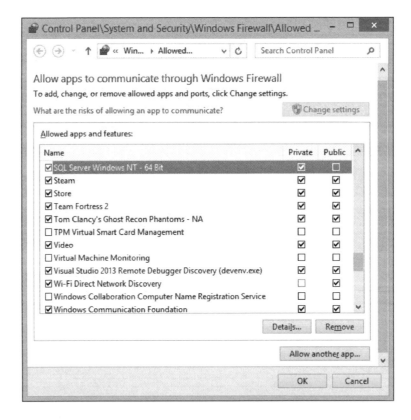

5. If your computers are in a home group instead of a domain network, add a SQL login to the remote database. This login should have full access to the `Northwind` database. Later, we will use this login to connect to this remote database as integrated security is not supported in a home group.

6. Now, on your local machine, open the SQL Server Management Studio and try to connect to the remote database. Write a query such as `select * from Products` to verify that you have set up the remote database properly. You should also verify that the `RowVersion` column has been added to the `Products` table. If you cannot connect to the remote database from your local machine or the `RowVersion` column has not been added to the `Products` table, you should fix it right now before moving on to the next section, following the instructions in this section.

Creating a new WCF service

Once you have the remote database set up properly, we will add a new WCF service to update a product in the remote database. We will reuse the same WCF service that we created for the `DistNorthwind` solution, but we will change the connection string to point to the remote database on the remote machine.

Follow these steps to add this new service:

1. On the local server, in Windows Explorer, create a new folder named `NorthwindRemoteService` under the `DistNorthwind` solution folder `C:\SOAwithWCFandEF\Projects\DistNorthwind`.

2. Copy `Web.config` and `bin` from the `NorthwindService` folder to the new `NorthwindRemoteService` folder.

3. Open the `Web.config` file in the new service folder, change the **Data Source** part within the `connectionString` node from **localhost** to the remote machine's name.

4. If your computers are in a home group instead of a domain network, change the connection string to use the SQL Server login instead of integrated security since connecting to the remote machine with integrated security is not supported in a home group.

5. Now, open IIS Manager and add a new application pool, `NorthwindRemoteAppPool`. Make sure it is a .NET 4.0 application pool.

6. Change the identity of this new application pool to a user that has appropriate access to the remote `Northwind` database. The service that is going to be created in the next step will use this identity to access the remote `Northwind` database.

If your computers are in a home group instead of a domain network, your app pool's identity doesn't need to have access to the remote database since the specified SQL Server login in the connection string will be used to connect to the remote database.

In IIS Manager, add a new application, `DistNorthwindRemoteService`, and set its physical path to the new `NorthwindRemoteService` folder. Choose the newly created application pool as this service's application pool. You can open `http://localhost/DistNorthwindRemoteService/ProductService.svc` in Internet Explorer to verify that the new service is up and running.

 If you get the error **Cannot read configuration file due to insufficient permissions**, you should give the identity of the new app pool read access to the `NorthwindRemoteService` folder.

1. To make it easier to maintain this new service, in the **Solution Explorer**, add a new solution folder, `NorthwindRemoteService`, to the solution and add the `Web.config` file and the `bin` folder of this new service to be under the new solution folder.

2. Also, in the **Solution Explorer**, right-click on the **NorthwindService** project item, select **Properties**, then click on the **Build Events** tab, and add the following to the **Post-build event command line** box below the original line of the `copy` command:

```
copy .\*.* ..\..\..\NorthwindRemoteService\bin
```

Again, this post-build event command line will make sure that the remote service folder will always contain the latest service binary files.

Calling the new WCF service in the client application

The new service is now up and running. Next, we will add a checkbox to the WPF client. If this checkbox is checked and the **Get Product Details** button is clicked on, we will get the second product from the remote database using the new WCF service. When the **Update Price** button is clicked, we will also update the price of the product in the remote database using the new WCF service.

Now, follow these steps to modify the WPF client application to call the new service:

1. Within Visual Studio, in the **Solution Explorer**, right-click on the **DistNorthwindWPF** project item and add a service reference to the new WCF service, `DistNorthwindRemoteService`. The namespace of this service reference should be `RemoteProductServiceProxy`, and the URL of the product service should be `http://localhost/DistNorthwindRemoteService/ProductService.svc`.

2. Open the `MainWindow.xaml` file, go to the design mode, and add a checkbox to indicate that we are going to get and update a product in the remote database by using the remote service. Set this checkbox's properties as follows:

   ○ **Content: Get and Update 2nd Product in Remote Database**

   ○ **Name: chkRemote**

3. Open the `MainWindow.xaml.cs` file and add a new class member:

   ```
   RemoteProductServiceProxy.Product remoteProduct;
   ```

4. In the `MainWindow.xaml.cs` file, copy the `GetProduct` method and paste it as a new method, `GetRemoteProduct`, in the same file. Change the `Product` type within this new method to be `RemoteProductServiceProxy.Product`, and change the `client` type to `RemoteProductServiceProxy.ProductServiceClient`. The new method should be as follows:

```
private string GetRemoteProduct(TextBox txtProductID,
  ref RemoteProductServiceProxy.Product product)
{
  var result = "";

  try
  {
    var productID = Int32.Parse(txtProductID.Text);
    var client =
    new RemoteProductServiceProxy.ProductServiceClient();
    product = client.GetProduct(productID);

    var sb = new StringBuilder();
    sb.Append("ProductID:" +
        product.ProductID.ToString() + "\n");
    sb.Append("ProductName:" +
        product.ProductName + "\n");
    sb.Append("UnitPrice:" +
        product.UnitPrice.ToString() + "\n");
    sb.Append("RowVersion:");
    foreach (var x in product.RowVersion.AsEnumerable())
    {
      sb.Append(x.ToString());
      sb.Append(" ");
    }
    result = sb.ToString();
  }
  catch (Exception ex)
  {
```

```
        result = "Exception: " + ex.Message.ToString();
    }

    return result;
}
```

5. Change the `btnGetProduct_Click` method to call the new service if the checkbox is checked, as follows:

```
private void btnGetProduct_Click(object sender, RoutedEventArgs e)
{
    txtProduct1Details.Text = GetProduct(
            txtProductID1, ref product1);
    if(chkRemote.IsChecked == true)
        txtProduct2Details.Text = GetRemoteProduct(
            txtProductID2, ref remoteProduct);
    else
        txtProduct2Details.Text = GetProduct(
            txtProductID2, ref product2);
}
```

6. Copy the `UpdatePrice` method and paste it as a new method, `UpdateRemotePrice`. Change the `Product` type within this new method to `RemoteProductServiceProxy.Product`, and change the `client` type to `RemoteProductServiceProxy.ProductServiceClient`.

The new method should be as follows:

```
private string UpdateRemotePrice(
    TextBox txtNewPrice,
    ref RemoteProductServiceProxy.Product product,
    ref bool updateResult)
{
    var result = "";
    var message = "";

    try
    {
        product.UnitPrice =
        Decimal.Parse(txtNewPrice.Text);

        var client =
        new RemoteProductServiceProxy.ProductServiceClient();
        updateResult =
        client.UpdateProduct(ref product, ref message);
        var sb = new StringBuilder();

        if (updateResult == true)
        {
            sb.Append("Price updated to ");
```

```
      sb.Append(txtNewPrice.Text.ToString());
      sb.Append("\n");
      sb.Append("Update result:");
      sb.Append(updateResult.ToString());
      sb.Append("\n");
      sb.Append("Update message:");
      sb.Append(message);
      sb.Append("\n");
      sb.Append("New RowVersion:");
    }
    else
    {
      sb.Append("Price not updated to ");
      sb.Append(txtNewPrice.Text.ToString());
      sb.Append("\n");
      sb.Append("Update result:");
      sb.Append(updateResult.ToString());
      sb.Append("\n");
      sb.Append("Update message:");
      sb.Append(message);
      sb.Append("\n");
      sb.Append("Old RowVersion:");
    }
    foreach (var x in product.RowVersion.AsEnumerable())
    {
      sb.Append(x.ToString());
      sb.Append(" ");
    }

    result = sb.ToString();
  }
  catch (Exception ex)
  {
    result = "Exception: " + ex.Message;
  }

  return result;
}
```

7. Change the `btnUpdatePrice_Click` method to call the new service, if the checkbox is checked. The new method should be as follows:

```
private void btnUpdatePrice_Click(object sender,
      RoutedEventArgs e)
{
  if (product1 == null)
  {
    txtUpdate1Results.Text = "Get product details first";
  }
```

```
else if (chkRemote.IsChecked == false
 && product2 == null
 ||    chkRemote.IsChecked == true
 &&    remoteProduct == null)
{
  txtUpdate2Results.Text = "Get product details first";
}
else
{
  bool update1Result = false, update2Result = false;

  using (var ts = new TransactionScope())
  {
    txtUpdate1Results.Text = UpdatePrice(
      txtNewPrice1,
      ref product1,
      ref update1Result);
    if(chkRemote.IsChecked == true)
      txtUpdate2Results.Text = UpdateRemotePrice(
      txtNewPrice2,
      ref remoteProduct,
      ref update2Result);
    else
      txtUpdate2Results.Text = UpdatePrice(
      txtNewPrice2,
      ref product2,
      ref update2Result);
    if (update1Result == true && update2Result == true)
      ts.Complete();
  }
 }
}
```

Testing the WCF service with two databases

Now, let's run the program to test the distributed transaction support of the WCF service with two databases. Follow these steps to perform this test:

1. Press *Ctrl + F5* to start the client application.

2. Check the **Get and Update 2nd Product in Remote Database** checkbox.

3. Enter 30 and 31 as the product IDs in the top two textboxes.

4. Click on the **Get Product Details** button to get the product details for the product IDs 30 and 31. Note that the details of the product 31 are now retrieved from the remote database. The price of the product 30 should be **28.89** and the price of the product 31 should still be **12.5** in the remote database.

   If you get an exception in the second product results' textbox, make sure that you have specified the correct connection string in the Web.config file of the new WCF service and you have added the RowVersion column in the Products table of the remote Northwind database.

5. If you see the price for the product 31 is not **12.5** but **13.5**, it is likely that you did not check the remote database checkbox. For this test, we need to involve the remote database, so you need to check the remote database checkbox and again click on the **Get Product Details** button before you continue the test.

6. Now, enter 29.89 and -14.5 as the new prices in the **New Price** textboxes and click on the **Update Price** button.

7. The updated result for the first product should be **True** and for the second product should be **False**. This means that the second product in the remote database has not been updated.

8. Click on the **Get Product Details** button to refresh the product details so that we can verify the update results.

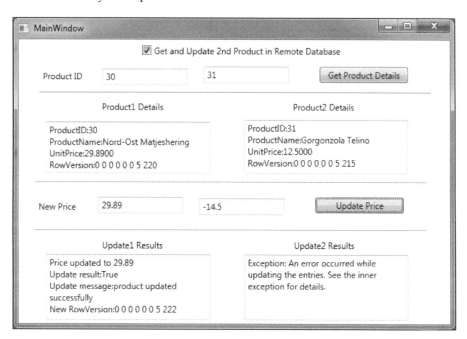

Just as in the previous test, we know that the second service call fails due to the invalid price; so, the second update is not committed to the database. From the refreshed product details, we know this is true (the price of the product 31 did not change). However, from the refreshed product details, we also know that the first update of the first service call has been committed to the remote database (the price of the product 30 has changed). This means that the first call to the service is not rolled back even when a subsequent service call fails. Each service call is in a separate standalone transaction. In other words, the two sequential service calls are not within one distributed transaction.

If you debug the code and examine the inner exception of the product service update exception, you will see that the error message is **The UPDATE statement conflicted with the CHECK constraint**. This is very important for us, as this proves that the update was made to the remote database but then it failed due to a constraint. In the *Testing the distributed transaction support with two databases* section, we need the remote database to get involved so that we can test the settings of MSDTC.

Enabling distributed transaction support

In the previous sections, we verified that the WCF service currently does not support the distributed transactions irrespective of whether there are two sequential calls to the same service or two sequential calls to two different services, with one database or with two databases.

In the following sections, we will learn how to allow this WCF service to support distributed transactions. We will allow the WCF service to participate in the client transaction. From another point of view, we will learn how to propagate a client transaction across the service boundaries so that the client can include service operation calls on multiple services in the same distributed transaction.

Enabling transaction flow in service binding

The first thing that we need to pay attention to is the bindings. As we learned in *Chapter 1, Implementing a Basic HelloWorld WCF Service*, the three elements of a WCF service endpoint are the address, binding, and contract (WCF ABC). Although the address has nothing to do with the distributed transaction support, the other two elements do.

We know that WCF supports several different bindings. Most of them support transactions except some HTTP bindings, such as BasicHttpBinding. In this chapter, we will use wsHttpBinding for our example.

However, using a transaction-aware binding doesn't mean that a transaction will be propagated to the service. The transaction propagation is disabled by default, and we have to enable it manually. Unsurprisingly, the attribute to enable the transaction flow in the bindings is called `transactionFlow`.

In the following section, we will do the following to enable the transaction propagation:

- Use `wsHttpBinding` on the host application as a binding
- Set the value of the `transactionFlow` attribute to `true` on the host application binding configuration

Enabling transaction flow on the service hosting the application

In this section, we will enable the transaction flow in bindings for both `ProductService` and `RemoteProductService`:

1. In the **Solution Explorer**, open the `Web.config` file under the `C:\SOAwithWCFandEF\Projects\DistNorthwind\NorthwindService` folder. Refer to the following line:

   ```
   <endpoint address="" binding="basicHttpBinding"
      contract="NorthwindService.IProductService">
   ```

   Change it to this line:

   ```
   <endpoint address="" binding="wsHttpBinding"
      contract="NorthwindService.IProductService"
         bindingConfiguration="transactionalWsHttpBinding">
   ```

2. Add the following node to the `Web.config` file inside the `system.serviceModel` node and in parallel with node services:

   ```
   <bindings>
     <wsHttpBinding>
       <binding name="transactionalWsHttpBinding"
           transactionFlow="true" receiveTimeout="00:10:00"
           sendTimeout="00:10:00" openTimeout="00:10:00"
           closeTimeout="00:10:00" />
     </wsHttpBinding>
   </bindings>
   ```

   In this configuration section, we have set the `transactionFlow` attribute to `true` for the binding, so a transaction is allowed to flow from the client to the service.

3. Make the same changes to the `Web.config` file under the
   `C:\SOAwithWCFandEF\Projects\DistNorthwind\`
   `NorthwindRemoteService` folder.

In the preceding configuration file, we have verified and left the bindings for both `ProductService` and `RemoteProductService` to `wsHttpBinding` and set the `transactionFlow` attribute of the binding to `true`. This will enable distributed transaction support from the WCF service binding side.

Modifying the service operation contract to allow a transaction flow

Now, the service is able to participate in a propagated transaction from the client application, but the client is still not able to propagate a distributed transaction into the service. Before we enable the distributed transaction support from the client side, we need to make some more changes to the service-side code, that is, modify the service operation to opt in to participate in a distributed transaction. By default, it is opted out.

Two things need to be done in order to allow an operation to participate in a propagated transaction. The first thing is to enable the transaction flow in operation contracts. Follow these steps to enable this option:

1. Open the `IProductService.cs` file under the `NorthwindService` project.

2. Add the following attribute definition before the `UpdateProduct` method:

```
[TransactionFlow(TransactionFlowOption.Allowed)]
```

In the preceding code line, we set `TransactionFlowOption` in the `UpdateProduct` operation to be `Allowed`. This means that a transaction is allowed to be propagated from the client to this operation.

The three transaction flow options for a WCF service operation are `Allowed`, `NotAllowed`, and `Mandatory`, as shown in the following table:

Option	Description
NotAllowed	Transaction flow is not allowed; this is the default value
Allowed	Transaction flow is allowed
Mandatory	Transaction flow must happen

Modifying the service operation implementation to require a transaction scope

The second thing that we need to do is to specify the `TransactionScopeRequired` behavior for the service operation. This has to be done on the service implementation project.

1. Open the `ProductService.cs` file under the `NorthwindService` project.

2. Add the following line before the `UpdateProduct` method:

    ```
    [OperationBehavior(TransactionScopeRequired = true)]
    ```

The `TransactionScopeRequired` attribute means that for the `UpdateProduct` method, the whole service operation will always be executed inside one transaction. If a transaction is propagated from the client application, this operation will participate in the existing distributed transaction. If no transaction is propagated, a new transaction will be created and this operation will be run within the new transaction.

> At end of this chapter, after you have finished setting up everything for transaction support and run the program, you can examine the ambient transaction inside the WCF service (`Transaction.Current`) and compare it with the ambient transaction of the client to see if they are the same. You can also examine the `TransactionInformation` property of the ambient transaction object to see if it is a local transaction (`TransactionInformation.LocalIdentifier`) or a distributed transaction (`TransactionInformation.DistributedIdentifier`).

We now need to regenerate the service proxy and the configuration files on the client project because we have changed the service interfaces. Remember that in your real project, you should avoid making any nonbackward compatible service interface changes. Once the service goes live, if you have to make changes to the service interface, you should version your service and allow the client applications to migrate to the new versions of the service when they are ready to do so. To simplify our example, we will just update the proxy and the configuration files and recompile our client application.

These are the steps to regenerate the configuration and proxy files:

1. Rebuild the solution. As we have set up the post-build event for the `NorthwindService` project to copy all the assembly files to two IIS directories, both `NorthwindService` and `NorthwindRemoteService` should now contain the latest assemblies with distributed transaction support enabled.

2. In the **Solution Explorer**, right-click on **RemoteProductServiceProxy** under the **Service References** directory of the `DistNorthwindWPF` project.

3. Select **Update Service Reference** from the context menu.

4. Right-click on **ProductServiceProxy** under the **Service References** directory of the `DistNorthwindWPF` project.

5. Select **Update Service Reference** from the context menu.

Open the `App.config` file under the `DistNorthwindWPF` project. You will find that the `transactionFlow` attribute is now populated as `true` because the code generator finds that some operations in the service now allow transaction propagation.

Understanding the distributed transaction support of a WCF service

As we have seen, the distributed transaction support of a WCF service depends on the binding of the service, the operation contract attribute, the operation implementation behavior, and the client applications.

The following table shows some possible combinations of the WCF-distributed transaction support:

Binding permits transaction flow	Client has transaction flow enabled	Service contract opts in transaction	Service operation requires a transaction scope	Possible result
True	Yes	`Allowed` or `Mandatory`	True	Service executes under the flowed-in transaction
True or false	No	`Allowed`	True	Service creates and executes within a new transaction
True	Yes or no	`Allowed`	False	Service executes without a transaction
True or false	No	`Mandatory`	True or false	SOAP exception
True	Yes	`NotAllowed`	True or false	SOAP exception

Testing the distributed transaction support of the new WCF service

Now that we have changed the service to support distributed transactions and let the client propagate the transaction to the service, we will test this. We will first change the distributed transaction coordinator and firewall settings for the distributed transaction support of the WCF service, then propagate a transaction from the client to the service, and test the WCF service for multiple database support.

Configuring the Microsoft Distributed Transaction Coordinator

In a subsequent section, we will call two services to update two databases on two different computers. As these two updates are wrapped within one distributed transaction, **Microsoft Distributed Transaction Coordinator (MSDTC)** will be activated to manage this distributed transaction. If MSDTC is not started or not configured properly, the distributed transaction will not be successful. In this section, we will learn how to configure MSDTC on both the machines.

You can follow these steps to configure MSDTC on your local and remote machines:

1. Open **Component Services** by going to **Control Panel | Administrative Tools** (or start dcomcnfg.exe from the **Run** dialog box (Windows + *R*)).

2. In the **Component Services** window, expand **Component Services**, then **Computers**, and then right-click on **My Computer**.

3. Select **Properties** from the context menu.

4. In the **My Computer Properties** window, click on the **MSDTC** tab.

5. Verify that **Use local coordinator** is checked and then close the **My Computer Properties** window.

6. Expand **Distributed Transaction Coordinator** under the **My Computer** node, right-click on **Local DTC**, select **Properties** from the context menu, and then from the **Local DTC Properties** window, click on the **Security** tab.

7. You should now see the security configuration for DTC on this machine. Set it as shown in the following screenshot:

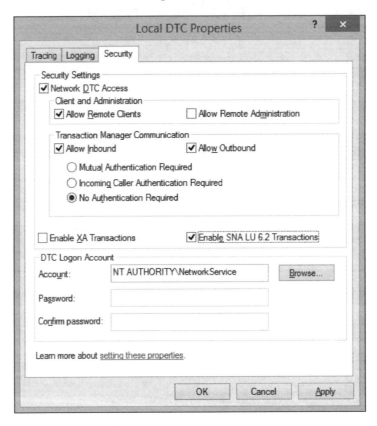

 You have to restart the MSDTC service after you have changed your MSDTC settings for the changes to take effect. You might also need to reboot your machine to let these changes take effect.

Also, to simplify our example, we have chosen the **No Authentication Required** option. You should be aware that not needing authentication is a serious security issue in a production environment.

Remember that you have to make these changes to both your local and remote machines.

Configuring the firewall

Even though the distributed transaction coordinator has been enabled, the distributed transaction may still fail if the firewall is turned on and hasn't been set up properly for MSDTC.

To set up the firewall for MSDTC, follow these steps:

1. Open the **Windows Firewall** window from the **Control Panel**.

2. If the firewall is not turned on, you can skip this section.

3. Go to the **Allow a program or feature through Windows Firewall** window.

4. Add **Distributed Transaction Coordinator** to the program list (`Windows\System32\msdtc.exe`), if it is not already in the list. Make sure the checkbox before this item is checked.

5. You need to change your firewall settings for both your local and remote machines.

6. You can also configure this through **Windows Firewall with Advanced Security** under **Control Panel** | **System and Security** | **Windows Firewall** | **Advanced Settings**.

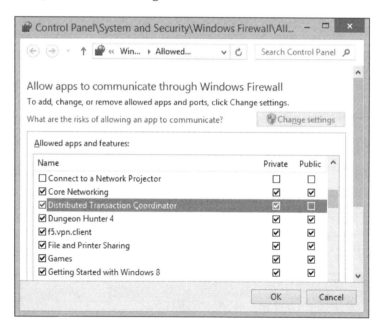

Now, the firewall will allow `msdtc.exe` to go through, so our next test won't fail due to the firewall restrictions.

You might have to restart IIS after you have changed your firewall settings. In some cases, you might also have to stop and then restart your firewall for the changes to take effect.

Propagating a transaction from the client to the WCF service

Now, we have the services and MSDTC ready. In this section, we will rerun the distributed test client and verify the distributed transaction support of the enhanced WCF service.

Testing the distributed transaction support with one database

First, we will test the distributed transaction support of the WCF service within one database. We will try to update two products (30 and 31). The first update will succeed, but the second update will fail. Both the updates are wrapped in one client transaction, which will be propagated into the service, and the service will participate in this distributed transaction. Due to the failure of the second update, the client application will roll back this distributed transaction at the end, and the service should also roll back every update that is within this distributed transaction. So, in the end, the first update should not be committed to the database.

Now, follow these steps to do this test:

1. Press *Ctrl* + *F5* to start the client application.
2. Enter 30 and 31 as the product IDs in the top two textboxes.
3. Make sure **Get and Update 2nd Product in Remote Database** is not checked.
4. Click on the **Get Product Details** button. The prices for these two products should be **29.89** and **13.5**, respectively.
5. Enter 30.89 and -14.5 as the new prices in the **New Price** textboxes.
6. Click on the **Update Price** button.

7. Click on the **Get Product Details** button to refresh the product details so that we can verify the results, as follows:

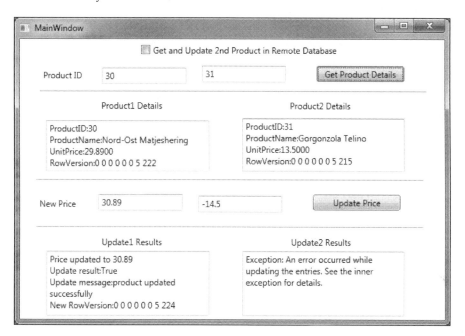

From the output window, we can see that the prices of both the products remain unchanged, which proves that the first update has been rolled back. From this output, we know that both the service calls are within a distributed transaction and the WCF service now fully supports the distributed transaction within one database.

Testing the distributed transaction support with two databases

Next, we will test the distributed transaction support of the WCF service with two databases or machines involved. As mentioned before, this is a true distributed transaction test, as MSDTC will be activated only when the machine boundary is crossed.

In this test, we will try to update two products (product 30 and 31). However, this time, the second product (product 31) is in a remote database on another machine. As in the previous test, the first update will succeed, but the second update will fail. Both the updates are wrapped in one client transaction, which will be propagated into the service, and the service will participate in this distributed transaction. Due to the failure of the second update, the client application will roll back this distributed transaction at the end, and the service should also roll back every update that is within this distributed transaction. The first update should finally not be committed to the database.

Now, follow these steps to carry out this test:

1. Press *Ctrl + F5* to start the client application.

2. Enter 30 and 31 as the product IDs in the top two textboxes.

3. Make sure **Get and Update 2nd Product in Remote Database** is checked.

4. Click on the **Get Product Details** button. The prices for these two products should be **29.89** and **12.5**, respectively.

5. Enter 30.89 and -14.5 as the new prices in the **New Price** textboxes.

6. Click on **Update Price**.

7. Click on the **Get Product Details** button to refresh the product details so that you can verify the results, as shown in the following screenshot:

From the output window, we can see that the prices of both the products remain unchanged, which proves that the first update has been rolled back. From this output, we know that both service calls are within a distributed transaction and the WCF service now fully supports the distributed transaction with multiple databases involved.

Now, to prove that the distributed transaction support works, click on the **Get Product Details** button to refresh `product1` (make sure **Get and Update 2nd Product in Remote Database** is still checked), enter two valid prices, such as `30.89` and `14.5`, and then click on the **Update Price** button. This time you should see that both products' prices are updated successfully.

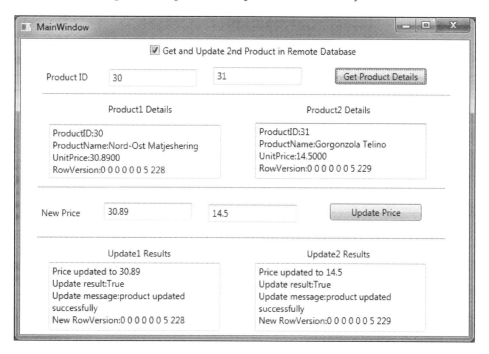

To see the status of all your distributed transactions, you can go to **Component Services** and select **Transaction Statistics**, as shown in the following screenshot:

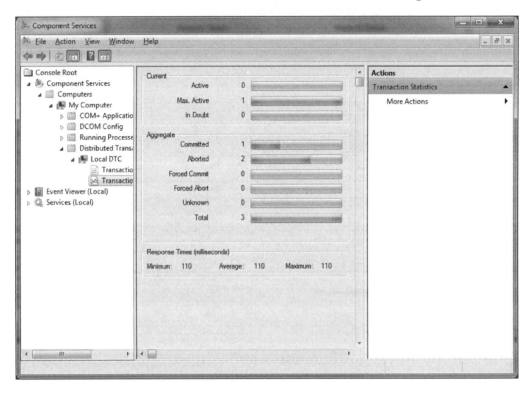

For the last successful test, you might not get an output as shown in the preceding screenshot, but instead still get an exception. If you debug your code inside the UpdatePrice operation of your product service (note that you need to step into your service code from the client's UpdateRemotePrice method), when you examine the update product exception, you might see one of the following error messages:

- **MSDTC on server 'xxxxxx' is unavailable**

- **Network access for Distributed Transaction Manager (MSDTC) has been disabled**

- **The transaction has already been implicitly or explicitly committed or aborted**

- **The MSDTC transaction manager was unable to push the transaction to the destination transaction manager**

- **The partner transaction manager has disabled its support for remote/network transactions**

This might be because you have not set your distributed transaction coordinator or firewall correctly. In this case, you need to follow the instructions in the previous sections to configure these settings and then come back and redo these tests. Remember that you may need to restart your machines (both the local machine and the remote machine) to let the changes take effect.

If you get an exception of the `OptimisticConcurrencyException` type inside the `UpdateRemotePrice` method, double-check your client proxy object within the `UpdateRemotePrice` method. You might have forgotten to change the client proxy from `ProductServiceProxy.ProductServiceClient` to `RemoteProductServiceProxy.ProductServiceClient`. Once you have corrected it, you should be able to perform this test successfully.

If you get a timeout exception while you are debugging, increase your client application's service binding settings of `sendTimeout` and `receiveTimeout` to a larger value such as 5 minutes and try again.

Trade-offs of distributed transactions

Now, you have learned how to turn on distributed transaction support for a WCF service. Before you dive into the world of distributed transaction in your real-work environment, you need to be aware that distributed transaction support will impact your applications in a few areas, sometimes maybe significantly.

The following is a list of some of the impacts of using distributed transactions:

- Distributed transactions might introduce more complexity to your applications
- Distributed transactions might decrease the performance of your applications
- Distributed transactions might increase the deadlock probability of your processes

You should analyze your requirements, consider all the pros and cons of turning the distributed transaction support on, and then make your own judgment for your applications.

Summary

In this chapter, we discussed how to enable distributed transaction support for a WCF service. We learned how to choose a binding for a transactional WCF service, how to enable transaction support for the binding, and how to opt in an operation to a transactional WCF service. Now, we can wrap the sequential WCF service calls within one transaction scope and include the distributed transaction into the WCF services. We can also update multiple databases on different computers, all within one single distributed transaction.

In the next chapter, we will learn how to convert an existing SOAP WCF service to a RESTful WCF service.

11
Building a RESTful WCF Service

In the previous chapters, we created a 3-layered WCF service, used LINQ to Entities in the data access layer, then turned on distributed transaction support for the service. In this chapter, we will convert this SOAP WCF service to a RESTful WCF service and create two Windows 8 apps to consume this RESTful WCF service.

In this chapter, we will cover the following topics while creating and testing the RESTful WCF service:

- SOAP versus REST
- WCF REST versus the ASP.NET Web API
- Creating the RESTNorthwind solution
- Creating the RESTful service
- Defining RESTful service contracts
- Implementing the RESTful service
- Modifying the configuration file
- Testing the RESTful service in a browser
- Testing the RESTful WCF service with a C#/XAML client
- Testing the RESTful WCF service with a JavaScript

SOAP versus REST

SOAP was originally an acronym for Simple Object Access Protocol. This acronym was dropped from SOAP Version 1.2 and now it is a communication protocol to exchange structured information in a decentralized, distributed environment. The SOAP protocol exclusively relies on XML, and all its messages are in the XML format. It was originally developed by Microsoft and became a W3C recommendation in 2003.

REST is an acronym for Representational State Transfer. It is an architectural style to retrieve/update resources within a distributed computer system. It relies on a stateless, client-server, cacheable communications protocol, and in virtually all cases, the HTTP protocol is used. REST was developed by W3C in parallel with HTTP 1.1, based on the existing design of HTTP 1.0.

SOAP is a resource-heavy choice to build services but it has the following advantages over REST:

- It is transport independent (REST supports HTTP only)
- It supports all WS-* standards (REST does not)

REST is more lightweight and has the following advantages over SOAP:

- It is more efficient (SOAP uses XML for all messages, but REST can use a much smaller message format)
- It is faster (no extensive processing is required)

In general, if you need to build a service for non-HTTP transport protocol or you need to support WS-* standards, use SOAP, otherwise use REST.

WCF REST versus the ASP.NET Web API

The ASP.NET Web API is a framework that makes it easy to build HTTP services to reach a broad range of clients, including browsers and mobile devices. The ASP.NET Web API is an ideal platform to build RESTful applications on the .NET Framework.

Though WCF is now mostly used to create SOAP services, it can also be used to build RESTful services from the very beginning. As a matter of fact, the ASP.NET Web API was initially developed under the umbrella of WCF and it was even called WCF Web API. As REST supports HTTP only and WCF is transport neutral, the WCF Web API was eventually moved outside of WCF and into ASP.NET.

WCF REST is again resource heavy but has the following advantages over the ASP.NET Web API:

- It supports multiple transport protocols and allows switching between them (the ASP.NET Web API supports HTTP only)
- It supports all WS-* standards (the ASP.NET Web API does not)

The ASP.NET Web API is more lightweight and has the following advantages over WCF REST:

- It is more efficient and faster
- It takes advantages of the HTTP protocol, such as caching, conditional requests, and status codes

Again in general, if you need to build a service for non-HTTP transport protocol (or multiprotocols), or you need to support WS-* standards, use WCF REST, otherwise use the ASP.NET Web API.

Creating the RESTNorthwind solution

In this chapter, we will create a new solution based on the LINQNorthwind solution. We will copy all of the source code from the LINQNorthwind directory to a new directory and then customize it to suit our needs.

Follow these steps to create the new solution:

1. Create a new directory named RESTNorthwind under the existing C:\SOAwithWCFandEF\Projects\ directory.

2. Copy all of the files under the C:\SOAwithWCFandEF\Projects\ LINQNorthwind directory to the C:\SOAwithWCFandEF\Projects\ RESTNorthwind directory.

3. Remove the LINQNorthwindClient folder. We will create a new client for this solution.

4. Change the solution file's name from LINQNorthwind.sln to RESTNorthwind.sln.

Now, we have the file structures ready for the new solution. Here, we will reuse the old service to demonstrate how to make an existing WCF service RESTful.

First, we need to make sure this old service in the new solution still works and we also need to create a new IIS application for the service:

1. Start Visual Studio and open the C:\SOAwithWCFandEF\Projects\ RESTNorthwind\RESTNorthwind.sln solution.

2. Click on the **OK** button to close the **projects were not loaded correctly** warning dialog.

3. From **Solution Explorer**, remove the LINQNorthwindClient project.

4. Open IIS Manager, add a new application RESTNorthwindService, and set its physical path to C:\SOAwithWCFandEF\Projects\RESTNorthwind\ NorthwindService. Choose the application pool NorthwindAppPool, which we have created in a previous chapter, as this service's application pool.

Now, you have finished setting up the service to be hosted in IIS. Open Internet Explorer, go to http://localhost/RESTNorthwindService/ProductService. svc, and you should see the ProductService description in the browser.

Creating the RESTful service

Now we have the solution ready and have hosted the service in IIS. Next, we will modify the existing NorthwindService to be RESTful. We will modify the service contracts, service implementation, and web config file.

Defining RESTful service contracts

In the existing NorthwindService, we have defined two operations for the service, GetProduct and UpdateProduct. To make them RESTful, we need to change their definitions using the following steps:

1. Add a reference of System.ServiceModel.Web to the service project, NorthwindService.

2. Open the IProductService.cs file in the project.

3. Add a using statement:

   ```
   using System.ServiceModel.Web;
   ```

4. Add the following line of code before the GetProduct method:

   ```
   [WebGet (UriTemplate = "Product/{id}" , ResponseFormat =
   WebMessageFormat.Json )]
   ```

   In the preceding line of code, we tell the WCF runtime engine that this operation will be a HTTP Get operation and the UriTemplate maps the parameter name, id, from the HTTP protocol to the service operation parameter, id. Also, the response will be in the JSON format.

5. Now, change the parameter type of the method, GetProduct, from int to string:

   ```
   Product GetProduct(string id);
   ```

This is because for a RESTful service call, the default HTTP protocol parameter will always be of the type `string`.

For the `UpdateProduct` method, we need to do a little more as it is a method with complex parameters. There are a few approaches to handle complex parameters for a RESTful WCF service, and here we will take the one that requires a request/response package for the method.

Follow these steps to define the service contract for the `UpdateProduct` method.

1. Add the following two classes to the `IProductService.cs` file for the request/response packages:

```
public class UpdateProductRequest
{
    public Product Product { get; set; }
}

public class UpdateProductResponse
{
    public bool Result { get; set; }
    public string Message { get; set; }
    public Product Product { get; set; }
}
```

The `UpdateProductRequest` class will be used for the input operation, which contains the `Product` information to be updated. The `UpdateProductResponse` class will be used for the output operation, which contains the result of the update, updated product information, and update message.

2. Now, add the following line of code before the `UpdateProduct` method:

```
[WebInvoke(Method = "POST", UriTemplate = "/UpdateProduct",
RequestFormat = WebMessageFormat.Json, ResponseFormat =
WebMessageFormat.Json)]
```

Here, we use POST as the web invoke method, and both the request and response will be in the JSON format.

3. Change the definition of the `UpdateProduct` method to be like this:

```
UpdateProductResponse UpdateProduct(UpdateProductRequest
request);
```

As you can see, we have passed in a `UpdateProductRequest` parameter, and the return result will be `UpdateProductResponse`.

The service contract definitions will be like this now:

```
using System;
using System.Collections.Generic;
using System.Linq;
using System.Runtime.Serialization;
using System.ServiceModel;
using System.Text;
using System.ServiceModel.Web;

namespace NorthwindService
{
    [ServiceContract]
    public interface IProductService
    {
        [WebGet(UriTemplate = "Product/{id}",
            ResponseFormat = WebMessageFormat.Json)]
        [OperationContract]
        [FaultContract(typeof(ProductFault))]
        Product GetProduct(string id);

        [WebInvoke(Method = "POST",
            UriTemplate = "/UpdateProduct",
                RequestFormat = WebMessageFormat.Json,
                ResponseFormat = WebMessageFormat.Json)]
        [OperationContract]
        [FaultContract(typeof(ProductFault))]
        UpdateProductResponse UpdateProduct(
            UpdateProductRequest request);
    }

    public class UpdateProductRequest
    {
        public Product Product { get; set; }
    }

    public class UpdateProductResponse
    {
        public bool Result { get; set; }
        public string Message { get; set; }
        public Product Product { get; set; }
    }
```

```
[DataContract]
public class Product
{
    [DataMember]
    public int ProductID { get; set; }
    [DataMember]
    public string ProductName { get; set; }
    [DataMember]
    public string QuantityPerUnit { get; set; }
    [DataMember]
    public decimal UnitPrice { get; set; }
    [DataMember]
    public bool Discontinued { get; set; }
    [DataMember]
    public byte[] RowVersion { get; set; }
}
[DataContract]
public class ProductFault
{
    public ProductFault(string msg)
    {
        FaultMessage = msg;
    }

    [DataMember]
    public string FaultMessage;
}
}
```

Implementing the RESTful service

Now, let's implement the service contracts. To reuse the existing code, here we will add two new methods to the existing `ProductService.cs` file as follows:

1. Open the `ProductService.cs` file in the `NorthwindService` project.

2. Add a new method, `GetProduct`, like this:

```
public Product GetProduct(string id)
{
  return GetProduct(Convert.ToInt32(id));
}
```

This new method actually just converts the input parameter to an integer, then calls the exiting method to get product details. Note that we didn't check whether the input is really an integer here. In a real situation, you should add appropriate error handling to this method.

3. Add another new method, UpdateProduct, like this:

```
public UpdateProductResponse UpdateProduct(
    UpdateProductRequest request)
{
    var product = request.Product;
    var message = "";

    var result = UpdateProduct(ref product, ref message);
    var response = new UpdateProductResponse()
        { Result = result,
          Message = message,
          Product = product };
    return response;
}
```

Again, this new method just calls the exiting method to update the product. As we couldn't have ref parameters for a RESTful WCF service, we will return the updated product in the response package.

Modifying the configuration file

For the NorthwindService to work as a RESTful WCF service, we need to modify the Web.config file. We need to change the binding and define the behavior of the service endpoint:

1. Open the Web.config file in the NorthwindService project.

2. Change the product service endpoint to be like this:

```
<endpoint address="" binding="webHttpBinding"
    contract="NorthwindService.IProductService"
    behaviorConfiguration="restfulBehavior">
```

3. Add a new node as a child node of behaviors, right after the existing node, serviceBehaviors:

```
<endpointBehaviors>
    <behavior name ="restfulBehavior">
        <webHttp />
    </behavior>
</endpointBehaviors>
```

Make sure that this new node is on the same level as the existing node `serviceBehaviors`, not nested within it.

Testing the RESTful service in a browser

We have finished modifying the existing `NorthwindService` to be a RESTful WCF service. Before building our own client to test it, let's test it with a browser.

To test the RESTful WCF service, first rebuild the solution, then open Internet Explorer and enter the following URL in the address bar of the browser: `http://localhost/RESTNorthwindService/ProductService.svc/Product/5`.

Depending on your browser's settings, you might be prompted to open/save the response file, or you might get the following content displayed on your browser:

```
{"Discontinued":true,"ProductID":5,"ProductName":
"Chef Anton's Gumbo Mix","QuantityPerUnit":"36 boxes","RowVersi
on":[0,0,0,0,0,0,7,252],
"UnitPrice":21.3500}
```

This shows the JSON-formatted details of the product with ID 5.

Now if you try to call the `UpdateProduct` method on the browser, you will get a response that says **Method not allowed**. As this is a POST method, we have to create a client to submit a POST request to the service to get the response, and in the next section we will create such a client.

Testing the RESTful WCF service with a C#/XAML client

Next, we will create two clients to test the RESTful WCF service. We will create a C#/XAML client to call the RESTful WCF service from the code behind the C# class and create another client to call the RESTful WCF service in JavaScript with jQuery and WinJS. We will create these two clients as Windows 8.1 apps. If you don't have Windows 8.1, you can create the first client as a WPF application, and the second client as an ASP.NET application in Windows 7.

Creating the C#/XAML client

First, let's create a C#/XAML client to call the RESTful WCF service from the code behind the C# class. You can follow these steps to create this client:

1. From the **Solution Explorer**, right-click on the solution item and add a new project. Go to **Visual C# | Store Apps | Windows Apps | Blank App (Windows)** as the template, change the name to `RESTNorthwindClientXAML`, and leave the location to be the default one (`C:\SOAwithWCFandEF\ Projects\RESTNorthwind`).

2. You might be prompted to get a developer's license to create a Windows app. Just follow the instructions to get a new one or renew an existing one and then continue.

3. Delete the `MainPage.xaml` file from this new project.

4. Right-click on the new project and add a new item. Choose **Visual C# | Basic Page** as the template and change the name to `MainPage.xaml`.

5. Click on the **Add** button to add this new page. A dialog window will pop up to ask you to add some missing files. Click on the **Yes** button on this dialog window to add those files.

Implementing the GetProduct method of the C#/XAML client

To test the RESTful WCF service, we will add a few controls to the main page of the test client and call the `GetProduct` method of the service to get product details for the entered product ID. You can follow these steps to implement this functionality:

1. First, from the **Solution Explorer**, right-click on the test client project
   `RESTNorthwindClientXAML`, and add a service reference to the project. Use
   `http://localhost/RESTNorthwindService/ProductService.svc` as the
   address and change the name to be `ProductServiceRef`. We are not going
   to call the service using this service reference, instead we are going to use the
   service interface that is imported to the client application with this service
   reference, so we don't need to redefine them in the client application.

   > Instead of adding a service reference to the client application or
   > redefining all of the service interface contracts in the client project, you
   > can also keep the interface in a standalone project and reference this
   > interface DLL in both the service implementation and client projects.

2. In the **Solution Explorer**, right-click on the client project item,
   `RESTNorthwindClientXAML`, select **Manage NuGet Packages… | nuget.
   org | Json.NET**, and then install Json.NET to the project. This will add a
   JSON reference and the JSON library to the project. We will need this library
   to serialize and deserialize the request and response of the RESTful WCF
   service calls.

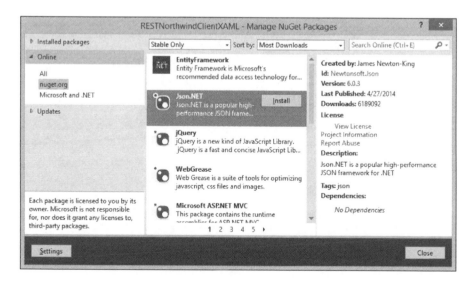

3. Now, open the designer of the main page and add the following items to the designer of the main page:

   ○ A text block named **lblProductID** with the text, **Product ID** and font size of 20 px

   ○ A textbox named **txtProductID**

   ○ A button named **btnGetProduct** with the content, **Get Product Details**

   ○ A text block named **lblProductDetails** with the text, **Product Details** and font size of 20 px

   ○ A textbox named **txtProductDetails**

4. Then, on the main page designer, double-click on the **Get Product Details** button and add an event handler for this button, as follows:

```
private void btnGetProduct_Click(object sender, RoutedEventArgs e)
{
    GetProduct();
}
```

5. In the `MainPage.xaml.cs` file, add the following three `using` statements:

```
using RESTNorthwindClientXAML.ProductServiceRef;
using System.Net.Http;
using Newtonsoft.Json;
```

6. Add the following two class member variables:

```
string service =
"http://localhost/RESTNorthwindService/ProductService.svc";
Product product;
```

The `service` variable holds the address of the RESTful WCF service and the `product` variable holds the product we will get from calling the RESTful WCF service. We will reuse both these variables when we update a product.

7. Now, add the following method to this file:

```
private async void GetProduct()
{
    var client = new HttpClient();
    var url = service + "/Product/" + txtProductID.Text;
    var response = await client.GetAsync(url);
```

```
var json = await response.Content.ReadAsStringAsync();
product = JsonConvert.DeserializeObject<Product>(json);
var sb = new System.Text.StringBuilder();
sb.Append("ProductID:"
        + product.ProductID.ToString() + "\n");
sb.Append("ProductName:"
        + product.ProductName + "\n");
sb.Append("UnitPrice:"
        + product.UnitPrice.ToString() + "\n");
sb.Append("RowVersion:");
foreach (var x in product.RowVersion.AsEnumerable())
{
    sb.Append(x.ToString());
    sb.Append(" ");
}
this.txtProductDetails.Text = sb.ToString();
}
```

Within this method, we first created a `HttpClient` object and then called the `GetAsync` method of this HTTP client object. As we have specified the response format to be JSON in the WCF service, this call returned a JSON string as a result. So we deserialized this string back to a `Product` object and printed out the product details on the UI.

Testing the GetProduct method of the C#/XAML client

We have finished implementing the `GetProduct` functionality of the test client. To test it, first set the `RESTNorthwindClientXAML` project as the startup project, press *Ctrl + F5* to run the client program, enter an integer to the **Product Id** textbox, and then click on the **Get Product Details** button. You will see that the product details are displayed on the bottom text block, as shown in the following screenshot:

Implementing the UpdateProduct method of the C#/XAML client

Next, we will implement the UpdateProduct functionality in the client, so we can call the RESTful WCF service to update a product.

1. First, we need to add some more controls to the page. Open the designer's main page in the RESTNorthwindClientXAML project and add the following items to the designer of the main page:
    - A text block named **lblNewPrice** with the text **New Price** and font size 20 px
    - A textbox named **txtNewPrice**
    - A button named **btnUpdatePrice** with the content, **Update Price**
    - A text block named **lblUpdateResult** with the text, **Update Result** and font size 20 px
    - A textbox control named **txtUpdateResult**

2. On the main page of designer, double-click on the **Update Price** button and add an event handler for this button, as follows:
    ```
    private void btnUpdatePrice_Click(object sender, RoutedEventArgs
    e)
    {
        UpdateProduct();
    }
    ```

3. Add the following method to the class to update the product:
    ```
    public async void UpdateProduct()
    {
        if (product == null)
        {
            this.txtProductDetails.Text =
                "Get product details first";
            return;
        }

        product.UnitPrice =
            Convert.ToDecimal(this.txtNewPrice.Text);
        var updateRequest =
            new UpdateProductRequest() { Product = product };
        var json = JsonConvert.SerializeObject(updateRequest);

        var rowVersionArray =
    ```

```
                product.RowVersion.Select(b => (int)b).ToArray();
        var jsonRowVersion =
                JsonConvert.SerializeObject(rowVersionArray);
        var start = json.IndexOf("\"RowVersion\":") + 13;
        var end = json.IndexOf(",\"UnitPrice\":");
        if (end > start && start >= 0)
        {
            var binaryRowVersion =
                json.Substring(start, end - start);
            json =
                json.Replace(binaryRowVersion, jsonRowVersion);
        }

        using (var client = new HttpClient())
        {
            client.BaseAddress = new Uri(service + "/");
            var response =
                await client.PostAsync("UpdateProduct",
                        new StringContent(json,
                            System.Text.Encoding.UTF8,
                            "application/json"));
            using (var content = response.Content)
            {
                var responseJson =
                    await content.ReadAsStringAsync();
                var updateResponse =
        JsonConvert.DeserializeObject<UpdateProductResponse>
                    (responseJson);
                product = updateResponse.Product;
                if (updateResponse.Result)
                    this.txtUpdateResult.Text =
                        "Price updated to "
                        + product.UnitPrice.ToString();
                else
                    this.txtUpdateResult.Text =
                        "Update failed: "
                        + updateResponse.Message;
            }
        }
    }
```

Inside this method, we first created an `UpdateProductRequest` object, then serialized this object to a JSON string. However, we had a problem with the row version here. By default, JSON.NET selects the binary converter to read and write an array of bytes. It uses the `WriteValue` operation on the `JsonWriter` class with the array of bytes that causes them to be written to as Base-64. So, the row version in the serialized JSON string was in the Base-64 string format. However, the RESTful WCF is expecting an array of integers, so we had to replace the Base-64 string-formatted row version with an array of integers.

You can also supply your own binary converter to JSON.NET, so it will serialize the row version as an array of integers.

After we corrected the row version, we again created a `HttpClient` object and called the `PostAsync` method to post the updated product to the service. This call again returned a JSON string to us as we have specified the response format to be JSON in the WCF service. We then deserialized this string to an `UpdateProductResponse` object and printed out the update result on the UI.

 You can also use `HttpWebRequest` to submit the post request to the service with a slightly different syntax.

Testing the UpdateProduct method of the C#/XAML client

Now we have finished implementing the `UpdateProduct` functionality of the test client. To test it, just press *Ctrl + F5* to run the client program, enter an integer to the **Product Id** textbox, and then click on the **Get Product Details** button to get back the product. Enter a new price in the **New Price** textbox and then click on the **Update Price** button. You will see that the product is updated with the new price. You can click on the **Get Product Details** button to verify that the product is updated correctly with the new price. You can also keep updating the price for the product, as the client always holds the latest product information.

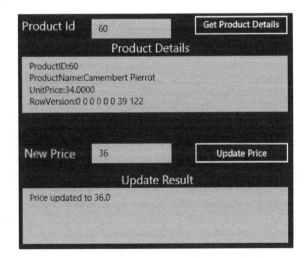

Testing the RESTful WCF service with a JavaScript client

In the previous sections, we created a C#/XAML client to call the RESTful WCF service from the code behind C# class. In the next sections, we will create a JavaScript client to call the RESTful WCF service. We will first call the service using jQuery and then using WinJS.

Creating the JavaScript client

You can follow these steps to create the JavaScript client:

1. From the **Solution Explorer**, right-click on the solution item and add a new project. Choose **JavaScript | Store Apps | Windows Apps | Blank App (Windows)** as the template, change the name to RESTNorthwindClientJS, and leave the location to be the default one (C:\SOAwithWCFandEF\ Projects\RESTNorthwind).

2. Again, you might be prompted to get a developer's license to create a Windows app. Just follow the instructions to get a new one or renew an existing one and then continue.

3. Now, first add some HTML controls to the default page. Just open the `default.html` file and replace the body node with the following code:

```
<br />
<p>REST Northwind JavaScript Client</p>
Product Id <input id="txtProductId" type="text" />
<input type="button" id="btnGetProduct" value="Get Product
Details" />
<br />
<textarea id="txtProductDetails" rows="7" cols="61"> </
textarea><br />
<br />
New Price <input id="txtNewPrice" type="text" />
<input type="button" id="btnUpdatePrice" value="Update Price"
style="width:156px;" />
<br />
<textarea id="txtUpdateResult" rows="7" cols="61"> </textarea>
```

4. Set the client project `RESTNorthwindClientJS` as the startup project, press *Ctrl + F5* to run this client, and you should see a similar UI as in the *Testing the UpdateProduct method of the C#/XAML client* section.

Testing the service with jQuery

We will first implement this test client with jQuery. We will install jQuery to the client project, call the service with jQuery to get product details, and then call the service with jQuery to update the product.

Installing jQuery to the client project

To use jQuery, we first need to install it to the project. Just right-click on the client project `RESTNorthwindClientJS`, select **Manage NuGet Packages...** | **nuget.org** | **JQuery**, and then install jQuery to the project.

Implementing the GetProductJQuery method

Now that we have the controls on the UI, we will write some jQuery code to call the `GetProduct` method of the service to get product details for the entered product ID. You can follow these steps to implement this functionality:

1. Open the `default.html` file in the `RESTNorthwindClientJS` project.

2. Add the following line of code to the head node of this file, right after the WinJS scripts are loaded and before the `default.js` script file is loaded (you should replace 2.1.1 with your project's jQuery version):

```
<script src="Scripts/jquery-2.1.1.js" type="text/javascript"></
script>
```

3. Then, open the `default.js` file, which is under the `js` folder.

4. Add the following two lines of code to the end of the file to define two global variables:

```
var product;
var service =
'http://localhost/RESTNorthwindService/ProductService.svc';
```

The first variable, `product`, holds the product object that we get back from the service. Later, we will update the price of this product and pass the updated product object to the service to update it. The second variable, `service`, holds the RESTful service endpoint address. We will connect to the service with this endpoint address.

5. Add the following JavaScript method after the preceding two global variables:

```
function FormatProduct() {
    var result = "";
    result += "ProductID:" +
            product.ProductID + "\r\n";
    result += "ProductName:" +
            product.ProductName + "\r\n";
    result += "QuantityPerUnit:" +
            product.QuantityPerUnit + "\r\n";
    result += "UnitPrice:" +
            product.UnitPrice + "\r\n";
    result += "Discontinued:" +
            product.Discontinued + "\r\n";
    result += "RowVersion:";
    for (var i = 0; i < 8; i++) {
        result += product.RowVersion[i] + " ";
    }
    return result;
}
```

As you will see soon, this method will be called to convert a product object to a string, so it can be displayed in a textbox on the UI.

6. Then, add the following JavaScript method to call the RESTful WCF service and get the product details for the entered product ID:

```
function GetProductJQuery() {
    jQuery.support.cors = true;

    $.ajax(
    {
```

```
            type: "GET",
            url: service + '/Product/' +
                        $('#txtProductId').val(),
            data: "{}",
            contentType: "application/json; charset=utf-8",
            dataType: "json",
            cache: false,
            success: function (data) {
                product = data;
                $("#txtProductDetails").val(FormatProduct());
            },
            error: function (msg, url, line) {
                $("#txtProductDetails").val(msg.responseText);
            }
        });
    }
```

Within this method, we use AJAX to call the RESTful WCF service. We pass in the product ID, get back the product object, format the product object to a string, and then display it on the UI.

7. Finally, we need to add these lines of code to attach the click event handler of the **Get Product Details** button to the GetProductJQuery method:

```
$(document).ready(function () {
    $("#btnGetProduct").click(GetProductJQuery);
});
```

Testing the GetProductJQuery method of the JavaScript client

We have finished implementing the GetProductJQuery functionality of the test client. To test it, first set the RESTNorthwindClientJS project as the startup project, then press *Ctrl + F5* to run the client program, enter an integer to the **Product Id** textbox, and then click on the **Get Product Details** button. You will see that the product details are displayed on the bottom text block.

Implementing the UpdateProductJQuery method

Now we can get back product details with jQuery; let's update it with jQuery:

1. Open the `default.js` file in the `RESTNorthwindClientJS` project.

2. Add the following JavaScript method to this file:

```
function UpdateProductJQuery () {
  jQuery.support.cors = true;

  if (product == null) {
    $("#txtUpdateResult").val("Get product details first");
        return;
  };


  product.UnitPrice = $("#txtNewPrice").val();

  $.ajax(
  {
      type: "POST",
      url: service + '/UpdateProduct',
      data: JSON.stringify({ Product: product }),
      contentType: "application/json; charset=utf-8",
      dataType: "json",
      success: function (response) {
          product = response.Product;
          if (response.Result)
              $("#txtUpdateResult").val(
                "Price updated to " + product.UnitPrice);
          else
              $("#txtUpdateResult").val(
                 "Update failed: " + response.Message);
      },
      error: function (msg, url, line) {
          $("#txtUpdateResult").val(msg.responseText);
      }
  });
}
```

3. Add this line of code to the `$(document).ready` code block to attach the click event handler of the **Update Price** button to the `UpdateProductJQuery` method:

```
$("#btnUpdatePrice").click(UpdateProductJQuery);
```

Testing the UpdateProductJQuery method of the JavaScript client

Now we have finished implementing the UpdateProductJQuery functionality of the test client. To test it, press *Ctrl + F5* to run the client program, enter an integer to the **Product Id** textbox, and click on the **Get Product Details** button to get back the product object. Then, enter a new price and click on the **Update Price** button. You will see the product price is updated with the new price. You can click on the **Get Product Details** button again to verify that the price is updated correctly.

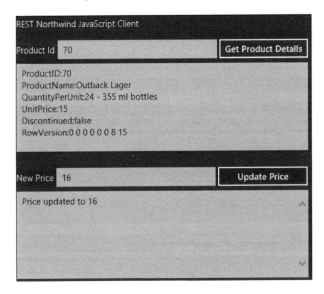

Testing the service with WinJS

The Windows Store app actually uses WinJS by default. So in this section, we will implement the GetProduct and UpdateProduct functionalities with WinJS.

Implementing the GetProductWinJS method

First, we will write some WinJS code to call the GetProduct method of the service to get product details for the entered product ID. You can follow these steps to implement this functionality:

1. Open the default.js file in the RESTNorthwindClientJS project.

2. Add the following JavaScript method to this file:

```
function GetProductWinJS(mouseEvent) {
    var xhrOptions = {
```

```
    url: service + "/Product/"
        + document.getElementById("txtProductId").value,
    headers: {
      "Content-Type": "application/json",
      "If-Modified-Since": "Mon, 27 Mar 1972 00:00:00 GMT"
        },
    data: {},
};
WinJS.xhr(xhrOptions).done(
    function (req) {
        product = JSON.parse(req.response);
document.getElementById("txtProductDetails").innerHTML =
            FormatProduct();
    },
    function (req) {
document.getElementById("txtProductDetails").innerHTML =
            toStaticHTML(req.response);
    });
}
```

As you can see, this method is very similar to the `GetProductJQuery`
method, except that we use `WinJS.xhr` instead of AJAX to call the service.
We also use the `document` object to get the objects on the UI.

3. We now need to attach the click event handler of the **Get Product Details**
    button to the `GetProductWinJS` method. Just find the following line of
    code in this file:

```
args.setPromise(WinJS.UI.processAll());
```

Replace it with the following line of code:

```
args.setPromise(WinJS.UI.processAll().done(function () {
    document.getElementById("btnGetProduct").addEventListener(
        "click", GetProductWinJS, false);
    })
);
```

Testing the GetProductWinJS method of the JavaScript client

We have finished implementing the `GetProductWinJS` functionality of the test client.
However, before we test it we need to comment out the following two lines of code,
otherwise the click events of the buttons will be fired twice:

```
$("#btnGetProduct").click(GetProductJQuery);
$("#btnUpdatePrice").click(UpdateProductJQuery);
```

Then, press *Ctrl + F5* to run the client program, enter an integer to the **Product Id** textbox, and click on the **Get Product Details** button. You will see that the product details are displayed on the bottom text block and that this time the service is being called through WinJS, not jQuery.

Implementing the UpdateProductWinJS method

Now we can get back product details with WinJS. Let's update the UpdateProductWinJS method with WinJS:

1. Open the default.js file in the RESTNorthwindClientJS project.

2. Add the following JavaScript method to this file:

```
function UpdateProductWinJS(mouseEvent) {

    if (product == null) {
document.getElementById("txtUpdateResult").innerHTML =
            "Get product details first";
        return;
    };

    product.UnitPrice =
        document.getElementById("txtNewPrice").value;

    var xhrOptions = {
        type: "POST",
        url: service + "/UpdateProduct",
        headers: { "Content-Type": "application/json" },
        data: JSON.stringify({ Product: product })
    };
    WinJS.xhr(xhrOptions).done(
        function (req) {
            var updateResponse = JSON.parse(req.response);
            product = updateResponse.Product;
            if (updateResponse.Result)
document.getElementById("txtUpdateResult").innerHTML =
                "Price updated to " + product.UnitPrice;
            else
document.getElementById("txtUpdateResult").innerHTML =
                "Update failed: " + updateResponse.Message;
        },
        function (req) {
document.getElementById("txtUpdateResult").innerHTML =
                toStaticHTML(req.response);
        });
}
```

3. Again, this method is very similar to the `UpdateProductJQuery` method, except that we use `WinJS.xhr` instead of AJAX to call the service. We also use the `document` object to get the objects on the UI.

4. Finally, add this line of code to the `args.setPromise(WinJS.UI.processAll().done` code block to attach the click event handler of the **Update Price** button to the `UpdateProductWinJS` method:

```
document.getElementById("btnUpdatePrice").addEventListener(

    "click", UpdateProductWinJS, false);
```

Testing the UpdateProductWinJS method of the JavaScript client

Now we have finished implementing the `UpdateProductWinJS` functionality of the test client. To test it, press *Ctrl + F5* to run the client program, enter an integer to the **Product Id** textbox, and click on the **Get Product Details** button to get back the product object. Then, enter a new price and click on the **Update Price** button. You will see that the product price is updated with the new price and this time the service is being called through WinJS, not jQuery. You can also click on the **Get Product Details** button again to verify that the price is updated correctly.

Summary

In this chapter, we changed the WCF service to be RESTful. We changed the definitions of the service, changed the configuration file of the service, and we tested this service with two Windows app clients. We also learned how to consume a RESTful WCF service with C#/XAML, jQuery, and WinJS.

In the next chapter, we will learn how to secure a WCF service.

12
WCF Security

At this point, we have learned how to develop a three-layer WCF service with LINQ to Entities. To further enhance our WCF service, in this chapter we will explore the security settings of a WCF service. We will host our `HelloWorld` WCF service using the basic and the Windows authentication with the HTTPS protocol.

We will cover the following topics in this chapter:

- WCF security components
- Hosting a WCF service with basic authentication
- Hosting the WCF service with Windows authentication

WCF security components

WCF security spans multiple components in the WCF architecture. The main aim of security in WCF is to provide integrity, confidentiality, authentication, authorization, and audit for the applications that are built on top of the WCF framework. A good WCF architecture splits these functions into the following pieces:

- **Transfer security**: This is responsible for providing message confidentiality, data integrity, and the authentication of communicating parties
- **Authorization**: This is responsible for providing a framework to make authorization decisions
- **Auditing**: This is responsible for logging the security-related events to the audit log

In this section, we will cover WCF authorization and auditing briefly; in the next section, we will discuss WCF transfer security in detail.

WCF authorization

Authorization is the process of controlling access and rights to resources, such as services or files. Unlike WCF service authentication, which is usually handled automatically by the communication framework, for WCF service authorization you will have to come up with your own strategy and infrastructure. You can choose one of the following authorization types to implement an authorization for your WCF service:

- **Role-based**: The user is authorized based on his/her role membership. Users belonging to the same role will share the same security privileges within the application.

- **Identity-based**: The identity model is an extension of the role-based authorization. The identity model enables you to manage claims and policies in order to authorize clients. You can verify claims contained within the users' credentials and compare the claims with a set of authorization policies to determine whether the user is authorized for an operation.

- **Resource-based**: Windows **access control lists (ACLs)** are used to secure individual resources. The caller will be impersonated, and the operating system will perform standard access checks using the original caller's security context when a resource is accessed.

Between these three methods, identity/claims is now preferred for WCF authorization. Starting from .NET 4.5, **Windows Identity Foundation (WIF)** makes it even easier to implement a claims-aware WCF service. For more information on WIF, you can refer to `http://msdn.microsoft.com/en-us/library/hh291066(v=vs.110).aspx`.

In this book, we will not discuss WCF service authorization any further, as it is fundamentally the same as the authorizations of any other type of application.

WCF auditing

WCF applications can log security events (success, failure, or both) by using the auditing feature. The events are written to the Windows system event log and can be examined using Event Viewer.

The benefits of WCF auditing include the following:

- Audits security events such as authentication and authorization failures
- Detects attacks that have occurred or that are in progress
- Helps debug security-related problems

You can configure the WCF service's security logging through the `ServiceSecurityAudit` behavior in the service configuration file. You can specify security audit levels for both message authentication and service authorization events.

For example, the following behavior configuration will enable a security audit for all events, for both the authorization and authentication of a WCF service:

```
<behavior name = "MySecurityAudit">
    <serviceSecurityAudit auditLogLocation = "Default"
       serviceAuthorizationAuditLevel = "SuccessOrFailure"
       messageAuthenticationAuditLevel = "SuccessOrFailure" />
</behavior>
```

WCF transfer security

In the rest of this chapter, we will focus on the transfer security part of WCF services. We will discuss WCF's transport-level and message-level security, transfer security modes supported by various bindings, and WCF authentications.

WCF security modes

WCF transfer security is also referred to as a security mode. There are two transfer security levels for WCF services—transport level and message level. You can also mix these two levels to create a mixed-level security mode.

The WCF security modes that are available are none, transport, message, both (transport and message), mixed (`TransportWithMessageCredential`, and `TransportCredentialOnly`).

Not every WCF binding supports every security mode. For example, `basicHttpBinding` supports transport, message, or mixed security modes, but not both, while `netNamedPipeBinding` only supports transport-level security (or none). The following table lists the most common bindings and their supported security modes:

Binding name	None	Transport	Message	Mixed	Both
basicHttpBinding	Yes (default)	Yes	Yes	Yes	No
netTCPBinding	Yes	Yes (default)	Yes	Yes	No
netNamedPipeBinding	Yes	Yes (default)	No	No	No
wsHttpBinding or ws2007HttpBinding	Yes	Yes	Yes (default)	Yes	No

Binding name	None	Transport	Message	Mixed	Both
wsFederationHttpBinding	Yes	No	Yes (default)	Yes	No
wsDualHttpBinding	Yes	No	Yes (default)	No	No
netMsmqBinding	Yes	Yes (default)	Yes	No	Yes

WCF transport security

WCF transport security is applied at the transport level on the byte stream below the message layer. In this case, a message does not have a security header and it does not carry any user authentication data. The transport security mode only provides point-to-point security between two endpoints, and it is the least flexible in terms of WS-Security usage because it is highly dependent on the transport layer. However, the transport security mode is the fastest in terms of performance and it gives the best interoperability with client applications.

The most common approach for the transport security mode is to combine it with **Secure Sockets Layer (SSL)** or HTTPS to encrypt and sign the contents of all the packets. We will secure a WCF service with transport security and SSL in the later sections of this chapter.

WCF message security

WCF message security is applied on the message level. With message security, the user credentials and claims are encapsulated in every message. The message security mode provides end-to-end security and it provides high flexibility from an authentication perspective. Since messages are directly encrypted and signed, having intermediaries does not break the security. You can use any type of authentication credentials you want; it is largely independent of the transport layer as long as both the client and the server agree.

WCF mixed security

WCF mixed security gives you the best of both transport security and message security. In this case, WCF transport security ensures the integrity and confidentiality of the messages, while WCF message security encapsulates the user credentials and claims in each message. The WCF mixed security mode allows you to use a variety of user credentials that are not possible when using strict transport security mechanisms, while leveraging transport security's performance.

WCF transport and message security

When WCF transport security and WCF message security are combined, the user credentials and claims are transferred at both transport layer and within the message. Similarly, message protection is provided at the transport layer and within the message. Note that this is not a common scenario, and the **Microsoft Message Queuing (MSMQ)** binding is the only binding that supports this mode.

Authentication options for transport security

The WCF authentication options depend on the transfer security mode being used. For this reason, the authentication choices are partly determined by the transfer security mode. The following are the available authentication options for the transport security mode:

- **None**: When using the None option, callers are not authenticated at all.

- **Basic**: The Basic option is available only with the HTTP protocol. The client is authenticated using the username and password against the Microsoft Active Directory service. Note that the username and password are transported using a Base64 encoded string, which is very similar to a clear string. Therefore, this is not a secure option at all if used by itself.

- **NTLM**: The NTLM option is also available with the HTTP protocol only. The client is authenticated using a challenge-response scheme against Windows accounts. NTLM authentication is well-suited for a workgroup environment and is more secure than basic authentication.

- **Windows**: When using the Windows option, the WCF service uses Kerberos authentication in a domain or the NTLM authentication when deployed in a workgroup environment. This option uses a Windows token presented by the caller to authenticate against the Active Directory. This is the most secure option compared to basic or NTLM authentication.

- **Certificate**: When using the Certificate option, the caller presents an X.509 client certificate that the WCF service validates by trusting the certificate (peer trust) or trusting the issuer of the certificate (chain trust). This option should be considered only when Windows authentication is not possible, as in the case of **business-to-business (B2B)** scenarios.

Authentication options for message security

For WCF services using the message security mode, authentication choices are different from the services using the transport security mode. The following are the available authentication options for the message security mode:

- **None**: When using the None option, callers are not authenticated at all.
- **Windows**: When using the Windows option, the WCF service uses Kerberos authentication when in a domain or the NTLM authentication when deployed in a workgroup environment. The Windows option uses the Windows token presented by the caller to authenticate against the Active Directory.
- **Username**: When using the Username option, the caller provides a username and password to the service. The service can then authenticate the caller against their Windows credentials or use a membership provider. This option should be considered only when Windows authentication is not possible.
- **Certificate**: When using the Certificate option, the caller presents an X.509 client certificate. The WCF service looks up the certificate information on the host side and validates it (peer trust) or trusts the issuer of the client certificate (chain trust). This option should be considered only when Windows authentication is not possible.
- **Issue Token**: When using the Issue Token option, the client and service depend on the **Secure Token Service (STS)** to issue tokens that the client and service trust.

Hosting a WCF service using basic authentication

In the previous sections, we learned the basic concepts and theories about WCF security. Now, we will do some practical work. We will host a WCF service with basic authentication and then consume this service in a client application.

Since with basic authentication the username and password are transmitted in a Base64 encoded text, SSL will be configured with this authentication mode to enhance the security of the service.

To keep the code simple and to focus only on the security side of the WCF service, HelloWorldService and HelloWorldClient will be used for this practice.

Setting up the service

First, we will set up a copy of `HelloWorldService` with no authentication.
We will enhance this service, as shown in the following sections, to enable
basic authentication and host it with the HTTPS protocol.

To set up the service, follow these steps:

1. You can refer to *Chapter 1, Implementing a Basic HelloWorld WCF Service,*
    and *Chapter 2, Hosting the HelloWorld WCF Service,* to get the `HelloWorld`
    solution ready.

2. Create a new folder, `HostIISSecure`, under `C:\SOAwithWCFandEF\`
    `Projects\HelloWorld\`.

3. Copy all the files from `HostIIS` to this new folder.

4. Start the IIS manager and add a new application,
    `HelloWorldServiceSecure`, pointing to this new folder.

5. Test it with this URL in a browser:
    `http://localhost/HelloWorldServiceSecure/HelloWorldService.svc`.

You should see the WSDL description page of `HelloWorldService`. Click on the
link to make sure that you can get the WSDL code of this new service.

Enabling the Basic Authentication feature

Basic Authentication is a feature of Internet Information Service. By default, the
module is not installed. In this section, we will install and enable this feature:

1. Open **Control Panel**.

2. Go to **Programs | Turn Windows features on or off**.

3. Now the **Windows Features** dialog window should pop up.

4. Navigate to **Internet Information Services | World Wide Web
    Service | Security**.

5. Check **Basic Authentication**.

6. Note that **Windows Authentication** is unchecked for now, as shown in the following screenshot. Later in this chapter, we will learn how to host this same WCF service with Windows authentication, in which case you will need to come back to this same place and check the **Windows Authentication** option:

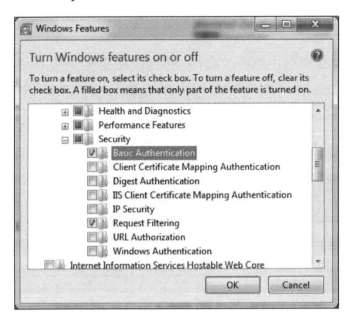

Configuring basic authentication on IIS

Now, the **Basic Authentication** feature is enabled on the computer, but the IIS application is still not using it. We need to configure the HelloWorldServiceSecure application to be authenticated with this feature, as follows:

1. Start the IIS manager.

2. Select the **HelloWorldServiceSecure** application.

3. In the **Features View** panel, double-click on **Authentication**:

4. In the **Authentication** panel, disable **Anonymous Authentication** and enable **Basic Authentication**. If you don't see the **Basic Authentication** option on your screen, close the IIS manager and then start it again to refresh the authentication options. The authentication of the service should be configured as shown in the following screenshot (anonymous authentication must be disabled because when negotiating with the server, most browsers will try for anonymous authentication first):

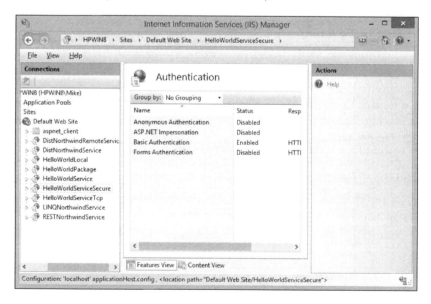

5. If your computer is within a domain while the **Basic Authentication** node is still selected, click on the **Edit** button in the right-hand side panel and enter your domain name in both the **Default domain** and **Realm** boxes (You should enter your domain name here (normally, your company's name), not your computer name. For example, if your computer's full address is `pcNameA.companyNameB.com`, enter `companyNameB` here.):

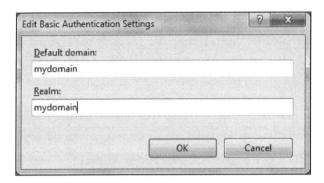

Now, if you browse to the original service address, you will be prompted to enter your credentials. After you have entered your Windows credentials, you will get an error as **The authentication schemes configured on the host ('Basic') do not allow those configured on the binding 'BasicHttpBinding' ('Anonymous')**. This is because the `HelloWorldServiceSecure` service is still configured to communicate using anonymous authentication. Next, we will modify the service configuration file to use basic authentication instead.

Configuring the HTTPS protocol

Before we modify the service configuration file, we need to do more on the IIS site. We will enable the HTTPS protocol for our website so that the client can communicate with our service via the HTTPS protocol. This is especially important for basic authentication, since with basic authentication, the username and password are transmitted in Base64 encoded text, which can be easily decoded to clear text.

To configure HTTPS for our service, follow these steps:

1. Start the IIS manager.

2. Select the root node in the left-hand side panel (it should be your computer's name).

3. Double-click on **Server Certificates** in the middle panel:

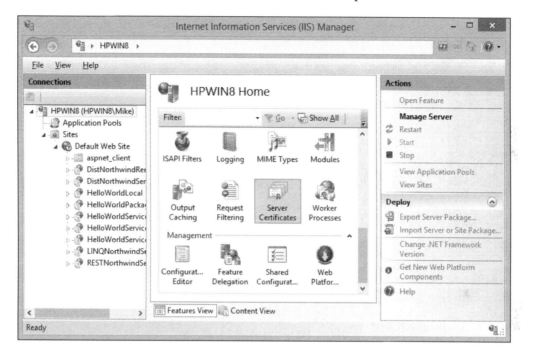

4. On the right-hand side, in the **Actions** panel, click on the **Create Self-Signed Certificate...** link:

5. The **Create Self-Signed Certificate** dialog window should appear on your screen. Specify a name, MyTestCert, for the certificate and click on the **OK** button to close the dialog window.

6. In the IIS manager, select the website of the `HelloWorldServiceSecure` application. By default, this should be **Default Web Site**. Make sure you select the website, not the **HelloWorldServiceSecure** application, as the binding settings apply to the whole website.

7. On the right-hand side, in the **Actions** panel, click on the **Bindings...** link.

8. If **https** is not in the list of the binding types, click on the **Add** button, or else select **https** from the list and click on **Edit**.

9. On the **Add Site Binding/Edit Site Binding** dialog window, specify the test certificate in the **SSL certificate** field:

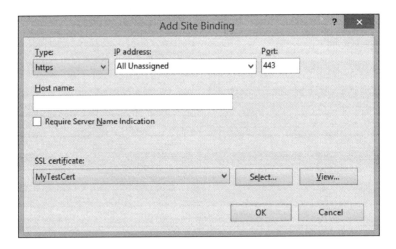

10. Click on the **OK** button to close the **Add Site Binding** dialog window and then click on the **Close** button to close the **Site Bindings** dialog window.

11. The bindings of your website should be similar to those shown in the following screenshot:

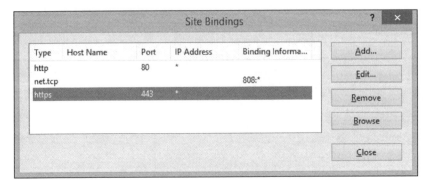

In your staging and production environments, you should create a signed certificate from a Certificate Authority such as VeriSign. Moreover, if SSL brings too much overhead in development time, you can host your service without SSL. It is recommended that you turn it on for security purposes when the service is deployed to the staging and production environments.

Configuring basic authentication on the service

Now, IIS is configured to use basic authentication, but the service is not. We need to configure the `HelloWorldService` service to be authenticated with the basic authentication:

1. Open the `HelloWorld` solution.

2. Add a new solution folder, `HostIISSecure`, to the solution.

3. Add the `C:\SOAwithWCFandEF\Projects\HelloWorld\HostIISSecure\Web.config` file to the new solution folder.

4. Add another solution folder, `bin`, under the `HostIISSecure` solution folder.

5. Add all the files under the `C:\SOAwithWCFandEF\Projects\HelloWorld\HostIISSecure\bin` folder to this new solution folder.

6. Open the properties of the `HelloWorldService` project and add the following statements to the post-built event of the project. This will make sure that the `HelloWorldServiceSecure` application will always have the latest service binary files as other hosting applications:

```
xcopy "$(AssemblyName).dll" "C:\SOAwithWCFandEF\Projects\
HelloWorld\HostIISSecure\bin" /Y
xcopy "$(AssemblyName).pdb" "C:\SOAwithWCFandEF\Projects\
HelloWorld\HostIISSecure\bin" /Y
```

7. Now, open the `Web.config` file within the `HostIISSecure` solution folder and make the following changes to this file:

   ° Change the service metadata attribute from `httpGetEnabled` to `httpsGetEnabled`.

   ° Add the following services node just after the `behaviors` node. This will define an endpoint with our specific binding configuration:

```
<services>
  <service name="HelloWorldService.HelloWorldService">
    <endpoint address="" binding="basicHttpBinding"
```

```
            contract="HelloWorldService.IHelloWorldService"
            bindingConfiguration="secureHttpBinding">
            <identity>
              <dns value="localhost" />
            </identity>
          </endpoint>
          <endpoint address="mex" binding="mexHttpBinding"
                    contract="IMetadataExchange" />
        </service>
      </services>
```

○ Add the following `bindings` node just after the new node that we just added. This will define the binding with basic authentication:

```
<bindings>
  <basicHttpBinding>
    <binding name ="secureHttpBinding">
      <security mode="Transport">
        <transport clientCredentialType="Basic" />
      </security>
    </binding>
  </basicHttpBinding>
</bindings>
```

○ Now, the `system.serviceModel` node should have four child nodes: `serviceHostingEnvironment` (existing node), `behaviors` (existing node), `services` (new node), and `bindings` (new node).

○ Save your `Web.config` file.

In your `Web.config` file, the `system.serviceModel` node should be as follows:

```
<system.serviceModel>

  <serviceHostingEnvironment >
    <serviceActivations>
      <add factory="System.ServiceModel.Activation.ServiceHostFactory"
        relativeAddress="./HelloWorldService.svc"
        service="HelloWorldService.HelloWorldService"/>
    </serviceActivations>
  </serviceHostingEnvironment>

  <behaviors>
    <serviceBehaviors>
      <behavior>
```

```
      <serviceMetadata httpsGetEnabled="true"/>
    </behavior>
  </serviceBehaviors>
</behaviors>

<services>
  <service name="HelloWorldService.HelloWorldService">
    <endpoint address="" binding="basicHttpBinding"
      contract="HelloWorldService.IHelloWorldService"
      bindingConfiguration="secureHttpBinding">
      <identity>
        <dns value="localhost" />
      </identity>
    </endpoint>
    <endpoint address="mex" binding="mexHttpBinding"
            contract="IMetadataExchange" />
  </service>
</services>

<bindings>
  <basicHttpBinding>
    <binding name ="secureHttpBinding">
      <security mode="Transport">
        <transport clientCredentialType="Basic" />
      </security>
    </binding>
  </basicHttpBinding>
</bindings>

</system.serviceModel>
```

The service is now ready. You can go to `https://[your_pc_name]/HelloWorldServiceSecure/HelloWorldService.svc` and see the WSDL of the service.

You will be prompted to enter your credentials. You should then enter your Windows login credentials here.

If you go to `https://localhost/HelloWorldServiceSecure/HelloWorldService.svc` (using `localhost` instead of your PC name in the URL), you will get a warning: **The security certificate presented by this website was issued for a different website's address**. You can ignore this warning and still see the WSDL of the service. However, in one of the following sections, when you add the service reference, you must use your PC name instead of `localhost`.

On the service WSDL page, you should see the following XML node:

```
<http:BasicAuthentication xmlns:http="http://schemas.microsoft.com/
ws/06/2004/policy/http"/>
```

This means that the service is now secured by basic authentication.

Testing the service with basic authentication

To test the secured service, we need a test client. In this section, we will create a console application to test the secured service:

1. Add a console application project, `HelloWorldClientSecure`, to the solution.

2. Right-click on the new project and select **Add | Service Reference...** from the context menu.

3. Enter `https://[your_pc_name]/HelloWorldServiceSecure/HelloWorldService.svc` as the address and `HelloWorldServiceRef` as the namespace. You will be prompted to enter your credentials. Enter your Windows login credentials here.

    If you get an error saying **An error (Details) occurred while attempting to find service** and the error details are **Metadata contains a reference that cannot be resolved**, you might need to give your IIS identity proper access rights to your `C:\Windows\Temp` directory.

    You might be prompted to enter your credentials up to three times while Visual Studio is trying to discover or enumerate all the services for the desired name on your machine. In my environment, it was trying to discover the service at three places: `HelloWorldService.svc/_vti_bin/ListData.svc/$metadata`, `HelloWorldService.svc/$metadata`, and `HelloWorldService.svc`.

    If you are prompted more than three times for your credentials and you still cannot add the service reference, make sure you are using the correct URL for the service. You might need to replace `localhost` with the system name of your PC, or you might need to include your domain name in the URL. This is because the host part of the URL must match the **Issued to** part of the self-signed certificate. You can open your certificate (from the IIS manager) to see the exact party name that this certificate is issued to and use this in your URL. In the following screenshot, the computer is not in a domain, so in this case, **Issued to** is the same as the computer name. If it is within a domain, the **Issued to** field should look similar to `MyLaptop.domain_name.com`. In this case, you should use `MyLaptop.domain_name.com` in the URL.

If your computer is within a domain, you also need to make sure that you have set your default domain and realm in your bindings settings. You can refer to the previous section, *Configuring the HTTPS protocol*, for more details.

4. Now, open the `Program.cs` file and add the following code to the `Main` method (remember to replace the user's credentials with your own):

```
var client =
    new HelloWorldServiceRef.HelloWorldServiceClient();
client.ClientCredentials.UserName.UserName = "your_user_name";
client.ClientCredentials.UserName.Password = "your_password";
Console.WriteLine(client.GetMessage("Basic Authentication
caller"));
```

5. Set the `HelloWorldClientSecure` project as the startup project and run the program. You should get an output that looks similar to the output shown in the following screenshot:

Hosting a WCF service with Windows authentication

In the previous sections, we learned how to host a WCF service with basic authentication. As you can see, with basic authentication, the client has to capture the user's credentials (the credentials are hardcoded, taken from a configuration file, or the user is prompted to enter them), and the credentials are transported in clear text unless HTTPS is configured.

This might be an acceptable approach if the clients are outside your domain, that is, from the Internet or extranet. However, for intranet clients, a better approach is to use Windows authentication so that you don't need to capture the user's credentials. Instead, you can use the user's network credential token and pass it to the WCF service. In this section, we will configure our WCF service to use this authentication mode.

As we have the IIS application and the test client for basic authentication ready, we will just modify them to enable Windows authentication. We can do this as follows:

1. Go to **Control Panel** | **Programs and Features** | **Turn Windows features on or off** and check **Windows Authentication** under **Internet Information Services** | **World Wide Web Services** | **Security**. See the previous section in this chapter (*Enabling the Basic Authentication feature*) for a screenshot.

 Windows authentication is not supported on the Windows Home version. You need to have Professional or above to have this option. You can go to **Control Panel** | **System and Security** | **System** to check your Windows version.

2. Go to **IIS manager** | **HelloWorldServiceSecure** | **Authentication**, disable **Basic Authentication** and enable **Windows Authentication**. If **Windows Authentication** is not in the list, close the IIS manager and then reopen it.

3. Start Visual Studio, open the `Web.config` file located under the `HostIISSecure` folder, and change the attribute value of `clientCredentialType` in the `binding` node from `Basic` to `Windows`.

4. Save the configuration file.

5. Expand the **Service References** folder in the **HelloWorldClientSecure** project, right-click on the **HelloWorldServiceRef** item, and select **Update Service Reference** from the context menu. The service reference will be updated without asking for additional credentials. This is because we are now using Windows authentication, so your current login token is passed to the service.

6. Open the client's config file, App.config, in the HelloWorldClientSecure project to verify that the attribute value of clientCredentialType in the binding node has been changed from Basic to Windows.

7. Open the Program.cs file in the HelloWorldClientSecure project and change the old code in the Main method as follows:

```
var client =
    new HelloWorldServiceRef.HelloWorldServiceClient();
client.ChannelFactory.Credentials.Windows.ClientCredential =
    System.Net.CredentialCache.DefaultNetworkCredentials;
Console.WriteLine(client.GetMessage("Windows Authentication
caller"));
```

8. Run the program again and you should get an output similar to the one shown in the following screenshot:

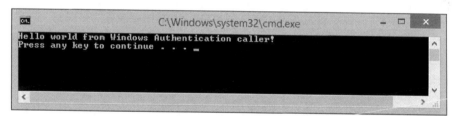

This output shows that the service is now hosted with Windows authentication and the client is passing the user's default network credential to the service. The current logged-in user's Windows token, instead of the user's name/password, is now transmitted over the network.

Besides setting the attribute value of clientCredentialType to Windows or Basic in the binding node of the service web configuration file, you can also set it to InheritedFromHost, which means that the WCF service will inherit the security settings of the hosting IIS application. This option will be very helpful if you would like to specify multiple authentication schemes on a single endpoint.

Summary

In this chapter, we learned the basic concepts of WCF security and hosted the `HelloWorld` service using basic authentication and Windows authentication. The .NET Framework gives you a variety of configuration settings for WCF security. You should examine your WCF service needs and pick the most appropriate settings for your organization.

In the next chapter, we will explore the basic concepts of WCF extension points and learn how to extend our `HelloWorld` service.

Extending WCF Services

13

As we have learned from previous chapters, WCF provides a unified programming model to build service-oriented applications. With WCF, you can build secure, reliable, transacted solutions that integrate well across different platforms and interoperate with existing solutions. The WCF programming model is very comprehensive, and yet, it is very flexible. You can extend this model to enhance the functionality or customize the framework for your specific needs. In this last chapter of this book, we will explore extension points of WCF services and learn how to extend a WCF service.

We will cover the following topics in this chapter:

- WCF runtime architecture
- Why extend a WCF service?
- WCF extension points
- Extending a WCF service
- Extending HelloWorldService

The WCF runtime architecture

The WCF runtime provides a set of classes responsible for sending and receiving messages. For example, formatting messages, applying security, transmitting and receiving messages by using various transport protocols, as well as dispatching received messages to the appropriate operations; all these fall within the WCF runtime scope.

The following diagram shows the WCF runtime (http://msdn.microsoft.com/en-us/magazine/cc163302.aspx):

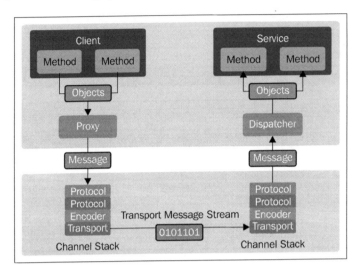

The sequence of a WCF service call might look as follows:

1. A client application calls a WCF service through a WCF proxy.

2. The proxy translates the call to one or more WCF messages.

3. The messages are passed through channels and transported to the service.

4. On the service side, the messages are transported through channels.

5. Service dispatchers pick up the messages, making calls to WCF services and then returning the results back to the client.

As you can see from this diagram, there are multiple layers and many entry points for a WCF service call. At almost every entry point, there is a possible extension interface that you, as a WCF developer, can extend. In fact, there are over 30 extension points in the WCF runtime. In this chapter, we will explore some common extension points and extend our HelloWorldService to log incoming/outgoing messages.

 For a comprehensive list of WCF extension points, look at the MSDN documentation on WCF extensions. Additionally, you might want to check out the blog at http://blogs.msdn.com/b/carlosfigueira/archive/2011/03/14/wcf-extensibility.aspx for WCF extension points. This blog explains many of the WCF extension points up to .NET Framework 4.0, but they are all also valid for .NET 4.5.

Why extend WCF services?

There are many reasons why you might need to extend a WCF service, such as the following:

- Message validation
- Parameter validation
- Message logging
- Message transformations
- Custom serialization formats
- Custom deserialization formats
- Output caching
- Object pooling
- Error handling
- Authorization
- Authentication
- Monitoring/auditing
- Service usage analysis/metrology

WCF extension points

The client and service runtimes expose various extensibility points that the developer can leverage. These extensibility points can be used to customize various WCF capabilities, such as encoding messages, intercepting parameters, or selecting the operations to invoke on the service side.

Client-side extension points

A client-side extension is also called a proxy extension. Some available client-side extensions are listed as follows:

- **Parameter inspection**: Performs custom validation, value modification, or special filtering for method parameters, before these method calls are translated to messages
- **Message formatting for serialization**: Customizes the serialization process by using a custom formatter object

- **Message inspection**: Implements cross-operation messaging features such as message logging, validation, or transformations functionality
- **Result processing**: Inspects the returned result, formats the message, and customizes the deserialization process after the service invocation is finished, but shortly before the result is returned to the client

The following diagram shows three extension points on the client side (`http://msdn.microsoft.com/en-us/magazine/cc163302.aspx`):

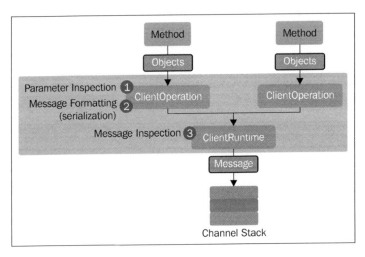

Service-side extension points

A service-side extension is also called a dispatcher extension. A service-side extension can be used to perform message inspection, message formatting, and parameter inspection. For the message formatting extension, it can customize the deserialization process for incoming messages and the serialization process for outgoing messages. In addition, there is an operation selector extension, which is to override the default operation selection behavior and an operation invoker extension to provide a custom operation invoker object.

The following diagram shows five extension points on the service side (`http://msdn.microsoft.com/en-us/magazine/cc163302.aspx`):

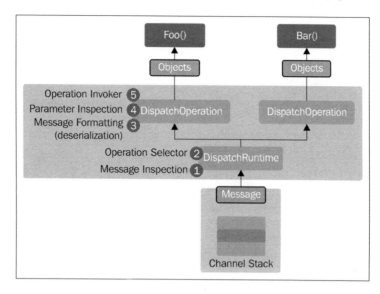

Extending a WCF service

As we have learned earlier, there are more than 30 extension points in the WCF runtime, but the most common situation is to customize the extension of a behavior. Discussion of all WCF extension points is beyond the context of this book, and from this point on, we will focus only on the behavior extension.

WCF behaviors are types that define how a WCF service behaves. A custom behavior can be applied to a WCF service to modify the default behavior and add custom extensions, to inspect and validate service configuration, or modify runtime behavior of the service.

To extend a behavior, `DispatchRuntime` and `DispatchOperation` need to be extended on the service side and `ClientRuntime` and `ClientOperation` need to be extended on the client side. This can be achieved by implementing corresponding interfaces such as `IParameterInspector`, `IDispatchMessageInspector`, and `IClientMessageFormatter`. These interfaces provide the necessary methods to allow parameters to be inspected, messages to be inspected, and to serialize and deserialize parameters to and from messages.

The following are standard procedures to extend a WCF behavior:

- Create an extension class, implementing the appropriate extension interface(s)

- Create a behavior class, implementing the appropriate behavior interface(s)

- Optionally create a behavior element class if extensions will be applied through a configuration file

- Add behaviors to the runtime through code, attribute, or configuration

WCF extension classes

To extend a WCF service, you first need to create an extension class. As each extension point is modeled by an interface, you need to choose the proper interface to implement when creating an extension class. An extension class can implement a service (dispatcher) interface, a client (proxy) interface, or in some cases, both interfaces. If the extension class implements both the client and service interfaces, this same extension class can be used to extend a WCF service on both the client and service sides.

All extension interfaces are defined in the System.ServiceModel.Dispatcher namespace. The following is a list of the commonly used extension interfaces:

- IParameterInspector: You can implement this interface to create a custom parameter inspector that can view and modify the contents of a call. The inspection can be done before or after the call in either client or service applications.

- IDispatchMessageFormatter/IClientMessageFormatter: You can implement this interface to create a custom formatter that serializes objects into messages and deserializes messages into objects for a particular operation.

- IDispatchMessageInspector/IClientMessageInspector: You can implement this interface to inspect or modify inbound or outbound application messages either prior to or after an operation is invoked.

- IDispatchOperationSelector/IClientOperationSelector: You can implement this interface to customize the selection of the operation to invoke.

- IOperationInvoker: You can implement this interface to control the conversion from an untyped object and array of parameters to a strongly typed method call on that object.

WCF behavior classes

In addition to an extension class, you also need to create a behavior class in order to extend a WCF service through behaviors.

There are four types of behaviors for a WCF service that you can extend:

- Service behavior
- Endpoint behavior
- Contract behavior
- Operation behavior

Each type allows you to apply extensions at different scopes. For example, `IServiceBehavior` can be applied at service, endpoint, contract, and operation level, but `IOperationBehavior` can only be applied at operation level.

Each type of behavior is modeled by a different interface. All interfaces contain the same set of methods, but each method has a different signature (with the exception of the `ApplyClientBehavior` method, as the service interface does not have this method). You need to choose the proper interface to implement when creating a behavior class.

The behavior class can also implement the attribute interface, so it can be applied through attributes in the code.

All behavior interfaces are defined in the `System.ServiceModel.Description` namespace. The following is a list of commonly used behavior interfaces with their scopes:

- `IServiceBehavior`: Service, endpoint, contract, and operation
- `IEndpointBehavior`: Endpoint, contract, and operation
- `IContractBehavior`: Contract and operation
- `IOperationBehavior`: Operation

WCF behavior element classes

If you want to add your extension class only through configuration, you need to create a behavior element class. A behavior extension element class represents a configuration element that contains subelements that specify behavior extensions, which enables the user to customize service or endpoint behaviors. You can override the `CreateBehavior` method and `BehaviorType` in this extension class to let the WCF runtime get the behavior extension definition through the `behaviorExtensions` element in the configuration file.

 If your WCF service is self-hosted, you can create your extension behavior in your host code. In this case, you don't need to create a behavior element class.

With a behavior element class, you can register your extension class in the config file (or `machine.config` file). It is strongly recommended that you use fully qualified assembly names when registering your extension types.

Applying the extensions

Once you have created the extension class, the behavior class, and optionally the behavior extension element class, you need to apply the extension to your WCF service.

The behaviors can be applied in three different ways:

- **Code**: The description of the service, endpoint, contract, and operation objects have a property with a collection of behaviors associated with that object. You can add your extension behaviors by using the code reference.

- **Configuration**: For service and endpoint behaviors, you can add your extensions via the `behaviors` section of the `system.serviceModel` node in the service configuration file.

- **Attributes**: For non-endpoint behaviors, you can create an attribute class, which implements one of the behavior interfaces, and then apply the attribute to the appropriate service element.

Extending HelloWorldService

Now that we have learned the basic concepts and theories of the WCF extension, let's do some practical work to further understand it. In this section, we will extend our `HelloWorldService` with a runtime behavior, inspecting and logging the incoming and outgoing messages of the service.

Setting up the service

First, we will set up a copy of `HelloWorldService` with no extensions. We will extend this service in the following sections to inspect and log all incoming and outgoing messages.

To set up the service, follow these steps:

1. You can refer to *Chapter 1, Implementing a Basic HelloWorld WCF Service,* and *Chapter 2, Hosting the HelloWorld WCF Service,* of this book to get the `HelloWorld` solution ready.

2. Create a new folder, `HostIISExtended`, under the `C:\SOAwithWCFandEF\Projects\HelloWorld` folder.

3. Copy all files from `HostIIS` to this new folder.

4. Start IIS Manager and add a new application `HelloWorldServiceExtended`, pointing to this new folder.

5. Test it with the following URL in a browser:
   `http://localhost/HelloWorldServiceExtended/HelloWorldService.svc`.

You should see the WSDL description page of the `HelloWorldService` service. Click on the link to make sure you get the WSDL of this new service.

Next, let's add this folder to the `HelloWorld` solution in Visual Studio:

1. Start Visual Studio and open the `HelloWorld` solution.

2. Add a new solution folder, `HostIISExtended`, to the solution.

3. Add the `C:\SOAwithWCFandEF\Projects\HelloWorld\HostIISExtended\Web.config` file to the new solution folder.

4. Add another solution folder, `bin`, under the `HostIISExtended` solution folder.

5. Add all files under the `C:\SOAwithWCFandEF\Projects\HelloWorld\HostIISExtended\bin` folder to this new solution folder.

6. Select the `HelloWorldService` project and go to the project's **Properties** page.

7. Add the following `copy` statements to the post-built events:

```
xcopy "$(AssemblyName).dll" "C:\SOAwithWCFandEF\Projects\
HelloWorld\HostIISExtended\bin" /Y
xcopy "$(AssemblyName).pdb" "C:\SOAwithWCFandEF\Projects\
HelloWorld\HostIISExtended\bin" /Y
```

This way it will make sure that the `HelloWorldServiceExtended` application will always have the latest `HelloWorldService` binary files.

Creating the extension project

To extend `HelloWorldService`, we need to create an extension class, a behavior class, and a behavior element class. We need to create an assembly for all of these classes so that later we can apply this extension to the WCF service.

You can follow these steps to create a project for this extension assembly:

1. Open the `HelloWorld` solution.

2. Add a new class library project named `HelloWorldExtension`.

3. Delete the `Class1.cs` file from this new project.

4. Add the following three references to the project:
   ```
   System.Configuration
   System.ServiceModel
   System.Web
   ```

5. Go to the project's **Properties** page.

6. Add the following `copy` statements to the post-built events:
   ```
   xcopy "$(AssemblyName).dll" ..\..\..\HostIISExtended\Bin /Y
   xcopy "$(AssemblyName).pdb" ..\..\..\HostIISExtended\Bin /Y
   ```

This way we will make sure that the `HostIISExtended` application will always have the latest extension binary files. As you will see in the following sections, the WCF runtime will search the `bin` directory of the host application to discover the extension class.

Creating an extension class

As we mentioned earlier in this chapter, to extend a WCF service, we first need to create an extension class to define the extension actions that will be applied to the WCF service. Follow these steps to create this extension class:

1. Add a new class named `MyMessageInspector` to the `HelloWorldExtension` project.

2. Add the following five `using` statements to the new class:
   ```
   using System.ServiceModel;
   using System.ServiceModel.Dispatcher;
   using System.ServiceModel.Channels;
   using System.IO;
   using System.Web.Hosting;
   ```

3. Make this class implement the `IDispatchMessageInspector` interface.

4. Add the following method to trace a message:

```
private Message TraceMessage(MessageBuffer buffer)
{
    var msg = buffer.CreateMessage();
    var appPath =
    HostingEnvironment.ApplicationPhysicalPath;
    var logPath = appPath + "\\log.txt";
    File.AppendAllText(logPath,
    DateTime.Now.ToString("G"));
    File.AppendAllText(logPath, "\r\n");
    File.AppendAllText(logPath,
        "HelloWorldService is invoked");
    File.AppendAllText(logPath, "\r\n");
    File.AppendAllText(logPath,
    string.Format("Message={0}", msg));
    File.AppendAllText(logPath, "\r\n");
    return buffer.CreateMessage();
}
```

 Here, we are logging to a file. You might want to log to the Windows event logs or a database in your own project. You can also take advantage of some logging frameworks such as Log4Net to do the logging.

5. Give the IIS identity of the `HostIISExtended` application write access to the `HostIISExtended` application folder (`C:\SOAwithWCFandEF\Projects\HelloWorld\HostIISExtended`), as the extended WCF service will write to a file in this folder. You can find out the IIS identity of the application from **IIS Manager | Application Pools**. In the application pool of the `HostIISExtended` application, go to **Advanced Settings | Process Model | Identity** (if you use the default application pool identity, which is **ApplicationPoolIdentity**, the corresponding Windows username for your application pool identity will be `IIS AppPool\<your application pool name>`).

6. Now, add the following two methods to call the method we just created so that we can log each incoming and outgoing message:

```
public object AfterReceiveRequest(
    ref Message request, IClientChannel channel,
    InstanceContext instanceContext)
{
```

```
        request =
            TraceMessage(request.CreateBufferedCopy(int.MaxValue));
            return null;
    }

    public void BeforeSendReply(
        ref Message reply,
        object correlationState)
    {
        reply =
        TraceMessage(reply.CreateBufferedCopy(int.MaxValue));
    }
```

In this extension class, we make it implement the `IDispatchMessageInspector` interface so that we can extend the service (dispatcher) to inspect the messages. Then, we have added two inspector methods to inspect the outgoing and incoming messages. In this case, we just log the messages, but you can even modify the messages according to your own requirements.

> As the body of the request/reply message can only be processed once, we have to pass a buffer of the original message to the `TraceMessage` method, create a new message from the buffer, and then return a new message to the original method, to ensure that the original methods do not get affected. Also, we make the `AfterReceiveRequest` method return `null` because we don't need to correlate between the two methods (the `correlationState` parameter in the `BeforeSendReply` method is the return result of the `AfterReceiveRequest` method).

The whole content of the `MyMessageInspector.cs` file is as follows:

```
using System;
using System.Collections.Generic;
using System.Linq;
using System.Text;
using System.Threading.Tasks;

using System.ServiceModel;
using System.ServiceModel.Dispatcher;
using System.ServiceModel.Channels;
using System.IO;
using System.Web.Hosting;
```

```csharp
namespace HelloWorldExtension
{
    class MyMessageInspector : IDispatchMessageInspector
    {
        private Message TraceMessage(MessageBuffer buffer)
        {
            var msg = buffer.CreateMessage();
            var appPath =
                HostingEnvironment.ApplicationPhysicalPath;
            var logPath = appPath + "\\log.txt";
            File.AppendAllText(logPath,
                DateTime.Now.ToString("G"));
            File.AppendAllText(logPath, "\r\n");
            File.AppendAllText(logPath,
                "HelloWorldService is invoked");
            File.AppendAllText(logPath, "\r\n");
            File.AppendAllText(logPath,
                string.Format("Message={0}", msg));
            File.AppendAllText(logPath, "\r\n");
            return buffer.CreateMessage();
        }

        public object AfterReceiveRequest(
            ref Message request, IClientChannel channel,
            InstanceContext instanceContext)
        {
          request =
          TraceMessage(request.CreateBufferedCopy(int.MaxValue));
          return null;
        }
        public void BeforeSendReply(
            ref Message reply,
            object correlationState)
        {
          reply =
            TraceMessage(reply.CreateBufferedCopy(int.MaxValue));
        }
    }
}
```

Creating a behavior class

Next, we need to create a behavior class. In this behavior class, we will apply the extension class to the WCF runtime.

Follow these steps to create the behavior class:

1. Add a new class named `MyMessageInspectorBehavior` to the `HelloWorldExtension` project.

2. Add the following five `using` statements to the new class:

```
using System.ServiceModel;
using System.ServiceModel.Description;
using System.ServiceModel.Channels;
using System.ServiceModel.Dispatcher;
using System.Collections.ObjectModel;
```

3. Make this class inherit `Attribute` and implement the `IServiceBehavior` interface.

4. Add the following method to apply the behavior:

```
void IServiceBehavior.ApplyDispatchBehavior(
    ServiceDescription serviceDescription,
    ServiceHostBase serviceHostBase)
{
    foreach (ChannelDispatcher cd in
                serviceHostBase.ChannelDispatchers)
        foreach (EndpointDispatcher ed in
                cd.Endpoints)
    ed.DispatchRuntime.MessageInspectors.Add
                (new MyMessageInspector());
}
```

5. We also need to implement the following two methods, though in this example, we don't do anything within them:

```
void IServiceBehavior.AddBindingParameters(
    ServiceDescription serviceDescription,
    ServiceHostBase serviceHostBase,
    Collection<ServiceEndpoint> endpoints,
    BindingParameterCollection bindingParameters)
{
    //do nothing
}
```

```
void IServiceBehavior.Validate(
    ServiceDescription serviceDescription,
    ServiceHostBase serviceHostBase)
{
    //do nothing
}
```

In this class, we make it implement the `IServiceBehavior` interface so that we can apply our extension behavior to the WCF runtime. We also make it inherit the `Attribute` class so that this extension behavior can be applied using attributes in code (though we are not going to take the code approach in this chapter).

The full content of the `MyMessageInspectorBehavior.cs` file will be as follows:

```
using System;
using System.Collections.Generic;
using System.Linq;
using System.Text;
using System.Threading.Tasks;

using System.ServiceModel;
using System.ServiceModel.Description;
using System.ServiceModel.Channels;
using System.ServiceModel.Dispatcher;
using System.Collections.ObjectModel;

namespace HelloWorldExtension
{
    class MyMessageInspectorBehavior : Attribute, IServiceBehavior
    {
        void IServiceBehavior.AddBindingParameters(
            ServiceDescription serviceDescription,
            ServiceHostBase serviceHostBase,
            Collection<ServiceEndpoint> endpoints,
            BindingParameterCollection bindingParameters)
        {
            //do nothing
        }

    void IServiceBehavior.ApplyDispatchBehavior(
        ServiceDescription serviceDescription,
        ServiceHostBase serviceHostBase)
    {
```

```
foreach (ChannelDispatcher cd in
            serviceHostBase.ChannelDispatchers)
    foreach (EndpointDispatcher ed in
            cd.Endpoints)
    ed.DispatchRuntime.MessageInspectors.Add
            (new MyMessageInspector());
    }

    void IServiceBehavior.Validate(
        ServiceDescription serviceDescription,
        ServiceHostBase serviceHostBase)
    {
        //do nothing
    }
  }
}
```

Creating a behavior element class

To apply the extension though configuration, we need to create a behavior element class. This class will tell the WCF runtime how to discover and apply the extension class to the WCF runtime.

The following steps create this behavior element class:

1. Add a new class named `MyMessageInspectorElement` to the `HelloWorldExtension` project.

2. Add the following `using` statement to the new class:

    ```
    using System.ServiceModel.Configuration;
    ```

3. Make this class inherit `BehaviorExtensionElement`.

4. Add the following code to define the behavior:

    ```
    public override Type BehaviorType
    {
        get { return typeof(MyMessageInspectorBehavior); }
    }

    protected override object CreateBehavior()
    {
        return new MyMessageInspectorBehavior();
    }
    ```

In this element class, we just override one property and one method of the `BehaviorExtensionElement` class. The `BehaviorType` property will tell the WCF runtime what type our extension behavior is, and the `CreateBehavior` method will tell the WCF runtime how to create the extension behavior class.

The full content of the `MyMessageInspectorElement.cs` file will be as follows:

```
using System;
using System.Collections.Generic;
using System.Linq;
using System.Text;
using System.Threading.Tasks;

using System.ServiceModel.Configuration;

namespace HelloWorldExtension
{
    class MyMessageInspectorElement : BehaviorExtensionElement
    {
        public override Type BehaviorType
        {
            get { return typeof(MyMessageInspectorBehavior); }
        }
        protected override object CreateBehavior()
        {
            return new MyMessageInspectorBehavior();
        }
    }
}
```

Applying the extension to HelloWorldService

The last step is to apply our newly created extension class to `HelloWorldService`. As we have created a behavior extension element class, we can apply this extension only through configuration.

1. Start Visual Studio.
2. Open the `HelloWorld` solution.
3. Open the `Web.config` file under the `HostIISExtended` folder.
4. Add the following `extensions` node to be a child node of the `system.serviceModel` node:

```
<extensions>
  <behaviorExtensions>
    <add name="myMessageInspectorBehavior"
```

```
        type="HelloWorldExtension.MyMessageInspectorElement,
            HelloWorldExtension, Version=1.0.0.0,
            Culture=neutral, PublicKeyToken=null"/>
    </behaviorExtensions>
</extensions>
```

Here, when specifying the extension element, we are fully qualifying it with the element name, name space, version, and culture. As we have said earlier in this chapter, this will make our extension more secure than just specifying its name. Here, we don't specify a public token, but to make it even more secure, you can assign a public key token to the element (first, you need to make your extension assembly strong-named, then put the public key token of the assembly here. See `http://msdn.microsoft.com/en-us/library/xwb8f617(v=vs.110).aspx` for more information about strong-named assemblies).

5. Add the following node as a child node of the `behavior` node:

```
<myMessageInspectorBehavior/>
```

So, the whole `behaviors` node should resemble the following:

```
<behaviors>
  <serviceBehaviors>
    <behavior>
      <serviceMetadata httpGetEnabled="true"/>
      <myMessageInspectorBehavior/>
    </behavior>
  </serviceBehaviors>
</behaviors>
```

This will apply the behavior extension that we have added in the preceding step to our `HelloWorldService` in this IIS application. This means that whenever this service is invoked, this extension will be applied. We will test this with a test program in the next section.

The following is the content of the `system.serviceModel` node:

```
<system.serviceModel>
  <serviceHostingEnvironment >
    <serviceActivations>
     <add factory=
        "System.ServiceModel.Activation.ServiceHostFactory"
        relativeAddress="./HelloWorldService.svc"
        service="HelloWorldService.HelloWorldService"/>
    </serviceActivations>
```

```
    </serviceHostingEnvironment>

    <behaviors>
      <serviceBehaviors>
        <behavior>
          <serviceMetadata httpGetEnabled="true"/>
          <myMessageInspectorBehavior/>
        </behavior>
      </serviceBehaviors>
    </behaviors>

    <extensions>
      <behaviorExtensions>
       <add name="myMessageInspectorBehavior"
        type="HelloWorldExtension.MyMessageInspectorElement,
             HelloWorldExtension, Version=1.0.0.0,
             Culture=neutral, PublicKeyToken=null"/>
      </behaviorExtensions>
    </extensions>

  </system.serviceModel>
```

Testing the extended HelloWorldService

Now that we have the service extension applied to the service, we can test it with a program. In this section, we will reuse our HelloWorldClient to test the service. We will verify that the extension has been applied to the service successfully through the Web.config file.

However, before testing it with the HelloWorldClient application, you need to rebuild the solution so that all the related library files will be created. After you have rebuilt the solution successfully, you can test it via a web browser first. Just go to http://localhost/HelloWorldServiceExtended/ HelloWorldService.svc, and you should see the WSDL description page of the extended HelloWorldService service.

Click on the link to make sure that you get the WSDL of this extended service.

If you didn't get the WSDL description page of the extended service and instead get an error page that says **Internet Explorer cannot display the webpage or This page can't be displayed**, it is because your IIS identity doesn't have write access to the HostIISExtended IIS application folder (C:\SOAwithWCFandEF\Projects\ HelloWorld\HostIISExtended). You can refer back to the previous section *Creating an extension class* for more details about this.

If you get a **The type 'HelloWorldExtension.MyMessageInspectorElement, HelloWorldExtension, Version=1.0.0.0, Culture=neutral, PublicKeyToken=null' registered for extension 'myMessageInspectorBehavior' could not be loaded** message, it is because you haven't rebuilt your solution. Rebuild the solution and try again.

Once you successfully get the WSDL of the extended service, you can follow these steps to test the service with the `HelloWorldClient` application:

1. In Visual Studio, open the `App.config` file from the `HelloWorldClient` project.

2. In the config file, change the address of the endpoint to `http://localhost/HelloWorldServiceExtended/HelloWorldService.svc`.

3. Now, rebuild the solution, set `HelloWorldClient` as the startup project, and run the program. You should see the same result as in *Chapter 1, Implementing a Basic HelloWorld WCF Service*.

4. Open Windows Explorer and go to the `C:\SOAwithWCFandEF\Projects\HelloWorld\HostIISExtended` folder. Here, you will find a `log.txt` file. Open it and you will see some logs like this:

```
8/6/2014 8:25:20 PM
HelloWorldService is invoked
Message=<s:Envelope xmlns:s="http://schemas.xmlsoap.org/soap/
envelope/">
  <s:Header>
    <Action s:mustUnderstand="1" xmlns="http://schemas.
microsoft.com/ws/2005/05/addressing/none">http://tempuri.org/
IHelloWorldService/GetMessageResponse</Action>
  </s:Header>
  <s:Body>
    <GetMessageResponse xmlns="http://tempuri.org/">
      <GetMessageResult>Hello world from Mike Liu!</
GetMessageResult>
    </GetMessageResponse>
  </s:Body>
</s:Envelope>
```

5. To debug the extension, you can first set a breakpoint within the `TraceMessage` method in the `MyMessageInspector.cs` class and then step into the extension from the client program, or attach to the `w3wp.exe` process and then run the client program to hit the breakpoint (you must be running Visual Studio as administrator to step into the extension class).

This test proves that our `TraceMessage` service extension method has been invoked by the service for all incoming and outgoing messages. As you can see in this example, we didn't change any code in the service, we are still using the same client program as before, yet the extension has been applied by changing a few lines within the configuration file. You can use the same mechanisms to plug in your extensions in your environment to any existing services at any time.

Summary

In this chapter, we learned the basic concepts of the WCF extension and extended service behavior of the `HelloWorld` service. In this sample extension, we just logged all incoming and outgoing messages, but in your environment, you can do much more than just logging messages. There are many extension points and you should examine the needs of your WCF service and pick the most appropriate extension points according to your application requirements.

This is the last chapter of the book. Through this book, we learned how to create, host, and debug a WCF service, whether on-premise or in the cloud. We also learned WCF exception handling and applied best practice to our WCF service development. As Entity Framework is now the standard data access ORM, we explored Entity Framework, LINQ to Entities, and replaced our data access layer with LINQ to Entities. We also learned WCF transaction management by using LINQ to Entities and configured the security for our WCF service. In addition to this, we upgraded our SOAP WCF service to a RESTful WCF service and created a Windows 8 app to consume this RESTful WCF service through C#/XAML, jQuery, and WinJS. Then, in this last chapter, we extended our WCF service to log all incoming and outgoing messages. At this point, you should be very comfortable in creating and configuring your own WCF service, customizing its transaction and security settings, and extending it if needed. I hope you can apply your WCF knowledge to your real work and enjoy it.

Index

conflicts detection, version column used
  conflicts, testing 196
  Products table, modeling 194
  test code, writing 194
  version column, adding 193
conflicts, version column
  testing 196
connection string
  adding, to configuration file 126
console application
  service hosted, consuming in 40
  service, hosting in 36-40
C#/XAML client
  creating 286
  GetProduct method, implementing
      of 287, 288
  GetProduct method, testing of 289
  UpdateProduct method,
      implementing of 290-292
  UpdateProduct method, testing of 292

D

data access layer
  about 90, 122
  adding 122
  calling, from business logic layer 124, 125
  connection string, adding to configuration
      file 126
  database, preparing 126
  database querying, GetProduct
      used 127, 128
  database update, UpdateProduct used 131
  GetProduct functionality, creating 206, 207
  GetProduct method, testing 129, 130
  LINQ to Entities, using 205
  project, creating 122, 123
  UpdateProduct functionality,
      creating 207-209
  UpdateProduct method, testing 132
data access layer project
  creating 122, 123
Data Access Object (DAO) 122
database
  preparing 126
  querying, GetProduct used 127, 128
  updating, UpdateProduct used 131

database package
  URL 126
database table
  program, running 157-159
  querying 154
  records, deleting 156
  records, inserting 156
  records, querying 154, 155
  records, updating 155, 156
  updating 154
data column
  used, for detecting conflicts 184
data contract
  about 10
  creating 93, 94
  properties 94
data model
  creating 147
  Entity Framework, installing 147
  generated LINQ to Entities classes 153, 154
  LINQ to Entities item, adding to
      project 148-152
data transfer object. See DTO
DbContext class 153
debugger
  attaching, for running WCF service
      process 82
debugging mode
  WCF service, starting in 80
debugging process
  starting 76
deferred execution
  about 162
  checking, with SQL Profiler 162-164
  eager loading, with Include
      method 171-173
  for aggregation methods 164
  for aggregation methods, within sequence
      expressions 165-169
  lazy loading, default 170, 171
  lazy loading, versus eager loading 169
deployment package
  creating 69, 70
  installing 71-73
  service, testing 73
  used, for publishing HelloWorldService 69

G

generated LINQ to Entities classes 153, 154
generated SQL statements
  viewing 159
  viewing, SQL Profiler used 161, 162
  viewing, ToString used 159, 160
GetProductJQuery method
  implementing 294-296
  testing, of JavaScript client 296
GetProduct method
  about 127
  creating, in data access layer 206, 207
  implementing 223
  implementing, of C#/XAML client 287, 288
  testing 129, 130
  testing, of C#/XAML client 289
  used, for querying database 127, 128
GetProduct operations
  testing 228, 229
GetProductWinJS method
  implementing 298, 299
  testing 299

H

HelloWorld project
  creating 13-18
HelloWorldService
  extending 330
  extension, applying to 339, 340
  publishing 61-63
  publishing, cloud website 67, 68
  publishing, deployment package used 69
  publishing, from Visual Studio 59
  publishing, from Visual Studio to
      on-premise computer 60
  publishing, to cloud 64
HelloWorldService, extending
  behavior class, creating 336, 337
  behavior element class, creating 338, 339
  extension, applying to
      HelloWorldService 339, 340
  extension class, creating 332-334
  extension project, creating 332

service, setting up 331
  testing 341, 343
HelloWorldService service contract interface
  defining 18, 19
  implementing 20
HelloWorld solution
  creating 13-17
host application, WCF service
  creating 21-23
  starting 27, 28
  testing 24
hosting, WCF 11
hosting website
  creating 60, 61, 85
host machine
  TCP WCF activation, enabling for 53, 54
HTTPS protocol
  configuring 312-315

I

IContractBehavior interface 329
identity-based, WCF authorization 304
IEndpointBehavior interface 329
IIS
  about 24, 41
  basic authentication, configuring
      on 310-312
  starting 44
  WCF service, hosting 219-221, 241
  WCF service, starting in 47
IIS application, HTTP protocol
  creating 46
IIS application, TCP protocol
  creating 54, 55
IIS Express
  about 24, 25
  WCF service, hosting 21
IIS hosting
  WCF service, debugging in 82-84
implicit transactions 196, 197
Include method
  about 177
  eager loading, using with 171, 172
IOperationBehavior interface 330
IServiceBehavior interface 329

P

parameter inspection 325
Plain Old CLR/C# Object (POCO) 152
Products table
  modeling, with version column 194
product variable 288
profile
  creating 65
program
  running 157-159
project
  creating, built-in WCF service
      template used 91
  LINQ to Entities item, adding to 148-152
proxy extension. *See* client-side
      extension points
proxy files
  generating 29, 30
publishing project
  creating 60, 61

R

records
  deleting 156
  inserting 156
  querying 154, 155
  updating 155, 156
reference
  adding, to BDO project 206
remote database
  configuring, on remote machine 253, 254
remote machine
  remote database, configuring on 253, 254
resource-based, WCF authorization 304
REST
  about 278
  versus SOAP 277, 278
RESTful service
  configuration file, modifying 284
  creating 280
  implementing 283, 284
  RESTful service contracts, defining 280, 281
  testing, in browser 285
RESTful service contracts
  defining 280, 281

RESTful WCF service
  C#/XAML client, creating 286
  GetProduct method, implementing of
      C#/XAML client 287, 288
  GetProduct method, testing of C#/XAML
      client 289
  JavaScript client, creating 293
  service, testing with jQuery 294
  service, testing with WinJS 298
  UpdateProduct method, implementing of
      C#/XAML client 290-292
  UpdateProduct method, testing of
      C#/XAML client 292
RESTful WCF service, with C#/XAML client
  testing 285
RESTful WCF service, with JavaScript client
  testing 293
RESTNorthwind solution
  creating 279, 280
result processing 326
role-based, WCF authorization 304
running WCF service process
  debugger, attaching to 82

S

Secure Sockets Layer (SSL) 306
Secure Token Service (STS) 308
sequential calls
  testing, to WCF service 249, 250
service
  basic authentication, configuring
      on 315-317
  error handling, adding to 134
  hosting, in console application 36-40
  hosting in IIS, HTTP protocol used 41
  hosting in IIS, TCP protocol used 49
  hosting, in managed application 36
  hosting, in Windows service 41
  layering 90
  setting up 331
  testing, own client used 104-108
  testing, WCF Test Client used 99-104
  testing, with basic authentication 318, 319
  testing, with jQuery 294
  testing, with WCF Test Client 217, 218
  testing, with WinJS 298

SQL Server Profiler 161
stored procedure
  adding, to model 178, 179
  calling 177
  mapping, to existing entity class 180-184
  mapping, to new entity class 178
  querying 179, 180
system-provided bindings
  BasicHttpBinding 8
  NetTcpBinding 8
  WSHttpBinding 8

T

TCP WCF activation
  enabling, for host machine 53, 54
test client
  creating 221, 222
test code, data column
  writing 187, 188
test code, version column
  writing 194
three extension points
  URL 326
ToString
  used, for viewing generated SQL
    statements 159, 160
trade-offs, of distributed transactions 275
transaction behavior
  testing, of existing WCF service 242
transaction behavior, testing
  client, creating to call WCF service
    sequentially 242-248
  multiple database support, testing of
    WCF service 252
  sequential calls, testing to WCF
    service 249, 250
  WCF service calls, wrapping in one
    transaction scope 251, 252
transaction flow options
  Allowed 264
  Mandatory 264
  NotAllowed 264

transaction flow, service binding
  allowing, through service operation
    contract modification 264
  enabling 262
  enabling, on service hosting
    application 263
transaction scope
  WCF service calls, wrapping in 251
TransactionScopeRequired attribute 265
transaction scope requirement
  service operation implementation,
    modifying to 265
transaction support
  about 196
  explicit transactions 198, 199
  implicit transactions 196, 197
transfer security levels, WCF services
  message level 305
  transport level 305
two databases
  distributed transaction support, testing
    with 271-275
two tables
  joining 173, 174

U

UpdateProductJQuery method
  implementing 297
  testing, of JavaScript client 298
UpdateProduct method
  creating, in data access layer 208, 209
  implementing 225-227
  implementing, of C#/XAML client 290-292
  testing 132
  testing, of C#/XAML client 292
UpdateProduct operation
  testing 102, 228, 229
UpdateProductRequest class 281
UpdateProductWinJS method
  implementing 300, 301
UpdateProductWinJS method,
    JavaScript client
  testing 301

Thank you for buying
WCF Multi-layer Services Development with Entity Framework
Fourth Edition

About Packt Publishing

Packt, pronounced 'packed', published its first book "Mastering phpMyAdmin for Effective MySQL Management" in April 2004 and subsequently continued to specialize in publishing highly focused books on specific technologies and solutions.

Our books and publications share the experiences of your fellow IT professionals in adapting and customizing today's systems, applications, and frameworks. Our solution based books give you the knowledge and power to customize the software and technologies you're using to get the job done. Packt books are more specific and less general than the IT books you have seen in the past. Our unique business model allows us to bring you more focused information, giving you more of what you need to know, and less of what you don't.

Packt is a modern, yet unique publishing company, which focuses on producing quality, cutting-edge books for communities of developers, administrators, and newbies alike. For more information, please visit our website: www.packtpub.com.

About Packt Enterprise

In 2010, Packt launched two new brands, Packt Enterprise and Packt Open Source, in order to continue its focus on specialization. This book is part of the Packt Enterprise brand, home to books published on enterprise software – software created by major vendors, including (but not limited to) IBM, Microsoft and Oracle, often for use in other corporations. Its titles will offer information relevant to a range of users of this software, including administrators, developers, architects, and end users.

Writing for Packt

We welcome all inquiries from people who are interested in authoring. Book proposals should be sent to author@packtpub.com. If your book idea is still at an early stage and you would like to discuss it first before writing a formal book proposal, contact us; one of our commissioning editors will get in touch with you.

We're not just looking for published authors; if you have strong technical skills but no writing experience, our experienced editors can help you develop a writing career, or simply get some additional reward for your expertise.

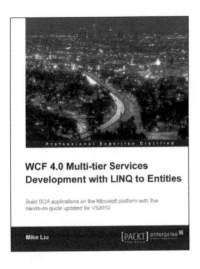

WCF 4.0 Multi-tier Services
Development with LINQ to Entities
===
WCF 4.0 Multi-tier Services Development with LINQ to Entities

ISBN: 978-1-84968-114-8   Paperback: 348 pages

Build SOA applications on the Microsoft platform
with this hands-on guide updated for VS2010

1. Master WCF and LINQ to Entities concepts by
   completing practical examples and applying
   them to your real-world assignments.

2. The first and only book to combine WCF
   and LINQ to Entities in a multi-tier
   real-world WCF service.

3. Ideal for beginners who want to build scalable,
   powerful, easy-to-maintain WCF services.

WCF Multi-tier Services
Development with LINQ
===
WCF Multi-tier Services Development with LINQ

ISBN: 978-1-84719-662-0   Paperback: 384 pages

Build SOA applications on the Microsoft platform in
this hands-on guide

1. Master WCF and LINQ concepts by completing
   practical examples and apply them to your
   real-world assignments.

2. First book to combine WCF and LINQ in a
   multi-tier, real-world WCF service.

3. Ideal for beginners who want to build scalable,
   powerful, easy-to-maintain WCF services.

Please check **www.PacktPub.com** for information on our titles

[PACKT] enterprise ❀
PUBLISHING   professional expertise distilled

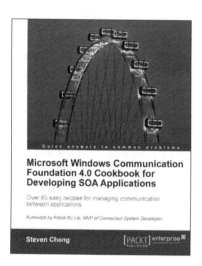

Microsoft Windows Communication Foundation 4.0 Cookbook for Developing SOA Applications

Over 85 easy recipes for managing communication between applications

Foreword by Frank Xu Lei, MVP of Connected System Developer

Steven Cheng   [PACKT] enterprise ❀

Microsoft Windows Communication Foundation 4.0 Cookbook for Developing SOA Applications

ISBN: 978-1-84968-076-9   Paperback: 316 pages

Over 85 easy recipes for managing communication between applications

1. Master WCF concepts and implement them in real-world environments.

2. An example-packed guide with clear explanations and screenshots to enable communication between applications and services and make robust SOA applications.

3. Resolve frequently encountered issues effectively with simple and handy recipes.

Microsoft Windows Workflow Foundation 4.0 Cookbook

Over 70 recipes with hands-on, ready-to-implement solutions for authoring workflows.

Foreword by Ryan Vice, Microsoft MVP for Connected Systems

Andrew Zhu   [PACKT] enterprise ❀

Microsoft Windows Workflow Foundation 4.0 Cookbook

ISBN: 978-1-84968-078-3   Paperback: 255 pages

Over 70 recipes with hands-on, ready-to-implement solutions for authoring workflows

1. Customize Windows Workflow 4.0 applications to suit your needs.

2. A hands-on guide with real-world illustrations, screenshots, and step-by-step instructions.

3. Explore various functions that you can perform using WF 4.0 with running code examples.

Please check **www.PacktPub.com** for information on our titles

34494515R00211

Made in the USA
Middletown, DE
23 August 2016